Narration in Light
Studies in Cinematic Point of View

George M. Wilson

The Johns Hopkins University Press
Baltimore and London

This book has been brought to publication with the generous assistance of the Andrew W. Mellon Foundation.

The Johns Hopkins University Press,
701 West 40th Street,
Baltimore, Maryland 21211
The Johns Hopkins Press Ltd, London

The paper in this book is acid-free and meets the guidelines for permanence and durability of the Committee on Production Guidelines for Book Longevity of the Council on Library Resources.

Library of Congress Cataloging-in-Publication Data

Wilson, George M.
  Narration in light.

  Includes index.
  1. Moving-pictures—Philosophy.   2. Moving-picture
plays—History and criticism.   I. Title.
PN1995.W584   1986   791.43'01'5   85-19765
ISBN 0-8018-3137-7 (alk. paper)

This book is dedicated to my mother, Kathleen H. Wilson, and to the memory of my father, George M. Wilson, Sr.

Contents

Acknowledgments

Chapter 6 originally appeared in *MLN*. Parts of chapters 1, 3, 4, and 10 were also published, in different forms, in *MLN*. Chapter 2 is a substantially altered and expanded version of the essay "*You Only Live Once: The Doubled Feature*," which appeared in *Sight and Sound* 46 (1977). I would like to thank the editors of these journals for their permission to draw upon these materials.

Figures 1–6 are from the Walter Wanger/United Artists release *You Only Live Once* (1937); figures 7–11 are from the MGM release *North by Northwest* © 1959 Loew's Incorporated; figures 12–17 are from the Universal release *Letter from an Unknown Woman* (1948); figures 18–23 are from the Paramount release *The Devil Is a Woman* (1935); and figures 24–28 are from the Warner Brothers release *Rebel without a Cause* (1955).

Three people have been crucial to the long evolution of this book. Mark Crispin Miller's comments, suggestions, and encouragement over the years have been consistently helpful and stimulating. More than this, however, the fact that a critic of Mark's perceptiveness and taste shared many of my interests in film has bolstered my sometimes shaky sense that those interests should be pursued. My brother Mark Wilson has discussed questions of film with me longer and more intensively than anyone else. It has been my chief test of the soundness of a given chapter to learn whether he found it plausible and interesting. My wife, Karen, has read through these chapters almost as often as I have, and she has done the most to reduce the number of errors and infelicities they contain. That our marriage has survived this process is a testimonial—but just one of many—to her patience, generosity, and affectionate supportiveness.

Nancy Thompson, who keeps the Hopkins Philosophy Department in its orbit, typed several versions of this material. My editor, Jane Warth, streamlined the manuscript, improving it greatly. Many other people have helped and encouraged me. I will mention John Belton, Michael Fried, David Hills, Dick Macksey, David Sachs, Jerry Schneewind, Bill Taschek, and Susan White, but the list could be much longer. Flannery and Gareth did absolutely nothing to speed the completion of the writing, but they did a great deal to make periods of distraction fun and lively. Finally, my parents, to whom this book is dedicated, started me in moviegoing when I was three and thereby laid the foundations for all that follows.

Narration in Light

Chapter 1

Film, Perception, and Point of View

Let's start from the beginning again, Jeff.
Tell me everything you saw . . . and what
you think it means.
from *Rear Window*

There are moments in some films which suddenly force us to reconsider, for at least an instant, our complacent ways of watching at the cinema. Here is one example that jolted me. In the Orson Welles film *The Lady from Shanghai*, two distinguishable series of shots are rapidly intercut. In one series, two male characters drive hurriedly toward an important destination. In the other, a female character, who is known to be at that time far distant from the men, learns of their journey and reacts angrily to this information. The following three-shot progression concludes the intercut series: (1) a shot from within the men's car reveals that a truck has abruptly pulled out onto the road ahead of them; (2) the woman's hand is shown reaching out and pressing an unidentified button; and (3) the men's car collides violently with the truck. Viewing these shots, it appears as if the pressing of the button has mysteriously caused the accident, but, at the same time, this impression of causality is difficult to reconcile with common sense and difficult also to integrate into our immediate sense of the film's narrative development at that juncture.

We could construct a number of hypotheses about this odd instance of apparent causation in the film. For example, we might suppose that it *is* a part of the tale that the woman somehow causes the crash, but, in so judging, we thereby assume that the world depicted in *The Lady from Shanghai* allows for causal connections that blatantly contravene the operations of the actual world. This assumption leaves us with hard questions about what we are and are not permitted to assume in making the world of the Welles story intelligible to ourselves.

Similarly, we might come to believe that, although we are meant to have the impression of the act causing the accident, we are not to conclude that this causal link is a genuine constituent of the film narrative; that is, that it is a fact of the story as determinate as the facts shown about the woman's action or the car's collision. Rather, it could be that this impression of causality has been created to make a kind of general, metaphorical statement, interjected here by the film maker, about, say, the uncanny power and influence of the woman over the men or, perhaps, about the film maker's own special power to impose arbitrarily upon our vision of the film's events. Thus, on this hypothesis, the impression of causality would have a status similar to that of the rising of the stone lions in Sergei Eisenstein's *Potemkin*.

Or again, to cite just one further possibility, we may come to judge that the appearance of causality at this point of the film is only an unfortunate effect of misjudged editing and take the shot of the woman's action to be the representation of a memory image or an hallucination experienced by one of the car's occupants immediately before the crash.

For present purposes, it does not matter which, if any, of these hypotheses is best. What does matter is that this relatively simple example illustrates two general points that will help to define the basic concerns of this book. First, if we are to make the most minimal sense of even a short series of shots like the one cited above, then we are forced to decide for ourselves a range of questions which plausibly belong to the topic of "point of view." We have just observed that we have to work out how our perceptual comprehension of the relevant film world is related to our normal modes of ordering and understanding perception in everyday visual experience. Discriminations have to be made, we noted, concerning the degree to which a given shot or shot series is meant to provide "direct" and "objective" visual information about the depicted world of the film. In addition, we saw that we are constantly required to keep track of the ways in which the sundry shots of the film are related to the perception and subjectivity of the characters it contains. Of course, in a large majority of cases, these decisions and discriminations are easy to make, but this only shows that these potentially complex matters have been settled (or seem to have been settled) by straightforward observance of familiar practices of narrative exposition in film or by a well-marked signaling of the special kind of apprehension for which the segment in question calls. Nevertheless, the potentiality for considerable epistemic complication always remains, and it is actually realized in some of the most interesting films ever made. Every film necessarily controls and limits the character of the visual access that we have to its fictional events, and sometimes the precise character of these limits and this control is both subtle and sophisticated. In any case, it is the various facets of this epistemic dimension of cinematic presentation which I wish to stress.

Second, it should be emphasized that local issues of perceptual understanding such as those suggested by our moment from *The Lady from Shanghai* are rarely answered by close inspection of just the shot or shot sequence that raised the issue in the first instance. Thus, in thinking about this example from Welles, one would need, in order to give any hypothesis a special plausibility, to relate the problematic series of shots to various elements in all or much of the rest of the film. For example, to establish that the woman's action did cause the car crash one would try to show how the attribution of strange causal powers to her is consonant with a number of other features and devices of the film which indicate that the unfolding of the narrative action is, in other ways, nonstandard. Building on this, one might look for a way in which her possession of such powers could be rationalized by, say, some peculiar moral or metaphysical status she seems to occupy. One might be able to delineate some quasi-allegorical structure that gives those powers a kind of emblematic point or purpose which transcends the narrow requirements of plot. In short, one argues that the film is best understood as deploying certain *global* strategies of narration within which the local perturbation, seen in a specified fashion, can be made to fit. These global strategies, especially in their more epistemic aspects, generate broad questions about how the film and its fictional world are to be apprehended and about how well we are situated to grasp whatever significance they may bear. Such questions belong, it seems to me, to a theory of filmic point of view.

The concept of point of view, as a construct of interpretation, is more familiar to us from literary theory and, admittedly, that concept is not as sharply delimited as one might wish. In film theory the situation is much worse.[1] Nevertheless, if there is a useful core concept to be discerned in both domains, then it is one that covers the different ways in which a form of narration can systematically structure an audience's overall epistemic access to narrative. Doubtless this characterization needs refinement and qualification, but the considerations we have before us already have given sense and substance to the expectation that such a concept can be elaborated for the case of cinema. This is the proposal I shall investigate throughout this book.

We can make this initial proposal more concrete and suggestive if we expand upon some of the dimensions of epistemic access which narrational strategies in film characteristically embody. It is a simple enough matter to generalize some of the reflections that the example from *The Lady from Shanghai* has already brought to light, and, in doing so, I shall sketch out some components of narrational focus which seem of central importance for our present investigations. Certainly, it should be obvious from even the following brief outline how a sizable variety of strategies of narration can arise under each of the headings I provide.

The proper viewing of a given film may require that members of its audience be situated at a certain *epistemic distance* from their usual habits of perception and common-sense beliefs. As noted, a spectator who is to achieve even a rudimentary understanding of a segment of film narrative must draw nonstop upon the incredible diversity of perceptual knowledge that we ordinarily and untendentiously assume we have about actual things and processes. This knowledge includes, of course, our more trustworthy beliefs about the nature and operation of the extracinematic world and about the ways they manifest themselves to us. It also includes, as a smaller but still important part, our prior knowledge of the techniques and conventions of film narrative and narration. In some films, such as *The Lady from Shanghai*, only part of this knowledge is meant to have application to the fictional world portrayed, while other strands of this knowledge are meant to be set in abeyance. It may be crucial to a correct viewing of such a film that our normal belief that things work in such-and-such a way is not fulfilled by *these things* appearing in *this* narrative. The result, when the strategy is successful, may be a view of our world as observed from a distanced metaphysical perspective. Therefore, assumptions about what features of our shared common-sense picture of the world are and are not projectable upon the world as pictured in a given film will help to constitute the viewer's epistemic base.

It is a different matter to inquire after the *epistemic reliability* of a film's narration. As a film proceeds, an audience's understanding of narrative developments depends not only upon its assimilation of the information with which it is directly presented but also upon its grasp of an imposing complex of inferences that it must make, consciously or unconsciously, from the visual manifolds that it is shown. (It actually underscores the present point that it is probably impossible to lay down a definite boundary between what is strictly seen and what is merely inferred.) A large and complicated part of the function of any film narration is to present immediately just enough material so that the desired inferences will reliably be drawn. But there is always an actual or potential gap between the inferences that will be made and the inferences that would, by some reasonable standard, be justified. Where a substantial disparity exists between the two classes, questions are implied either about the narration's power to construct a satisfactory fictional narrative or about the audience's acceptance of that power. Any film narration, whether trivial or intricately

4

problematic, is marked by implicit assumptions about the relations be-tween actual and justifiable inferences made on its basis. In chapter 2 we shall look closely at a film whose narration is, in a surprising fashion, systematically unreliable in this sense.

Finally, questions can also always be raised about the relations between the information that the audience progressively acquires concerning dra-matic issues in the film and the information that one or several characters is shown to possess about the same topic. In other words, our epistemic alignment with the characters may vary from case to case. A number of different kinds of relation are possible here, and there are a number of different ways in which the narration can set them up. As a rule, the audience enjoys an epistemic position superior to that of the fictional agents. The perception of these agents, after all, is confined within a line of narrative action which they cannot survey. However, this advantage may exist in limited respects only, and, in more extreme cases, no significant audience privilege may exist. Once again, the assumptions that underlie these relations of proximity to and distance from the characters help to shape the total way in which they enter the appraising spectator's con-sciousness. These are examples of questions about the *epistemic authority* of the film narration. We often can give a general characterization of the kinds of facts about the narrative which the narration is authorized to show, or we can specify certain significant overall constraints that exist upon the way in which that range of facts is shown. The remarks above concern themselves with the authority of the narration defined in relation to the situation of the characters, but, as we shall see, other poles of definition may be used as well.

The types of narrational assumption which are picked out within these three categories are not intended to exhaust the factors that pertain to cinematic point of view. Even allowing for a vagueness in that concept which leaves plenty of room for stipulation about what it is to include, this first, short taxonomy can and should be enlarged. Throughout this book, additional factors will be identified. Nevertheless, my claim that these three wide categories are key ingredients in a reasonable conception of point of view in film will be developed and defended in later chapters. In particular, most of the point-of-view distinctions I shall propose in chap-ters 3 and 5 can be seen to arise out of a deeper examination of epistemic distance, reliability, and authority. Reflection on these narrational dimen-sions will, therefore, recur.

For the time being, it is enough if I have made it plausible that a range of material lies at hand which promises to form the basis of a theory of cinematic point of view and that the existence of such a theory might allow us to describe some fundamental properties of our experience of film. Surely, one wants to say, film does more than tell a story that is rendered in a visual medium, and it expresses more than whatever meaning might be ascribed to the elements of the action of the story thereby rendered. An important part of the "more" to which one wants to appeal is the idea that film guides us to a way of seeing its fictional constituents, and the meaning a spectator discovers in these constituents is not detachable from the determinate point of view from which they have been shown. The difficult task is to find the means of characterizing explicitly our sense of those determinate points of view. It should be completely unattractive to declare that this intuitively central feature of film perception is either ineffable or inexplicable.

The thought that some notion of cinematic point of view is essential to the analysis of serious films is hardly a novel one. From D. W. Griffith and Vachel Lindsay to the present, many film makers and writers on film have tried to adumbrate the special narrative potential of film with the help of phrases such as "way of seeing," "form of vision," and, of course, "point of view." Among recent film theorists, V. F. Perkins seems closest to this kind of position. In summarizing his views about what is involved in our understanding of narrative film, he also invokes the very concepts just mentioned. "What we have here [in analyzing film] is primarily a way of seeing; the direct registration and embodiment in a 'secondary world' of a point of view."[2] By itself, this remark would not distinguish him from many other theorists, but he goes on to assert that a way of seeing is associated with a set of "assumptions" that a film incorporates, and these assumptions are said to be concerned with "the nature of the spectator's relation to narrative."[3] The primary vehicle by means of which the relevant assumptions are expressed is, for Perkins, a "norm" or "schema" of narrational "selection." I take it that these very brief proposals offer us a skeletal form of the conception of cinematic point of view to which I have lately attempted to add a little flesh.

The general thesis Perkins and I share—that a coherent stretch of narration embodies assumptions about how its narrated content is to be transmitted to an audience and about how the audience is to respond, cognitively and emotively, to that content—has a long and respectable ancestry. It yields a rough definition of the traditional idea of a *rhetoric* of narration. Seen in this light, the shared thesis implies that a theory of point of view in film should find its place within a broader account of the rhetoric of film narration, where the object of this rhetoric is not so much (at least in the first instance) the formation of belief and desire, but the shaping of perception itself.

The existence of such a rhetorical dimension to film is suggested by the following considerations. The film maker is constantly trying to find strategies in virtue of which an envisaged significance can be *made visible* to an audience. This is the fundamental level of communication in film. The film maker wishes to bring it about that a viewer sees, for example, a series of events as causally connected, sees a character's behavior as manifesting certain states of mind, or sees that behavior as directed at an objective of which the agent may or may not be aware. More ambitiously, the film maker may want the viewer to see the lives of the characters as ordered by chance, by social forces, or by divine intelligence. However, as these last examples particularly remind us, one's conception of what, in a given situation, *is* genuinely visible to a suitably placed observer, is likely to be problematic for others. I have in mind here the myriad disagreements, some practical, others systematic and philosophical, about what is and can be given in perception. For example, some believe that it is only the physical properties of an agent's behavior that we literally observe; others, on an opposite extreme, believe that it is possible just as literally to see God's grace imminent in some of that human activity. Hence, the film maker's beliefs about such matters may be quite different from the counterpart beliefs of most of his or her audience. When this is so, the very possibility of the sort of cinematic communication which is intended is threatened from the beginning. The task is then to construct a form of narration that can evoke, at least for the duration of the film, the necessary concordance of vision—a tacit agreement about the kinds of perceptual intelligibility that the portrayed action may be understood to have. In most films, the film maker presupposes a commonplace perspective that is automatically and unthinkingly available to a standard, contemporary audience. The narrational strategies that are employed are correspondingly conventional and undemanding. But in more sophisticated films, the solutions to these problems are far from trivial, and they involve extensive and delicate manipulation of perceptual habits and expectations. The methods of narration which constitute the concrete realization of these solutions are aimed at encouraging some of our perceptual dispositions and suppressing others. They often instruct us in new ways of integrating visual experience.

Several interlocking sorts of assumptions are therefore at risk when such a filmic communication is proposed. First, there are assumptions about the character of what potentially can be shown and seen in the prospective narrative action. These are assumptions about the visual "meaning" that the action might be expected to bear. Second, there are assumptions about how that action would be likely to be seen, in the absence of proper mediation, from the ordinary, perceptual standpoints that viewers bring to the theater. And third, there are assumptions about the narrational means appropriate for bridging a predicted discrepancy between the perception of the film which is desired and the likely upshot of a normal, untutored view of things. In this last case, it is assumed that the systematic inclusion, exclusion, ordering, and making salient of successively presented visual content through framing, editing, *mise en scène*, and so forth can significantly shift the aspects under which the narrative may be perceived and can do so in such-and-such a specific fashion. When the cinematic enterprise has been successful, all of these assumptions are embodied or expressed in the complicated assortment of factors which guides the viewer to a transformed outlook on the fictional world.

Even if we allowed that every feature of any such transformation may count as an effect of filmic rhetoric, we would be less inclined, I think, to count all of these effects as falling under the heading of "point of view in film." Because every element in a film's narration will probably have some influence upon our seeing something under some or another aspect, there is a danger that, without more refined specification, the embryonic concept of point of view will collapse into the wider concept of visual narration in the cinema. The concept of point of view should impose a categorization upon the domain of visual narration in actual films, a categorization that depends upon the structuring properties of the film's *overall* rhetorical organization, properties that determine the base from which an ideally perspicuous viewer assigns epistemic significance and value to the image track throughout its course. In prose fiction, the "epistemic base" is identified in terms of the narrator, and many of the familiar classifications of literary point of view are concerned with the mediated or unmediated epistemic relations that the narrator bears to the narrated events. However, as I shall argue in later chapters, it is dubious that fiction film generates any comparably general and central concept of a narrating figure. This means that the required notion of an "epistemic base" has to be described more directly and, in a sense, more abstractly. When I characterized the relationships between film narration and audience upon which the categories of epistemic distance, reliability, and alignment depend, I was thereby attempting to give the beginnings of a description of this orienting base.

When one thinks about a particular film, it may be difficult to state explicitly and accurately just what assumptions within these and related categories are operative in its narration. But this is to admit no more than that it may require a good deal of careful and detailed interpretative work to do so (although I believe that these factors often play a large role in determining our intuitive sense of a film's significance, even when we are far from being able to give a verbalized account of them). It suffices for now if it seems reasonable that such assumptions can control and thereby be manifest in the fine-grained articulation of screen imagery and *mise en scène*. After all, it is this articulation that governs shot by shot the kinds of perceptual access the spectator has to the events of the story, and the assumptions discussed above all have to do with modes of access to the film narrative. However, if the question of *how* these assumptions can be manifested still seems obscure, the analyses of individual films which make up much of this book should, by extended example, clarify the issue considerably. It is a part of the job of textual analysis to delineate the way that content (in the broadest possible sense) is expressed or implied within a work. This is one of the sites at which theory and practical criticism necessarily intertwine.

The line of argument I have constructed has been designed to motivate the general contention that a theory of cinematic point of view is both possible and desirable. As such, I am afraid that the conclusions drawn thus far are so abstract as to leave little feeling for the substantial content such a theory might have. This situation will be largely rectified, especially in chapters 3 and 5, when a set of more concrete point-of-view distinctions has been drawn. It will become apparent there that the structure of these distinctions is notably akin to the more familiar structure of point-of-view distinctions in literature. Even in the absence of this forthcoming elaboration, it can be seen that each of the epistemic dimensions of distance, reliability, and authority has an analogue in prose narration, and the literary analogue has traditionally been thought of as generating categories of point of view in the verbal medium. The reader should therefore find himself or herself on a path with more familiar landmarks the more these first proposals are worked out.

However, the existence of these analogies is double-edged, and the analogies need to be handled with tact and care. It simply will not do to import the relevant literary theory and apply it to the domain of film. We shall find, especially in chapters 2 and 3, that the possibilities subsumed under epistemic reliability permit a kind of systematically unreliable film narration which is both like and unlike unreliable narration in literary fiction. Both showing and telling may be unreliable, but the differences between these two ways of narrating are so great that the nature of unreliability in each instance has to be worked out on its own. Still, returning to the reassurances of the previous paragraph, I take it that reliable versus unreliable narration is a distinction of point of view.

An improved conception of point of view should do much to improve our impoverished sense of the possibilities of narrative and its presentation in film. Perhaps it is the confused idea that film is the most "direct and immediate" way of narrating a story which has led most viewers, professional and otherwise, to suppose that the requirements of plot exposition confine a film's significance to the dramatic progression of the action. It is as if we had a temporalized form of the following phenomenon. When the perspective focus of a painting is located within the frame but at a significant distance from the picture's horizontal midpoint, spectators are tempted to place themselves at a suitable position at the opposite side of the painting so that they create for themselves the impression of facing directly into the receding space of the focal point. If they succumb to this temptation, however, the proper balance of the composition will be destroyed. The lateral focus becomes *the* perceptual node around which the other spatial elements and relationships are configured rather than, as it was meant to be, a dynamic accent subordinate to patterns whose salience is visible only from a centered position before the canvas.[4]

It is similarly easy and natural to be situated "off center" in watching a sophisticated, narrative film. Viewers dispose their attention toward the "focus" of the story's ultimate resolution. They are perceptually set to follow the evolution of those plot conflicts that are marked out to be the subject of an audience's most immediate and engaged regard. Indeed, it is the normal goal of narrative strategies to make this temptation effectively irresistible.[5] However, there are narrative films—and I shall discuss several of them—in which central aspects of their interest and significance bear only an *oblique* relationship to the forms of dramatic closure they employ. In these instances, the strong narrative orientation of viewer awareness and expectation tends to block the obliquely situated prospects entirely from view. That is, various factors that either appear on the screen or are implied but not shown in the film and that are peripheral to the strict development of the basic tale may be assigned a weight in the narration in such a way that the chief issues raised by the drama come to be modified, displaced, or otherwise reappraised. It is not too much to say that when this counternarrative weighting is apprehended, the whole gestalt of the film often seems to shift. The original example from *The Lady from Shanghai* already suggests what can be at issue here, but the phenomenon will be recurrently illustrated in detail. For example, if the warnings of narrational unreliability in *You Only Live Once* (see chap. 2) are duly noted, the apparent bathos of its legend of social justice will be transformed. And if one is not blind to the function of the numerous visual puns and textual play in *The Devil Is a Woman* (see chap. 8), then the complex inflections of subjectivity in that film will become intelligible. Unfortunately, in cases such as these it is quite probable that the subtly weighted patterns of visual content which ought to qualify or subvert the linear dynamics of plot will be experienced in a fragmentary way, usually as odd obstructions to the direct fulfillment of the narrative's most obvious ends. The problem for the viewer of such a film is to locate a "centered position" from which the oblique strands of narrational strategy can come together in a configuration that reorganizes his or her perception and comprehension of the fictional events. There is no set of rules for achieving such a position, but a just appreciation of fruitful questions about point of view can do a lot to shift one's angle of perception toward a more fortunate perspective.

These last remarks are meant to introduce my reason for devoting so much space in this book to the study of individual films and to rationalize the type of film I have chosen to examine. Each film that is discussed here at any length was, with one exception, produced by a major American studio in the period from 1934 to 1959. They are all examples of what has been dubbed "classical narrative film" and, on the whole, they observe the constraints on form, style, and subject matter which this phrase suggests.[6] The general claims of the more theoretical chapters primarily apply to films within this somewhat loosely defined class. It is essential that we cultivate a lively sense of the subtlety, complexity, and variety which classical narrative and narrational strategies allow. The films discussed all provide surprising and even radical instances of the type of "oblique" perspective recently described. In some ways, these films are central test cases for a theory of point of view. The way they work is either difficult or impossible to explicate within the usual accounts of cinematic rhetoric. One reason for skepticism about the possibility at this time of a genuinely systematic theory of point of view is due to our lack of a good understanding of what our theory ought to explain. From *You Only Live Once* through *Rebel without a Cause*, each film discussed teaches us something distinctive about the data that want accounting for. Moreover, if we lack a satisfactory conception of the possibilities that the more conventional forms allow, we are likely to become disoriented when theory is supposed to encompass narrative and quasi-narrative films that overtly make a sharp break with established canons of exposition in film. The sheer diversity of possibilities quickly threatens to become unmanageable. Further, many modernist films are best understood, in part, as reactions against the traditional patterns of narrative and narration that popular commercial film has so heavily relied upon. It is hard to make out the premises of an alternative mode of narration if the assumptions it means to repudiate are themselves not understood.

I have also wished to institute an intimate interplay between theory and critical practice, to exhibit the continuous dialectic that ought to exist between the two. Too often in recent film theory one discovers lengthy and extremely abstract disquisitions on, for example, the relation of film to reality, the languagelike character of film presentation, whose Platonic purity is almost totally unsullied by illustration or evidence. These lofty theoretical edifices rise so grandly over the plain upon which the disorderly mass of actual films is strewn that it is often obscure just what issues are being addressed and how the results of so much theory-building labor are connected with anything one cares about in film. For one thing, one can learn a lot from good films concerning the questions it is useful to ask about films in general or about films of such-and-such a type. Any reasonably thorough analysis of a worthwhile film leads immediately to problems of significant generality. If it is maintained that film F expresses content C (if I may state the point too crudely), then the critic is committed to the thesis that film elements and structures of certain identifiable types which occur in F can play the sort of expressive role that the critic thinks he has discriminated as the basis of C. But then, if he has any theoretical bent at all, he will want to be able to formulate the way in which this arises as an expressive possibility of film. The methodological point is elementary, but it is frequently hard to carry out in practice, and it is widely ignored. This stricture was employed in reverse in selecting the films discussed in this book. All of these films make matters of perception a subject that they, with a high degree of self-consciousness, internally explore. Thus, they are especially well-suited to guide us in a study of point of view.

The remoteness of so much contemporary theory from its natural data has had unfortunate consequences for the study of older American films. Many writers, especially those influenced by Marxist or psychoanalytical versions of semiotics, talk as though "classical narrative film" were a determinate mechanism whose operations and output are, by and large, well-understood. The products of this mechanism are held to be varieties of "bourgeois illusionism," and the contents of the cinematically instantiated illusions are treated as determined, via the film machinery, by the dominant ideology of the time. A part of the silliness of these doctrines stems from an utterly indiscriminate use of the notion of "determination" and a wild inflation of the concept of "ideology." But another source of the trouble is an inflexible commitment to accepting the structures of representation and narrative elaboration in Hollywood films at face value while subjecting the resulting critical superficialities to a semiotic, Marxist, or psychoanalytic gloss. Admittedly, for most such films this does not matter much, but for the nonnegligible class of more challenging studio films the results have been disastrous. It is as if these theorists believed that the ruthless determinism of ideology left no room for the play of inventiveness, sensibility, and irony within the more formative features of a film's framework.

One thing that one might reasonably mean by the term *ideology* is this. It is to refer to the vast range of more or less unconscious habits of perception, attention, and attitudinal formation which have been unknowingly inculcated through social and cultural conditioning, especially as these habits inflect our social and political actions and beliefs. *If* one were to understand *ideology* in this way, then the films discussed here provide "critiques of ideology" in the most immediate sense possible. This is a consequence of the fact that they make available the sort of "oblique" perspective previously mentioned. These films all have a standard interpretation that will be absolutely foregrounded for any spectators who unresistingly watch them from their preestablished positions in ideological space. But each of the films also offers the possibility of *seeing* how the whole of its action and the filmic presentation of that action could have been more thoroughly and coherently perceived in an altogether different vein if one's inertia in that space had not been so total. One can literally learn to see that which was strictly invisible to us as long as even "simple observation" was imbued with the ideological forms and habits that the contexts of our lives make standard.

The critical outlook described in the penultimate paragraph may be extreme, but many other authors on film have also felt that the oppression of "dream factories" and the mass entertainment market has been so exiguous that the merits that exist in some of these mainstream films could only be matters of intermittent personal style or the piecemeal injection of subversive comment. One does not have to be a Romantic advocate of the thought that there is a mysterious infusion of authorial personality or vision into a work to believe that a number of film makers, thinking about the givens and conditions of their enterprise, were able to find ways of exploiting the very real limitations imposed upon them to design films of sustained and serious richness. Others have argued this before, but I argue it here once more with a special eye to its relevance for larger questions about point of view and narrational strategy in film.

Having so often conjured up the worthy ambition of building a theory of point of view in film, I should explain that my ambition in the ensuing chapters is somewhat more modest. This book is intended as a collection of studies *toward* the development of an adequate account of cinematic point of view. Moreover, these studies are of two types. In chapters 3, 5, 7, and 10, I pursue some of the theoretical argumentation that has been introduced in this chapter while adding other considerations that expand the topic. The remaining chapters, as mentioned previously, consist of close viewings of five exemplary films. Although I believe that the more theoretical chapters constitute an advance over current thinking, they do not pretend to any completeness with regard either to subject matter or rigorous formulation. Indeed, in many places, I have been as interested in raising questions and issues as I have been in advancing positive theses. Still, I have tried to give a wide survey of many of the kinds of distinctions which need to be introduced and, perhaps more importantly, to explain why, in terms of real problems confronted in thinking about actual films, some such distinctions are required. Beyond this, I have also tried to explicate some of the larger considerations about filmmaking and film viewing which permit the distinctions to be drawn.

The importance of a concept of cinematic point of view is not for me the result of an abstract analysis of the levels of narrative film or of some other line of theoretical reasoning. Rather, the importance of such a concept is that, in trying to give a refined and accurate account of films of the stature of those discussed in these pages, one repeatedly feels the need to employ some suitable notion of point of view. However, no version of the needed concept exists, and it is manifest that the formulation of the distinctions to be drawn is, by no means, an easy task. This, in any case, is the incentive to theory that I have had, and it has the advantage, at a minimum, of imposing numerous constraints upon the investigations it elicits. There are always all those remarkable properties of marvelous films to which the theoretical upshot has to be, in the end, responsible. So the films discussed in this book and other films of similar merit can teach us where to look for problems and about what solutions would look like if we found them. The number of genuine solutions in this work to the most general problems it considers is smaller than I had hoped for, but I am unreservedly convinced that the constant give-and-take between criticism and

14

theory that these chapters are meant to exemplify is essential to the healthy practice of both.

Chapter 2 is an analysis of Fritz Lang's 1937 film *You Only Live Once*. It seems desirable to have before our eyes as soon as possible a detailed and extended example of the phenomenon of perceptual shift in film, an example that also sharply motivates a major question about point of view. The peculiar logic of Lang's narrational strategies in this film is, although complex, unusually clear-cut, and it is therefore reasonably easy to delineate. At the same time, when one considers some of the larger implications of those strategies one is forced back upon some of the general topics broached in this chapter. Hence, in chapter 3 we shall be better prepared to return to the charms and diversions of a more abstract discussion.

The impending analysis of *You Only Live Once* is essential to the theory that will ensue. For this film, rightly viewed, lays out a narrational possibility of classical film which might antecedently seem nonexistent. The analysis proves that a certain theoretical question needs an answer. However, to repeat a point I have underscored before, the special mode of epistemic access in this (or any) film is not separate from the dramatic material to which the narration gives access. Therefore, I shall examine the film as a whole in some detail without attempting, in that immediate context, to lift out explicitly the lessons about point of view I wish to draw. Those lessons occur in chapter 3. In one way or another, I have kept to this division of labor throughout the book; that is, the stretches of practical criticism are relatively self-contained. This has the added advantage of making the analyses of individual films more easily available to readers whose predilection for theory may be slight. Nevertheless, all of the films that are here subjected to intensive scrutiny lead into problems so provocative that theory is hard pressed to respond. I am confident of the provocations I establish, less certain of the general responses I supply.

Chapter 2

Fritz Lang's
You Only Live Once

You Only Live Once is one of Fritz Lang's most widely admired American films and is thought to be among the finest of the so-called social consciousness films of the 1930s.[1] Some critics have found it a worthy vehicle for certain philosophical themes of human freedom and determinism. It is also praised for its technical excellence, richness of visual texture, and generally moving depiction of the story's star-crossed lovers. These judgments are, I believe, largely accurate as far as they go; the trouble is that they do not begin to go far enough. In particular, I argue that *You Only Live Once* exhibits kinds of structural and stylistic complexity which carry it into areas of concern that the usual remarks fail entirely to reflect. To see how this is so, clearly and in some detail, is a matter of some importance. What I take to be the main thematic concerns are of considerable interest on their own. Even more interesting, perhaps, are the peculiar strategies and devices by means of which these thematic materials are expressed. The narrational methods of this film constitute the formal exemplification of new and surprising reflections about the general character of cinematic narration in the fiction film. In this chapter, I shall attempt to uncover the concrete operations of these strategies; in chapter 3, I shall examine some of their broader implications. Finally, I wish to show that, understood in the context of the subtle framework that organizes the film's significance, certain of its segments and aspects that have seemed seriously flawed appear in a new and more satisfactory light—the ending, for example, which is often thought to be a disastrously maudlin lapse.

That ending seems to endorse a religious belief in redemption and release after death. Given what has become the standard "philosophical" reading of the film, it is hard not to find that conclusion unacceptable. This reading is summed up and emphatically asserted by Lotte Eisner at the outset of her analysis of the film in her book on Lang. She claims that "*You*

Only Live Once is Lang's Song of Songs, his American equivalent of *Destiny*. Man is trapped by fate: the loving woman cannot halt her lover's inexorable destiny; her involvement makes things worse and she must finally perish with him."[2] Indeed, it has become the most popular cliché, in discussions not only of this film but of Lang's career in general, to describe Lang as the cinematic visionary of some vague form of fatalism, the director whose characters are invariably trapped without hope by forces that far outrun their understanding and powers to resist. It is undeniable that in *You Only Live Once* the question is explicitly raised as to whether Eddie Taylor's career is to be seen in this way. However, the viewer has at least two immediate reasons for hesitating before giving a simple affirmative to the question. First, as I have meant to suggest, if Eddie's story is meant as a pat illustration of the workings of "inexorable destiny," the final religious vision seems especially gratuitous. Why should death, for anything this film has shown us, undercut the grim processes of Fate? Second, there are characters, notably Joan's cynical sister, who give voice to the rudimentary brand of fatalism or determinism that so many critics wish to ascribe to the film as a whole.[3] But the sister is pretty clearly designed to be a foil to Joan's automatic optimism and activism, traits she exercises most particularly in Eddie's behalf. Actually, the film goes to some lengths to introduce and lay stress upon the *variety* of perspectives from which Eddie and his behavior can be viewed. We shall explore this point extensively in our analysis. In any case, it seems odd to accept so readily this one view of the matter out of the several that are put forward.

The oddness of this interpretation is strongly reinforced when it is observed that the problematic character of any single perspective on the action is one of the film's principal preoccupations. The issue is stated quite explicitly, although with unwitting irony, by Father Dolan, the prison priest. He tells the warden's skeptical wife that "we all see through the same pair of eyes, but we don't all see the same thing." This is but one instance of such a reference in a film that seems obsessed with the various facets of perception and blindness. Through the visuals and the dialogue, we are repeatedly introduced to questions concerning sight and the failure to see, pictures and picturing, and the various senses of the word *vision*. Later, we shall explore the way in which Father Dolan's weighty words seem to carry an ironic application to him and the role he seeks to play.

However, we do best to begin with the possibility that this remark about what people do or do not see applies, with equal irony, to us as members of the film's audience. A striking and peculiar aspect of the film is the way in which it signals the possibility of manipulating our perception of its action. At several points, in several ways, the audience is led into making a mistake of perceptual judgment after which a wider context is revealed in terms of which the judgment is shown for the mistake it is. The basic pattern is exemplified within narrower and broader contexts, but two sequences initially stand out in that they are relatively isolated and well-defined within the film and that they seem, at first impression, particularly gratuitous. The sequences are these:

A. In what turns out to be Eddie Taylor's boarding room, the scene opens with a tracking shot in medium close-up. This reveals a sequence of objects which the audience already identifies with Eddie: a picture of Joan and his fatal, initialed hat. As the camera completes the track, a person is discovered lying on a bed. Because of an overall physical resemblance to Eddie and through the associations with the objects, we think for an instant that this person *is* Eddie. However, it is his criminal associate Monk. As we realize this, there is a cut to a medium shot of the whole room, and we see that Eddie is also present, standing at the back of the room looking out of the window (see fig. 1).

B. At the time of Eddie's trial, a scene opens with a close-up of a newspaper whose giant headlines announce that Eddie has been found innocent. Beneath the headlines is a picture of Eddie, warm and smiling. But next the camera slowly pans left, showing a second front page, which proclaims that his jury is deadlocked and pictures him with a blank, neutral expression. This time, when Lang cuts back to a broader perspective, we see that these are two of three press pages hanging on the wall of an editor's office. The third headline states that Eddie is guilty, and the picture shows him scowling and dangerous. To the left of this front page is a horseshoe. The editor is waiting for the jury's verdict to come down. The phone rings; the editor listens and silently picks out the "guilty" version with his pointer. Of course, we have first thought that Eddie has been released, but the scene as a whole corrects our quick impression (see fig. 2).

Both these scenes involve specific patterns, which we shall explore shortly, but, more simply, they raise a type of question we should be prepared to pursue. A and B are rudimentary but classic illustrations of the potential unreliability of film. On the one hand, film can focus our attention on the patterns of visual significance that segments of the visible world embody. To many, this has seemed the central promise of film. On the other hand, in providing such a focus, a selection is necessarily made from a wider setting: a setting that may contradict the significance the narrower focus has implied. And this has seemed the central danger of film—its most characteristic way of lying. *A* and *B* stand like small flags to the danger and warn us to ask whether the same moral applies to the wider contexts of the film.

A question that informs at least the whole middle section of the film is that of Eddie's guilt or innocence. Did he or did he not rob the bank? Lang has gone to rather special pains to raise this as a question for the audience. During his final fruitless visit to the Ajax Trucking Company, Eddie is established to be both frustrated and violent. He says explicitly that his old life of crime is all he can turn to. When the hold-up scene is presented, although we see the figure of the robber, we are carefully kept from knowing if it is Eddie Taylor. Of course, that Eddie's hat is in the robber's possession heightens our suspicions. These doubts do not even appear to be resolved until the beginning of the last third of the film.

At this point, during the prison break, the mystery seems to be cleared up. The police have found the stolen armored truck, with Monk's drowned body slumped in the front seat. They conclude that Eddie is innocent, and the audience, their sympathetic hopes finally substantiated, conclude the same thing. It may seem that by keeping the audience in doubt so long, Lang is simply playing for certain effects of suspense and irony; but this is incorrect. The point is to raise in the audience's mind, in a clear and definite way, the problem of what Eddie has done and who he really is. Moreover, it is just at the point where these questions seem answered that we are implicitly required to take them up again, more seriously and rigorously than before. We are asked to reconsider what it is that we have seen and what, from that, we know.

The issues here are complicated, and it is helpful to break them down into three categories. First, there is the logic of the evidence we have. The audience can play a game of detection with the facts it has been given. We find that (1) the evidence that purports to exculpate Eddie is radically insufficient, and (2) there is incriminating evidence that is altogether bypassed in the explicit presentation.

We begin with a point of logic. The fact that Monk is found in the submerged truck can be presumed to show that he was involved in the crime. However, it does not show that Eddie was not also involved. It is to be remembered that the proposition Monk had made earlier to Eddie involved collaboration on a hold-up. Thus, it becomes a prima facie possibility that Eddie and Monk committed the robbery together. Nevertheless, this possibility can seem foreclosed by the fact that we have seen the robbery and saw only one person engaged in the crime. Here we are forced to examine the details of this crucial scene.

It opens with a crane shot, which moves in on a pair of eyes surveying the situation in front of the bank. The eyes shift nervously across the scene. In addition—and this is of special importance—the eyes peer out of the rear window of a parked car. When we are later shown the inside of this car, everything is presented in a close-up of the action in the front seat. A suitcase is shown first, filled with a robber's tools. Next, a hand removes a gas mask from the case and replaces it with Eddie's hat. As the camera pans right someone is shown behind the steering wheel, but the face has been completely hidden by the gas mask. Throughout this extended shot, the camera is held so tightly on the action that it is impossible to make out what, if anything, is happening in the back of the car. The eyes we first saw looking from the rear window are not explained.

The suggestiveness of this shot is amplified by two later sequences, each of which contains shots of restlessly shifting eyes. In both cases, the eyes are clearly Eddie's. During Eddie's prison interview with Joan, and during the first stage, in his cell, of his escape from prison, his eyes dart back and forth over a threatening situation in the same manner that we have seen before.

Let us return for a moment to the robbery sequence. The person in the gas mask steps out of the car and bombards the street with grenades. Their explosion fills the area with almost impenetrable clouds of gas. We see the robber complete the hold-up under the cover of this gas, but it so cloaks the action and the sequence is so shot and edited that it is impossible to tell whether any other person is collaborating with the man we see.

The sequence that follows, which shows the getaway in the stolen armored truck, underlines the point that I have been making. We see the truck as it is driven furiously around a detour sign and down a small side road. But here the idea that we shall follow the action is firmly checked. The camera remains fixed at the crossroads in the heavy rain as we hear the sound of the truck crashing into an unseen body of water. If Eddie was in the truck and has managed to escape, we have been forbidden to know.

I have mentioned the unexplained eyes in the hold-up car, but another incriminating suggestion is made by a different fact. The second scene of the film begins with a close-up of a suitcase, which Joan is packing for Eddie, containing the things he will need in his life outside prison. This suitcase and the one holding the robber's gear appear to be one and the same. That Eddie's hat has been found at the scene of the crime figures significantly in the development of the plot. Much is made of this as evidence of his guilt, although he offers his own explanation of why it was there. Within the story, nothing is said about the matter of the suitcase;

but, for the audience, the two related close-ups of what seems to be the same object equally deserve and do not receive an explanation.

Thus, if the audience pursues the logic of the evidence, the later "proof of innocence" is completely unsatisfactory. I am not suggesting that we know Eddie is really guilty, but rather that we simply are in no position to judge. The facts we are given are flatly and disturbingly ambiguous. Actually, Lang seems to make fun of the way in which people treat the question of evidence. After the robbery, Eddie shows Joan a newspaper picture of his hat with the initials exposed. The caption claims that if the owner of the hat is identified, the murderer will be found. It is plain here that the ridiculously circumstantial nature of this inference is being mocked. And yet, when Eddie is cleared, a ticker tape carries the message that because Monk has been found in the truck, Eddie must be innocent. We are much more inclined to accept this inference, but we have just examined the way in which it is as willfully circumstantial as the first. "Thus and so, therefore Eddie is guilty." "Thus and so, therefore Eddie is innocent." In each case, these brusque pronouncements are intentionally absurd.

The second category of consideration concerns the suggestiveness of imagery embedded in the robbery and getaway sequences. *You Only Live Once*, as I mentioned earlier, is filled with references to the difficulty of seeing and of seeing clearly, and these two sequences are no exception. The holdup and getaway are persistently obscured by violent rain; the eyes in the car are forced to search through a thick curtain of rain. These difficulties are multiplied enormously, both for characters in the film and for the audience, when the scene is choked by the heavy layer of poison gas. In a similar vein, just before the robbery begins we see people in the immediate vicinity of the bank, including guards and passers-by. But the only person who is in a position to see the whole development of the robbery is a blind beggar selling pencils beside the bank's main doors. Such imagery evokes the idea that it will be difficult, if not impossible, to perceive what will happen.

The third and final category of evidence involves the relation between this whole question of Eddie's possible guilt and the two instances of explicit perceptual manipulation, sequences A and B, previously discussed. In sequence A, the pattern of perceptual mistake and recognition has the following form. The audience (a_1) mistakes Monk for Eddie; and then (b_1) recognizes that this person is Monk; and finally (c_1) sees that Eddie is also present, at the back and looking out of the window. Within the larger movement of the events connected with the robbery exists the definite possibility that exactly this pattern is recapitulated: (a_2) at the time of the hold-up, we are inclined to think that the robber is Eddie; (b_2) when the "proof" is discovered we realize that the robber is Monk after all. But I have argued at considerable length that the evidence of the film, taken as a whole, permits the possible inference that (c_2) both Monk and Eddie are present at the crime, with Eddie looking out of the back window of the car. The film is perfectly balanced between the standard reading and the inference to c_2. With this perfect, ambiguous balance, it has the beauty of a steel trap.

The implications of sequence B should by now be fairly clear. We first see the newspaper that shows us what we want to see: the smiling Eddie is innocent. A moment later, society delivers its judgment: the scowling Eddie is guilty. The right answer, however, is given by the front page in the middle, the page we tend to overlook. The jury ought to be deadlocked. Neither the jury in the film nor the "jury" in the audience is in a position to render a verdict on Eddie Taylor's essential guilt or innocence. Each group does make a judgment and both are wrong to do so. They are wrong in opposite ways and both are wrong equally. The horseshoe at the end of the row of papers marks a conclusion that the film amply justifies. It is merely a matter of luck as to which of the possible verdicts will be reached.

I have indicated several times that the audience desires and half expects that Eddie is innocent. In this connection, it is important that *You Only Live Once* works so smoothly and so well within the conventions of a thirties "social consciousness" film. A depression audience, especially, was prepared to believe that a sympathetic proletarian boy such as Eddie would be unjustly crushed by the implacable social machine. The honest openness that a young Henry Fonda so easily conveys reinforces the impression. If we are emotionally involved with the plight of the two attractive lovers trying to find a safe, comfortable place together, we care even more that he should not be irremediably a criminal. Both Fonda and Sylvia Sidney, in view of their earlier roles, were particularly well suited to evoke the appropriate responses. Lang has carefully calculated that his audience, whose predictable concerns and expectations are encouraged by the familiar narrative apparatus, will see the story of Eddie and Joan with a warm concern. Secure that the audience will condemn the prejudice and false perspective of society within the film, Lang employs a gamut of cinematic devices to guide us down the path of our own prejudices and false perspectives. At this point, the perfect steel trap has been closed on its viewer. If we recall that, a few years before the film was made, Fritz Lang had fled the Nazi regime after having been offered control of the German studios, it is hardly surprising that he should have been thinking deeply about the power of films to shape and control the factors in terms of which we see the world. *You Only Live Once* translates such reflection into a distinctively American idiom and style.

We have already touched upon the point that the film draws a direct connection between the way that people are seen by others and the way that they have appeared in films. Sequence *B* played upon this point in a grimly funny way. Most obviously, there are sections where the plot development turns on this connection. Eddie is recognized as an exconvict by the owner of the Valley Inn, where the couple plan to spend their honeymoon, because he has seen Eddie's picture in one of the old crime magazines that he collects. We watch, from the innkeeper's visual perspective, as he thumbs through a regular gallery of vicious-looking criminals until, among these, he locates a "mug shot" of Eddie. This situation is repeated toward the end of the film. Joan's identification by the manager of the Star Motel brings about their capture. Squinting through his spectacles, he recognizes her from her photograph on a wanted poster, which, by an odd coincidence, hangs on a wall of his room. He repeatedly compares the picture with his view of Joan herself, who stands, as though fixed in another picture, framed by the crossbars of his apartment window. His placing of her image seals the couple's doom (see fig. 3).

At other points, the issue is dealt with in similar ways. When Eddie is released from prison, the scene opens with a close-up of his face set in a blank, impassive expression. Warden Wheeler mechanically delivers his customary farewell speech beginning, "Now, you've been my guest exactly three time before." As he speaks, we join him in looking at the prison pictures in Eddie's file and gain the impression from this that it is more the pictures that he is addressing than Eddie himself. In all of this there is the suggestion that our perception of other human beings may be dangerously schematized into a crude mode of picturing them. One central visual motif in the film is made up of shots in which either Eddie or Joan is depicted within some framing rectangle inside the screen's frame. For example, when Eddie and Joan first come together after his release, they kiss through a wall of bars that separates them. Following a medium long shot that establishes the embrace, there is a closer shot of Eddie's face framed in the bars and then a reverse shot in which Joan is shown in the same way. Similarly, after the robbery, when Eddie arrives at their house, the utter desperation of his features is again framed by the crossbars of the window through which he peers. The culmination of this chain of imagery occurs in a famous shot at the end of the film. Trapped by the police, Joan and Eddie are reduced to two faceless forms caught in the cross hairs of a state trooper's rifle sight. Doubtless, many of these last cited shots are meant as images of entrapment, but, nonetheless, they echo the more subtle theme of picturing and the consequences of being so pictured. In this way, questions are posed about the precise nature of the entrapment Joan and Eddie suffer.

It is a simple transition from questions about the pictures *in* the film to the same questions about the pictures that constitute the film we are watching. We have already seen how well these questions apply. Nevertheless, Lang introduces a scene in which this link is invoked, subtly and effectively. When Eddie, after his trial, is being removed to the penitentiary, there is an unusual sequence outside the courthouse. It opens with a high-level long shot that shows him being led down the courthouse steps and confronted by an angry mob. In the middle of the crowd is a newsreel camera, which is filming his departure (see fig. 4). This is followed by a ground-level shot, which reveals the excited fury of the crowd and, during this shot, the newsreel camera begins to pan. The panning is completed exactly at the spot where the lens of this camera faces directly into Lang's camera shooting the scene. Subsequently, there is a cut to a close-up of Eddie's face. "Go ahead, take a good look, you monkeys," he yells. "Have a good time! Get a big kick out of it! It's fun to see an innocent man die, isn't it?" The connection established between the camera that is identified with the crowd's point of view and the camera that is identified with ours indicates that Eddie's words are thrown out as much to us as to the people in the scene.

A related device is employed in the strange episode in which Eddie and Joan meet in prison after his conviction. They are separated during their interview by a heavy iron door and are able to see each other only through a small window in the door. As they begin to talk, Lang crosscuts between their faces, each seen from the other's point of view through the window. Consequently, each face is framed within the screen frame by the rectangular borders of the window. The characters are backlit in a soft, luminescent manner so that they appear to each other and to the audience like glowing figures in a Hollywood close-up (see fig. 5). This, I believe, is the intended effect. We are given a sequence that consists of shots representing other shots: namely, close-ups focused on the faces of the stars. At this point in their relationship, Joan and Eddie are almost completely estranged. Seeing each other here, their emotional distance is so great that they fail, in any deeper sense, to see each other at all. And this estrangement, this sense of their strangeness to each other, communicates itself to us. Classical film theory has held that a close-up of the human face is the

Narration in Light

Fig. 1. Conclusion of the shot that reveals Eddie (Henry Fonda) in the background, with Monk on Eddie's bed in the foreground.

Fig. 2. The three "faces" of Eddie Taylor are displayed on the front pages of the *Daily Bulletin*.

Fig. 3. Joan (Sylvia Sidney) framed by the crossbars of the motel manager's window.

Fig. 4. Eddie on the courthouse steps after his trial. Note the motion-picture camera toward the middle of the frame.

26

Fig. 5. Eddie coldly stares out at Joan when she visits him in prison—another instance in which a principal is framed within the film frame.

Fig. 6. Joan and Eddie are reflected in the frog pond at their honeymoon inn.

paradigmatic way in which a subject's inner life may be cinematically exposed. But this series of metaphorical close-ups works on us in just the opposite way. Eddie's face is harsh, angry, withdrawn, and inscrutable. There is a crucial ambiguity about how Joan is to be understood, and this is perfectly rendered by the wild and pathetic countenance she presents in this scene. In conjuring up this film image of the film image itself, Lang warns the audience again that it may reveal much less than it appears to do.

Up to this point, I have concentrated on the central strategy of the film, the central ambiguity on which it turns. However, much of the film's emotional core resides in the manner in which this ambiguity is made to ramify across its whole duration. In particular, each of the three central characters appears as strangely doubled; psychologically doubled characters in the trap the film springs. Eddie, Joan, and Father Dolan can each be seen in at least two distinct ways.

The basic ambiguity of Eddie Taylor should now be obvious enough. On the one hand, he may be the essentially innocent victim of fate and injustice which, on the level of plot, he appears to be. On the other hand, he may be a fundamentally weak and emotionally dishonest man who will blatantly use the woman he loves when he is cornered in dangerous circumstances brought about by his own criminal actions. I do not believe that we are meant to doubt that, in some way, Eddie is in love with Joan. What is in question is the character and importance of that love. If he committed the robbery and massacre, then he lies to Joan about this. And he comes to her trusting, as he did before, that she will extricate him from the situation he has created. It is definitely established that a similar pattern of events has transpired before. Prior to his third conviction, we learn, Eddie and Joan had planned to marry, and then he robbed a bank with his gang. It is through Joan's intervention with the public defender (who is in love with her) that he is released, after only three years, from the sentence he was serving for this job. These are the circumstances that obtain when the film opens. In any case, for all we know, the situation, although even more grave, may be the same all over when Eddie arrives in the rain after the robbery we have seen.

One important fact about Eddie that is not obscure is his own proclivity to view himself as a product of forces he cannot master. In this, he is partially aligned with the outlook of those least sympathetic to him and in opposition to the views of Joan and Father Dolan. The warden tells Eddie that he has a reasonable chance to make good when he leaves prison. To this Eddie responds, "I will," and then in a more ominous tone, "if they let me." Evicted with his new bride from the Valley Inn, he buries his head in his hands and tells Joan, "I knew that something like this would happen," and characteristically she has to rescue him from despair. Later, after Eddie shoots Father Dolan and is wounded himself, he is met by Joan in an empty boxcar. "They made me a murderer," he says, and, in a despair that Joan once more rejects by taking action, he adds, "I'm through." Naturally, in terms of the standard interpretation of the film, these and similar remarks by him that express a pessimistic determinism can be accepted as correct. But, like so much else in the film, their status is doubtful. If Eddie is guilty of the robbery, his conception of himself in this regard seems more like a self-generated excuse for his frailty in the face of obstacles and temptation.

In sequence B, we noted the motif of Eddie's three faces emblemized in the newspaper photographs. Throughout the film, each of these faces intermittently appears. For instance, his first appearance in the film is given in a close-up of the "neutral" Eddie. We are invited to scrutinize this unrevealing face to find an answer to questions about his character which have already been raised. In the early scenes with Joan, the "good" Eddie seems definitively to emerge. This impression is so strong that one is put somewhat off balance by the coldness and viciousness with which the formerly "good" Eddie turns on Joan after his conviction. This face, the face of a "dangerous" Eddie, is not simply to be dismissed. In the end, the "real" Eddie Taylor still lies beyond our grasp.

Joan's case involves additional complications, and certain new patterns need to be established. The most obvious understanding of her is that she is simply the loving, loyal, and devoted wife who commits herself completely to the emotional bond with her husband. The loving devotion she displays is certainly complete, but there is also the clear-cut implication that there may be something blind, something a little out of control, about the extremity of her commitment.

Joan is one of the two characters who unequivocally "see goodness" in Eddie and, on the basis of this, put their faith in him. However, this *may* tell us much more about her than it does about him. In the film's opening scene, she walks in on the district attorney and the public defender, who are discussing the forthcoming case of a woman apparently faced with a serious charge. Joan cheerfully announces to them that the woman is innocent. "I believe her story," she declares, although there is no reason to suppose that she has the slightest grounds for her belief. Indeed, as she goes on to explain, her vision of the criminal justice system is that the district attorney should put people in jail in order for the public defender to get them out again—presumably just as he, at her instigation, has now arranged for Eddie's freedom.

This happy faith in Eddie and in the idealized machinery of social justice is repeated when Eddie turns to her for help after the robbery. First, there is a hint of "blind" faith in the way she believes the story that he tells her. Eddie provides her with only the flimsiest explanation for his dilemma and then demands from her a declaration of belief, which she immediately supplies, despite that what has happened seems a repetition of what had happened three years before. Second, her ideas about how the legal system ought to work come into play. When Eddie first arrives, he wants the car keys so that he can make an escape. She informs him that he ought to turn himself in so that his innocence will be established.

EDDIE: Are you crazy?
JOAN: Don't you see, its the only thing to do. Anything else will only make you look more guilty.

Eddie thinks, with some reason, that these tactics will result in the electric chair. But Joan responds that this is "looking at things all wrong." She stresses that, in asking what she does of him, she is asking him to believe in her and in her way of "looking at things." Of course, her way of looking at things does involve a dire misperception of the actual state of affairs, and Eddie is convicted and sentenced to death.

There is a repeated suggestion in the dialogue that we really do not understand what is going on inside Joan and even that there is something a little crazed about her. The district attorney asks the public defender what Joan thinks that she *sees in* Eddie and no reply is forthcoming. A little later, the public defender asks Father Dolan what it is that Joan *feels for* Eddie and again the question is not really answered. It is extremely striking how often the thought that Joan is crazy arises throughout the film. Joan's sister tells her that she is "crazy," crazy in particular to believe in Eddie. Joan responds cheerfully that she is "wacky" and that furthermore she "loves being wacky." When Eddie is released from prison, she tells him that he is looking at her "as if she were a maniac." And later they discuss her love for him as a matter of her being "all mixed up." Another character speaks of her having "lost her senses," and so on. The immediate context of these lines is often light, but other patterns in the film give them a more serious edge.

The famous scene in which Joan and Eddie see the frogs at their honeymoon inn is relevant to these issues. Eisner describes this as "one of the most lyrical love scenes in the cinema."[4] Lyrical it may be, but it is extraordinary not to notice that it is one of the most bizarre love scenes in all of cinema as well.

The sequence opens with an establishing shot of the newlyweds descending a stairway from the inn to a lovely, artificial pond outside. The second shot is from their point of view on the stairs as they look down upon the pond and spot a solitary frog sitting on a lily pad. This is answered immediately by what is roughly a point-of-view shot *up* from the pond looking back at the couple on the stairs. It is as if there were some, as yet undefined, perspective in that region that needs to be acknowledged. What that perspective might be becomes clearer as the sequence proceeds. When Joan and Eddie pause halfway down the stairs, he describes what is liable to happen to frogs in a world less idyllic than the present setting: they have their legs torn off by prankish little boys. At the end of this odd commentary, Joan cries, "There's another one!" and there is a cut to a close-up of a second frog that has appeared on the pond. Joan and Eddie creep up to the bank of the pond to take a more intimate look at the pair of frogs now on the scene, and their closer look elicits a somewhat disconcerting close-up of the two frogs, as it seems, staring back at them. The arrival of the frog couple makes it possible for the conversation to take a more suitably romantic turn. Lang cuts back to a medium long shot, from across the pond, of the human couple, and we hear:

EDDIE: Know something about frogs? If one dies, the other dies.
JOAN: That's funny. Why?
EDDIE: I don't know. Except they just can't live without each other.
JOAN (tenderly): Just like Romeo and Juliet.
EDDIE: No kidding, that's how they are.

They thus come to form a conception of the frogs as a tragic young couple in love, and the film responds visually to the sentimental anthropomorphism by showing Joan and Eddie's image reflected in the water upside down (see fig. 6). This is followed by a shot of one of the frogs jumping back into the water. Joan speculates that the frogs "see something in each other that no one else can see," and Eddie agrees that maybe this is so. However, the frogs' splash ends this section of their self-projecting reverie. As the lines above are delivered, the camera returns to the shot of their topsy-turvy reflection in the water, but this time their image is completely obliterated by the splash. In the ensuing series of more conventional shots, Eddie and Joan begin to talk about their reasons for loving each other. Eddie really dismisses the question by turning it back on Joan, and this is the exchange in which she confesses to having been "all mixed up" about him. Finally, as the musical sound track swells romantically, Eddie lifts Joan into his arms, kisses her, and carries her up the stairs back toward the inn. Suddenly, at the very conclusion of this shot of them, the music shifts; it is abruptly transformed into a cold and unearthly strain. For the last time, there is a cut back to a close-up of the two frogs (together again on a lily pad) while *they* watch inscrutably the ascent of their erstwhile companions. The sequence closes with a shot of Joan and Eddie's departure.

The key elements in this strange segment are the following. It is, of course, perfectly plain that Joan and Eddie are projecting their own vision of themselves onto the unresponsive, froggy subjects before their gaze. Especially telling, in this *and* the wider context of the film, is Joan's hypothesis that the frogs see in each other what no one else can see. A distinct hint of the possible distortions in the way in which Eddie and Joan see both the frogs and each other is provided by the shots of their inverted reflections, and the fragility of this vision is potentially implied by the destruction of their images when the one frog dives, by pure chance it seems, into the water. Still more disturbing, in an elusive way, is the continued impression that is developed—that somehow the frogs have their own unknowable point of view on the action before *them*. We ordinarily believe that a frog's visual perspective is almost wholly alien to us—an experience of things whose form and significance is beyond our grasp. Hence, when Joan and Eddie's perspectives are, as it were, set alongside those of the frogs, the juxtaposition imbues their seemingly more familiar romantic views with a sense of weirdness, opaqueness, and absolute isolation. Both the alien vision of the frogs and the sentimental human outlook seem equally in arbitrary relation to the dim facts of the actual world. Joan and Eddie certainly do see something in each other, but they do not seem to know just what that is. The disturbing mystery of that fact is highlighted in this nuanced and amazing scene.

This scene also figures in an important way later on. When Eddie is scheduled to die, it emerges that Joan has taken his story about the frogs with a grim earnestness. She asks Father Dolan to tell Eddie that she "remembers about the frogs," and this is her signal that she plans to act out the story by committing suicide. We see her preparing to take poison at the presumed moment of Eddie's execution, and she is saved only by his last-minute escape. There is a recurrent hysterical note to Sylvia Sidney's performance throughout the film that sustains the question about the balance of her thought and feeling, and, in this scene especially, the note is sounded with force and clarity.[5]

The examples already cited indicate that at the foundation of Joan's beliefs and motivations is a dominating vision of marriage and romantic love. The way she sees Eddie Taylor seems founded on the role that he is supposed to play within that vision. When they are first married, we are given a shot of a little shrine of flowers she has built around the marriage certificate. Everything connected with her love and marriage seems transmogrified for her by her vision. When they inspect a modest house that they plan to buy, she enthuses that "it is the swellest place [she] has ever seen." Later, she states that their baby is "the best baby that ever lived." After she and Eddie decide to buy the house, she gets on a bus by herself and begins to make out a budget for their future life. Ironically, as she systematically sets down her envisaged domestic schedule, she is seated beneath the bus company's schedule of arrivals and departures. As she enters each item in her plans, she raises her eyes and fixes them blissfully into space as though her vision were already enveloped in the future she is anticipating.

In the last third of the film, her initial faith in the broader social order has collapsed, and the fundamentals of her deepest emotional investments are laid bare. All of her desperate activity is devoted to the protection of her man and the maintenance of the family that they now form with their newborn son. When Joan goes to the Star Motel to deliver her child into the temporary care of her sister, we get our first close look at her behavior and demeanor since she and Eddie have gone on the run together. Throughout the scene, she seems dazed, disoriented, and in a state of excited confusion. She is so absorbed with the child and concerned about Eddie's fate that she is unable to make emotional contact with her sister or the public defender. When he asks her what the child is named, she looks startled and puzzled. "Why . . . we just call him 'Baby,' " she answers, as if the existence of *anything* outside the demands of their primitive family life were, at this point, irrelevant and unintelligible.

The audience that would see Eddie through her sympathetic eyes has reason to beware. She can be read as a character whose perception of the world is clouded by a larger vision, which she will cling to at any cost, until, quite literally, the end. Just before she dies in Eddie's arms, she opens her eyes, looks into his and says, "I'd do it *all* over again, darling." The sentiment is again conventionally romantic, but in the total setting of the film it has an unconventional ring, both pathetic and a little sinister.

Father Dolan is the other central character who sees redeeming virtue in Eddie. At the beginning of this chapter I quoted his remark that "we all see with the same pair of eyes, but we don't all see the same thing." I suggested that this might apply ironically to him, and, indeed, within the film's strategy of ambiguity, he is also a "doubled" character. The straight significance of the figure of the benevolent prison priest hardly needs to be detailed, but signposts that point to a different kind of significance do.

Father Dolan makes his claim in a discussion of Eddie with Warden Wheeler's wife shortly before Eddie's prison break. She has asserted that she believes that Eddie was "born bad," but the priest repudiates the thought: "Mrs. Wheeler, I can't agree with you. Every man, at birth, is endowed with the nobility of a king. The stain of the world soon makes him forget even his own birthright. Perhaps, that's why they invented death. Just to give us another chance at remembering who we were before we are born again." The warden cuts in on this: "Well, I hope, when Taylor dies tonight, he won't be born again. He's caused enough trouble in *this* world." Father Dolan's proposal that death is a rebirth, which provides a second chance to reclaim the lost birthright, is presumably a statement of how *he*, like the other speakers, sees the world through *his* pair of eyes. It has the consequence, as Eddie has noted much earlier, that Father Dolan sees some good, not just in him, but in everyone. But how are we meant to assess the validity of this view?

As one takes stock of the priest's appearances in the film, it is noticeable that he is presented as having a persistent penchant for getting things wrong or, at least, half right. When he is first introduced, he is the umpire in a prison baseball game and makes the call as one of the players slides home. It seems to be a bad call, or so the other prisoners think as they subject him to a loud booing. It also provides the occasion for a piece of sleight of hand. Among the crowd are two persons who are playing checkers surrounded by a small audience watching them. When this group turns its attention to Father Dolan's faulty umpiring, one of the players, unnoticed by anyone else, makes a cheating move—another minor lesson to us on the topic of audience attention. Father Dolan then leaves his umpire post to escort Eddie in his departure from the penitentiary. As they walk together, he stops and cheerily tosses out a new ball for the baseball game and then goes on to make what amounts to another call: he tells Eddie that he is a good man and predicts his success beyond prison walls. When, at the end of the scene, the public defender asks him what Joan feels for Eddie—love or pity?—the priest gives the sanguine reply that it is assuredly something more than pity. No doubt he is right about this, but by implying that it is a simple matter of love, he misses the key issues about Joan's feelings, which the public defender certainly wishes to raise.

Father Dolan reappears in the film when Eddie reappears in prison.

Narration in Light

Eddie persuades Joan to smuggle in a gun, and Father Dolan accompanies her as she attempts to bring it in. He tells her that when she sees Eddie for this final time, she will have to behave like "a good soldier." Unaware that she is bearing a pistol, he does not realize that she could not be a better "soldier" than she is already. The concealed gun trips a metal detector, and at this point the priest grasps the real situation; to protect Joan he tells the guards that the warning has been triggered by a penknife he carries, and then he leads her to his office and takes away the gun. Joan asks him if he will look after Eddie and he responds, "Yes, I will be with him to the end." This claim is also true, but unfortunately he cannot know that it is his end, not Eddie's, to which his words will properly refer.

Still later, after Father Dolan has delivered his homily about the goodness of man, the prison alarm signals Eddie's attempted escape. The priest goes with the warden to the scene of confrontation and, as they grapple with the danger, the news of Eddie's pardon arrives. Father Dolan offers to take the pardon down to Eddie and to convince him to give up his hostage. He argues that it is only he that Eddie will trust. As he makes his way through a dense night fog, which obscures both Eddie's sight and his, Eddie, mistrustful and panicky, shoots him through the heart.

This episode is followed by one that contains a curious commentary on his death. After the escape, Eddie arrives at a diner from which he will telephone Joan. Before he enters, however, we see a row of derelicts sitting at the counter discussing the recent events at the prison. The comments of the first two men merely establish that this is the topic of conversation. Out of the blue, the third man announces, "I knew a man once who shot his own dog right through the heart." The fourth man asks what this has to do with the murder of the priest, and the third man replies, "Oh, I don't know. It just came to mind." What he has done, of course, for the audience at least, is to hint at the alternative view of Father Dolan. His all-embracing, good-hearted faith in Eddie Taylor is placed on a par with the dumb, trusting belief of a dog for his master. The reward for such pure, unreflective trust has been a bullet in the heart. Just as Joan can be seen as significantly blinded by her romantic vision, so also Father Dolan may be similarly blinded by the Christian vision that guides his life.

It is this same religious vision that literally appears to Eddie in the moment before he dies. Joan has already died of a gunshot wound, and, as he holds her corpse in his arms, Eddie is also fatally wounded. Before his eyes, the light in the forest miraculously brightens, and he hears Father Dolan's voice calling his name. "You're free, Eddie," the voice calls out. "You're free. The gates are open." This seems a sign of the rebirth that the priest had spoken of before. The last shot of the film is from Eddie's point of view, and it represents the last sight Eddie has. Heavenly rays of light break through the tangle of trees and illuminate the muddy slope in front of him. An angelic (studio) choir floods the sound track with strains of beatific exaltation. It is this conclusion that so many critics have felt to constitute a saccharine betrayal of the whole tone of the film. This judgment, however, represents a failure to discern the development of those themes that have been traced throughout this chapter.

We have strong reason to suppose that Eddie's dying vision may be only the ultimate misperception that culminates the vast chain of misperceptions which has led him to his death. I have stressed again and again how much of the narrative development depends upon various failures of perception; how characters may appear deceptively to each other and to us. There is a compelling logic to the possibility that we are seeing in the end the last hope, the last pitiful illusion of a dying and defeated man. One characteristic that both Joan and Father Dolan share is that they, with their otherwise different outlooks, are continually expecting that an unhappy past and present will be redeemed by the realization of some promise for the future which they trust. One pattern that the film depicts (especially concerning their relation to Eddie) is the repeated disappointment of these beliefs. Thus, the film opens with an imposing shot of the Hall of Justice, an institution within which Joan is introduced and to which she exhibits a profound, optimistic allegiance. By the end of the film, the connotations of that first impressive view have been, even for her, totally shattered. But Father Dolan is the natural spokesman for a position that extends the promise of future redemption and release beyond the death of the individual. And this is the equally imposing view that the film's final shot portrays. If the initial invocation of the assurance of social justice has been shown to collapse, what possibly can guarantee the concluding assurances of a supernatural love and justice, which, beyond all experience, redeems the past at last?

Certainly there are sequences in the film that seem specifically designed to promote a certain skepticism about this matter. For example, in sequence A (Monk visits Eddie in his room), when Eddie stands looking out the window, he is listening to a revivalist band, which is singing the hymn "If you love your mother, you will meet her in the sky." Admittedly, this odd touch is pretty enigmatic, but it is striking that at the outset of the processes that end in his destruction, Eddie hears a particularly puerile version of the basic idea that Father Dolan will articulate later. Further, in the scenes that surround the one in which Joan and Eddie are shot, we are given information that potentially affects our reading of the concluding scene. As Joan and Eddie flee across the countryside, Eddie confesses that he is haunted by a vision of Father Dolan, that he always sees the priest's face before him. Therefore, the fact that he is pursued by this particular illusion has already been planted. Furthermore, it is partly another and fatal misperception that leads the couple into the police trap in which they are gunned down. While they are driving what ought to be the last stretch before the Canadian border and freedom, Joan notices with apprehension something that glistens in the woods ahead. We subsequently infer that what she has seen is a reflection, in the dawn light, from the police cars that lie in wait down the road. But Eddie reassures her, saying that the light is only the morning star, and she accepts the claim. The morning star is a traditional symbol of new hope and, as such, it aptly symbolizes their expectations as they draw nearer to the northern frontier. The hope, however, is again an illusion. Their death is what that distant light reflects. This pattern, then, cannot be ignored when Eddie's "vision" is considered. Like the film as a whole, the vision is strictly ambiguous. It may be genuine or it may be horribly false, but we surely cannot accept without question a heavenly promise of life after death in a film whose title is, after all, *You Only Live Once.*

I hope that this discussion cuts close to the film's central core by making salient its simultaneous depiction and demonstration of the fundamental ways in which people fail to grasp the underlying significance of what they see. *You Only Live Once* is structured by an interlocking network of characters and events, which expresses, with significant variations, the nature of this failure and its human consequences. The film systematically portrays a hierarchy of human relationships: relationships of love, marriage, and family; relationships to employers and spiritual advisors; relationships to the state and the social order. All of these relationships are represented as being perpetually threatened by the failure of people bound together by these ties to see and understand the others in a full and satisfactory manner. I have concentrated upon the more subtle elaboration of these issues with respect to the main characters, but, of course, some important points are presented quite directly. For Eddie Taylor, however he is ultimately to be judged, *is* caught within the prejudiced public picture of his character. And once he is so caught, the wheels of justice are geared up to crush him down regardless of what the actual facts might be. The self-satisfied, gourmandizing warden sees him as a fit subject for such a crushing and evinces more concern for his execution schedule than for any question of Eddie's welfare. The prison doctor saves Eddie from his self-inflicted wounds, but only so that the schedule can be maintained. Eddie is fired from the Ajax Trucking Company because, as an excon, he cannot be trusted to keep *its* schedule of deliveries. When it appears that he does not fit into the working order of things, the workings of that order fling him out definitively. Even when his exclusion is complete, the processes of public projection and fantasy do not end. An inflamed mob gathers to watch and revile him with uncontrolled fury. One short vignette indicates the way in which the small crimes of the "honest" populace are ascribed to him and Joan, and, in another, obvious victims of the depression imagine that the fleeing pair must be living high upon their outlaw gains. Lang's overall vision here seems one of despair. The sighted blind will find themselves a genuinely human situation only by chance if, indeed, they find themselves a place at all. This treatment of these aspects of the film is too brief, but I hope that enough has been said to indicate how they are to be located within the film's total framework.

Most striking is the way in which the film's audience is implicated within these concerns. The narration explores with elaborate care the ways in which film may enhance and complicate our difficulties of seeing the world accurately by leading perception and conviction astray with methods of its own. The film's power cannot be fully felt until the viewer recognizes that the dramas of misperception enacted on the screen have been replicated still one more time in his or her theater seat. Realizing this, we come to recognize that *You Only Live Once* has a kind of complexity and a kind of insight that we, unsurprisingly, are likely not to see.

Chapter 3

Coherence and Transparency in Classical Narrative Film

If the foregoing discussion of *You Only Live Once* is broadly correct, then the narration of that film is as systematically unreliable as the narration of a novel such as Ford Madox Ford's *The Good Soldier* or Albert Camus' *The Fall*. And yet, even after one has examined the film in some detail, it is unclear how its general strategy of unreliability is to be described. Obviously, there are many ways in which the narration *is* perfectly reliable— if this were not so the results would be incoherent. After all, the very existence of an intelligible course of fictional events in film depends at several levels upon our being able to take what is shown on the screen as a reliable indicator of what has and has not transpired within the story. This means that we must sort out a variety of factors that play a role in film narration. Moreover, unlike the novels mentioned above, *You Only Live Once* does not present itself as the product of a narrator portrayed by the film, and hence the source of its unreliability is not referable to the erratic and self-interested personality of such a figure. In a sense that is not easy to explicate, the source of unreliability in this film seems to be the very mechanism of classical film narration itself. In the terms introduced in chapter 1, certain assumptions that we normally make and are expected to make about how film narration constructs a narrative are shown within Lang's film to be unsound or, at a minimum, seriously problematic. However, the argument of that chapter left off precisely at the point of calling for a better understanding of possibilities such as these. So the relevant issues need to be rejoined. *You Only Live Once* is a classical narrative and it is more. The problem is to place its quite specific strategies and techniques within the wider spectrum of the norms of traditional film narration, norms whose letter it obeys and whose spirit it deeply violates. The payoff of such an inquiry will be more than a generalized review of this unusual film. It will yield a partial and provisional overview of a range of standard and not-so-standard modes of classical cinematic point of view.

Whatever may be the case in ordinary perceptual situations, we tend to assume, in watching a traditional film, that seeing is believing. And indeed, in a narrow but significant sense, *You Only Live Once* is in accordance with that assumption. That is, the film is *not* unreliable in virtue of presenting on-screen events and situations that, in the terms dictated by the fiction, did not or may not have occurred. The audience is entitled, throughout the film, to accept as given all of the information that it has been directly shown. Admittedly, there are issues, important for an account of point of view, about when the occurrences in a stretch of narrative have been shown "directly." Correlatively, there are also issues about the range and types of information an audience is entitled to accept as given within a particular film. I shall return to these topics later in this chapter, but they do not provide the route to an understanding of the specific unreliability of the narration in Lang's film.

Much of the complexity of *You Only Live Once* depends upon questions about the ways in which larger segments of narrative information fit or fail to fit together. The film plays upon some firmly rooted expectations about the completeness and overall consistency that the total narration should, it is thought, exemplify. The macrostructure of classical film narration does offer a guarantee of global reliability, a type of reliability that both presupposes and extends the shot-by-shot reliability of that which is directly shown. As in many other traditional forms of narration, there is a promise to depict a set of events, acts, and situations which will turn out to have an internal *explanatory coherence*. In the course of the narration, a host of central and subordinate questions of ground-level dramatic significance are raised and set to the fore. These typically include: Why did this event take place? Why and how was that action performed? Who performed that action? What consequences for the future will this event or action have? As a first approximation, classical narration, cinematic and other, offers the warrant that (1) the chief dramatically significant questions do have answers that the text will supply, and (2) the narrational material that gives these answers will be suitably, if perhaps not overtly, identified. For instance, it is a familiar fact that the most commonplace film narration may incorporate segments in which distorted and inaccurate perceptions, fantasies, and memories of one of the characters are registered on the screen. One elementary way in which the principle in (2) is observed is the practice of signaling the subjectivity of the implicated shot or shots to the viewer so that its explanatory value can be properly assessed. I shall discuss later some of the more interesting ways in which (2) can be made to operate.

First, however, there is a qualification to our initial statement of what is involved in this type of narrational coherence which is both important to keep in mind and hard to formulate adequately. Consider the recurrent device of mystery and suspense of withholding within a scene or series of scenes the character of certain weighty actions or the identity of their agent. Instances of such a device ought not to be counterexamples to a convention of explanatory coherence. In the completed story it will be shown to be exactly the point that these are temporary withholdings only, provisional obstructions that will receive their own dramatic rationale somewhere later in the narrative. The suspense of uncertainty has been elicited to provide the occasion for the large or small drama of revelation that it engenders, a moment of the action that itself resolves some strands of the narrative problematic. In the simplest cases, the hidden information is subsequently revealed, and the doubts of characters and audiences are terminated. These are not the cases that most threaten the unqualified conditions in (1) and (2). But, alternatively, there are cases in which the missing information never emerges at all (for example, Otto Preminger's *Anatomy of a Murder* and Michelangelo Antonioni's *Blow-up*), and yet even here the gist of the convention, correctly understood, remains intact. That is, the ultimate withholding is so placed in the narrative complex that it acquires a dramatic rationalization of its own. The audience is emotionally and/or epistemically aligned with a character who desires to solve the puzzle that the lack of information produces, but he or she is forced to discover that this is a desire that can never be satisfied. This culminating realization is precisely the dramatic resolution that his or her quest for an unveiling of the enigma receives. The audience and/or the character learn something about the character's personal limitations or about the limitations of the character's situation in an epistemically recalcitrant world. Hence, the requirement of explanatory coherence should be framed to say either that an answer will be supplied and marked as such, or the absence of an answer will be rationalized by other constituents of the narrative and narrational structures.

This background helps to define the nature and the depth of the systematic unreliability of *You Only Live Once*. The question of Eddie's guilt or innocence and the further questions about his character which it raises make up the pivot around which all of the dramatic action and reaction turns. And yet, despite conventional surface gestures of resolution, these questions, as we have seen, are never really answered.

Although the film gives the appearance of fulfilling the norms of a classical closed narrative, it does not do so. In particular, there is *no* internal rationalization of its explanatory indeterminacy of the kind mentioned above. Moreover, this is a film that implicitly acknowledges that its seeming closure is only superficial. In this sense, the narration exhibits itself as unreliable. The unreliability of *You Only Live Once* differs in this way from what might be deemed the unreliability of many modernist films such as Alain Resnais' *Last Year at Marienbad*, Ingmar Bergman's *Persona*, and Luis Buñuel's *Belle de Jour*. These films all explicitly fail to satisfy a wide variety of classical strictures on narrational form, and, as a result, it frequently seems impossible to know "what really is going on" in them. Actually, however, it is probably more accurate to say that the classical strictures do not have a definite application in this realm. In these instances, although standard aspects of a classical narrative apparatus are invoked, the apparatus is either shown to break down (*Persona*) or it is never really assembled in the first place (*Last Year at Marienbad*). Modernist films are not strictly to be counted as examples of unreliable narration, because the concept of "unreliability" presupposes in this context a notion of the truth about the fictional world of the film—truth about which the narration may then be unreliable—which the history of events in these films is deliberately too fractured to support.

It should be pointed out that in *You Only Live Once* the unreliability is not assigned to a fictional narrator who is somehow portrayed within the totality of the film's narrational systems. Seymour Chatman, in *Story and Discourse*,[1] is one author who recognizes a category of unreliable narration in film. He distinguishes two subtypes of the category, but both involve the presence of a *narrator* who is unreliable. In the first, a voice-over narrator, who may or may not be a character in the plot, describes and interprets, usually retrospectively, the action that is shown. However, the showing of the action proves that the commentary is false or misleading. Chatman cites a scene in Robert Bresson's *Diary of a Country Priest* as an example, but the voice-over narrator in Stanley Kubrick's *Barry Lyndon* illustrates the possibility more clearly and elaborately.[2] In Alfred Hitchcock's *Stage Fright*, Chatman's example of the second type, and also in Akira Kurosawa's *Rashomon*, stretches of the film are understood to be rendering visually the contents of a verbal account that one of the characters is delivering, an account that is partly or wholly untrue. Both of Chatman's types, however, rest upon the unreliability of a *secondary* verbal narration and do not envisage the possibility that the *primary* visual narration[3] of the film could be the source of unreliable representation. Indeed, in Chatman's types,

Narration in Light

the origin of unreliability is located by the film within its larger structures, and the ultimate truthfulness of the visual presentation is not only preserved but usually affirmed. By contrast, the subversive strategies of *You Only Live Once* strike at the core of the rhetoric of classical film narration. Even when the objectivity and autonomy of the film's world remain unscathed, as they do in this film, and even when the conventions of narrative coherence and closure are apparently maintained, as they are here, viewers are not protected from perceptual manipulation so extreme that they are likely to be mistaken about the dramatic questions that the narrative has posed.

And yet, if the secondary world depicted by a film is only a construction that the cinematic narration effects, how can that narration be unreliable about what it has itself constructed? In chapter 1, I made a brief first inventory of some of the epistemic assumptions that a film may embody and, within the category labeled "epistemic reliability," sketched the considerations that bear upon the present question. No film narrative is solely a function of what, in some narrow sense, is literally shown on the screen. It is determined also by an enormous and ill-defined collection of inferences, element-to-element connections, and identifying classifications that the audience makes and is supposed to make on the basis of the contents of the image track. If this narrow sense of the "literally shown" is drawn loosely enough, then it is probably true to say that everything that is literally shown to happen in *You Only Live Once* is an actual occurrence in the narrative chain. The unreliability in question—call this "rhetorical unreliability"—derives instead from the fact that the spectator is led to draw conclusions from parts and aspects of what he sees even though the screen equally displays information that, taken together with a general knowledge of the probabilities of the actual world, ought to serve to undercut some of the prompted inferences. In the terms of chapter 1, the film exploits what is here a sizable gap between the inferences that viewers actually tend to make and the inferences that, given all that is shown and not shown, it is justifiable to make. Several factors help to open up this gap: beliefs about the Hollywood formulae that are operative; moral and social convictions that are activated; and hopes for and expectations about the hero and heroine of such a film. These all help shape patterns of attention and inattention in the viewing of this film.

This last point suggests another observation to be made. In a lot of instructional writing about filmmaking, the would-be director or editor is advised to form a scene by choosing a series of shots which yields the best and clearest perspective on the action for the spectator. (We shall consider more closely a famous instance of such advice later in this chapter.) It can seem, on first reflection, that this kind of prescription is, although vague, obvious to the point of triviality, but our conclusions concerning *You Only Live Once* illustrate sharply a crucial ambiguity that all such instructions contain. There are at least two broad readings of the advice that is tendered. First, it might be that an edited sequence is to provide a series of views which corresponds to what an ideally mobile but humanly motivated spectator would *want and expect to see* by way of satisfying his or her interest in the action. But second, the claim could also be that the edited series of views should present what this spectator ideally *ought to see* if the questions that focus his or her interest are to be answered *correctly*. Obviously, the visual routes through a scene or a whole narrative which these two suggestions prescribe will not, in general, coincide. Furthermore, the point is not confined just to editing but to the whole collection of methods through which a narration is devised. The possibility of such a divergence partially defines a generalized strategy of unreliable cinematic narration. There is always a question about any film as to whether it is addressed more to what its audience wants and expects to see than to any real examination of the chief questions that it poses. Probably the most common complaint against the more "serious" Hollywood offerings—the social-problem films made by the major studios, for example—is that they announce an investigation and present a wish-fulfilling spectacle instead. The project of unreliable narration, the project that *You Only Live Once* paradigmatically carries out, is to embody this sort of discrepancy while, at the same time, discovering means to acknowledge and analyze the implications of that fact.

It is useful, I think, to reserve the concept of "unreliable (primary) narration" for films that involve the kind of systematic but unobtrusive critique of the superficial coherence of their narration that has been discussed in the last few paragraphs. But, if this terminology is adopted, it should be stressed that films may be classed as reliably narrated even when the material that establishes their internal coherence occurs *opaquely* in relation to the more obvious features of the narrative progression. Nothing in the idea of the explanatory coherence of a narrative requires that the material that is responsive to the dramatically significant questions of the film has to be deployed in a familiar or easily discernible way. It does not require that the standard mechanisms of narrative closure must be reliable indices of genuine resolution. On the contrary, the very real possibility that this will not be the case is something that any account of classical narrative and narrational forms in film should face.

Let us return to another theme of chapter 1. The thought that a film shows us the answer to, for example, "Why did Kane act as he did?" is the thought that a viewer can perceive *in* the film's action, as it is narrated, a reason for Kane's behavior. It is the thought that a certain explanatory connection can be made visible in the film. As long as fairly simple and well-understood action is in question, as long as a multitude of common-sense types of explanation is held in place, and as long as a variety of established cinematic conventions is presumed to be operative, then the thought may not seem a difficult one. (Although the simplicity and clarity of these easy cases are often the result of solutions to problems of film exposition which were, for earlier film makers, exceedingly hard.[4]) On the one hand, philosophers have suggested grounds for a general skepticism about our ability to perceive or to know through perception either causal connections or the psychological states of others. These forms of skepticism imply, among other things, broad restrictions upon our ordinary notions of what is visible to us. But, even if we set these philosophical doubts to one side,[5] it is itself a truism of commonsense that we are frequently unable, no matter how much has been observed, to make out the true causes of an event or the motivations that really prompted an agent to his act. So how, out of the diverse range of possibilities that arises, is *the* intended explanation of Kane's behavior to be foregrounded on the screen? Suppose, in addition, that a film maker wishes to establish new explanatory connections in the face of the audience's known disposition to see things otherwise. Or suppose that the film maker wishes to repudiate widespread practices of closure which yield, as it seems to him, only the false semblance of an honest explanation. Naturally, when these and similar suppositions obtain the foregrounding problem becomes enormously more difficult. Narrative and narration must together achieve a structure that appropriately weights the favored explanatory factors and traces out their relevance to the dramatic questions they purport to answer. But if it is a part of the point that these factors are not immediately open to perception, then the system of weighting and the network of tracing may themselves be less than obvious to first inspection. The factors are present but presented only opaquely.

John Ford's *The Searchers* provides an excellent example of a film whose narration is rhetorically reliable but whose underlying explanatory coherence is, in the indicated sense, opaque. Because a fine reading of this film already exists,[6] and because not all of the considerable complexity of this film is directly needed, I shall confine the following discussion, for the most part, to the outlines of its narrative and narrational dialectic.

However, I wish to say enough about this film's strategies to illustrate clearly the substance and point of the present notion of opacity; to show how and why a backgrounded coherence can, piece by piece, be formed in film. In a sense, the dialectic of *The Searchers* reverses that of *You Only Live Once*. In the former, the main dramatic issue can seem, at the level of plot, not to have been answered at all. The unresolved mystery of the central character appears only to be reinforced in the film's closing shots. However, in this instance, the somewhat cryptic nature of the ending is a signal to the spectator that he or she has failed to put together the right pieces of the puzzle, the pieces in terms of which the conclusion does have a deep explanatory significance.

The principal question of *The Searchers* is this: Why does Ethan hate the Indians with such a crazed and unbending intensity, and why is this hatred so strong that he regards Debby's marriage to Scar as a defilement sufficiently offensive to justify his continued attempt to kill her? The question certainly remains open when the final action of the film takes place, but that action seems to make matters even more obscure. First, Ethan, the character who most obsessively hates the Indians or, at least, whose hatred is most openly expressed, discovers amidst the confusion of the Rangers' raid that Scar has already been shot by Marty. Finding him dead, Ethan takes Scar's scalp—takes, in other words, precisely the revenge of the Comanches, whom he so much abhors. Second, immediately after this act, Ethan catches sight of Debby fleeing from the Comanche village and sets off in pursuit after her. However, instead of killing her as he had heretofore so plainly intended, he takes her up into his arms to return her to a place in the white community. Third, as the family to whom Debby is delivered passes into the protective enclosure of their home, Ethan stands awkwardly at the door for a moment as if he were mysteriously barred from entering himself, and then he turns away to leave forever.

Looked at in one way, these events could adequately resolve some hypothetical version of *The Searchers* that lacked the intense complication of Ethan's presence. Revenge against the Comanche tribe has been obtained, and there has been a restitution of the original order of family, community, and race. These ostensible satisfactions help to deflect attention from the fact that this final harmony has been purchased through a heightening of the enigma of Ethan and the meaning of his search. The key to the enigma lies in the recognition that Ethan's scalping of Scar, despite its apparent gratuitousness and despite the truncated manner in which it is portrayed, is for Ethan *the* act that culminates the search. The problem is to make out the pattern that it completes.

The pattern is woven, as Ethan himself rightly but too rigidly declares, out of the bonds of kinship. The first premise of the narrative is that he has returned, solitary and growing older, to claim his blood kinship to his brother and his brother's family, and to assert his wider natural kinship to the community of Texacan settlers to which the family belongs. Ethan means to abandon his rootless, wandering, and adventurous life as a warrior and, perhaps, an outlaw; to close a career that has been attached to causes and enterprises, such as the defense of the Confederacy, which are now long dead. He seems to believe that the simple fact of blood and racial kinship establishes his right to inclusion and acceptance despite the more blatant fact that he is shown throughout as a disruptive outsider who shares almost nothing of the values, attitudes, and customs of the people to whom he has come back. On this score, it emerges through small accumulations that Ethan's real kinship, his deep psychological and spiritual affinity, is to the Indians he passionately detests. There is a way in which Ethan's true brother is Scar, a point that is underscored, for example, by the symmetrical presentation of their immediate if hostile mutual understanding when at last they meet. This is the key to the true closure of the film.

Ethan is the one white man in the film, with the exception of his lunatic double, Mose Harper, who speaks the Comanche language and understands much of the tribe's social practices, religion, and psychology. He has a strangely intimate knowledge of the ways that they will act and respond, and he unselfconsciously employs some of their war stratagems himself. His dress and behavior incorporate elements derived from the Indians; for example, the odd sign language that accompanies a number of his verbal explanations. Most important, perhaps, is that the iron code of implacable revenge that informs the whole long search is a code he shares, not with the white settlers, who do not understand its stark inflexibility, but with the Comanches and specifically with Scar. (It is revealed late in the film that Scar's massacre of Ethan's family was part of a set policy of vengeance in retaliation for an earlier white attack on his tribe in which he lost two sons.) Much of this is presented directly but without much emphasis; the remainder is fixed by implication and ellipsis. Since Ethan's kinship to the Indians founds the explanatory coherence of the film, its unstressed and merely implied character founds the opacity of the narration.

Here is an example of the subtlety with which the relevant connections are suggested. When Marty and Ethan stop at a cavalry post to inspect a small group of white women who have been recaptured from the Comanches, they start to enter the room where the women, driven insane by their captivity, are being kept. As Ethan advances toward the excaptives, one of them, frightened by his entrance, screams hysterically and her scream freezes him in his place. He remains near the threshold of the room while Marty uncharacteristically comes forward and past him (the Comanches, we learn later, call him "He who follows") to take charge of their task. Later, as they leave, there is a dolly forward into a close-up of Ethan's puzzled and troubled scrutiny of the woman who screamed. Presumably, since she is not disturbed by Marty and the attending cavalrymen, it is to some quality in Ethan that she reacts. In view of the fears from which she suffers, she seems to have the delusory but nonetheless insightful impression of an Indian presence embodied somehow in Ethan.

The outward manifestation of that presence is most pronounced before and during the Rangers' attack on Scar's people. Ethan is the man who acts skillfully and silently as the Rangers' advance scout, studying the disposition of the Comanche village below the bluff. When he returns with a report of what he has seen, his explanation is again oddly accompanied by an abbreviated sign language that illustrates his words. Furthermore, when he signals the Rangers to prepare for attack, he employs a muffled bird cry, a cry that is particularly notable because it so distinctly echoes the signal that his brother heard shortly before the onset of the Comanche raid. Clearly, a set of circumstances and a point of view have been reversed: Ethan occupies the earlier position of the unknown Comanche scout who watched, with a perspective similar to the one Ethan (and the film viewer) now has, the trapped objects of incipient destruction. Ethan, so to speak, has become that scout. With this, the exposition of the explanatory premises is complete.

Marty fires the shot that kills Scar, the Rangers descend, and Ethan takes his revenge. Working through the patterns sketched above, Ethan's act of vengeance does have its own veiled sense and that, in turn, makes sense of the events that ensue. The explosive and distorted violence of the scalping uncovers for Ethan what his search and his hatred have been about. The significance of this resolution of his obsession is unequivocal, unavoidable, and unrepressible. No act could better display the unacknowledged psychic kinship that he bears to the Comanches and to their modes of thought and feeling. It lays bare to him the source of his constant and irremediable isolation from the white settlers who themselves instinctively hate and fear the "savage" Indians. It reveals to him the reason that there is no community to which he can belong. This moment of realization, marked by his dazed turmoil when he emerges from the tent where Scar lies dead, is partially an occasion of release. For he *is* at last released from the false objects he has projected for his anger, and he is therefore released to take Debby in his arms once more. Still, the realization that he makes entails that he cannot cross the threshold that Debby and the others cross. He knows himself to be caught between, and alien to, the two cultures that are internalized within him, these cultures that are tearing at each other in fierce and uncomprehending conflict.

The strategy of the narration of *The Searchers* is to define a set of variables which forms an explanatory counterstructure correcting for the superficial lack of closure in the plot. As developments in the narrative leave the objective of Ethan's search progressively more doubtful, the narration of scattered parts of the search show more and more about Ethan's true character and about the wider context of the Comanches' situation. These lines intersect in the resolution just described at the juncture where the film's explanatory coherence otherwise threatens to collapse.

One type of device that is used to single out the required variables is encountered in both *The Searchers* and *You Only Live Once*. In the latter film, sequences *A* (Monk and Eddie are shown to have met at Eddie's apartment) and *B* (the guilty verdict is announced in the newspapers) serve as *rhetorical figures of narrational instruction*. Roughly, sequence *A* demonstrates a possibility of deliberately inducing a visual misidentification and introduces a pairing of characters which will have a transformed recurrence, easy to miss, later in the film. Sequence *B* reminds the viewer of the constant potential availability of a larger viewpoint and the importance of this when hopes and fears are guiding perception. In such a scene or shot or limited series of shots the primary function of the local narration is to establish a stressed configuration of audio-visual elements which adumbrates features of the way in which the global narration is to be read. It provides instruction in the forms of perceptual intelligibility that the film proposes and flags the segments where the realization of these forms principally occurs.

The symmetrical opening and closing shots of *The Searchers* make up together a rhetorical figure of this kind. In the opening shot, the camera tracks *out* from inside a settler's home, through the doorway, and onto a view of the wilderness in which Ethan, for the first time, appears. The camera tracks in the opposite direction, in the film's closing shot, from the wilderness outside, back through a doorway, and *into* a similar but different home. When the camera attains the counterpart of its initial position in the film, it halts, and Ethan is seen retreating from the porch, and the door closes on his departure. This pair of shots picks out at least three image types that are played upon throughout the film.

The image of the door is repeated several times as such, but analogous shots through the entrance to a teepee or the arched mouth of a cave occur as variants. The image emblemizes the protection (which may be violated) of a home, a living space, a primitive mode of shelter. These are fixed as the basic sites of interpersonal community, whether relatively complex or rudimentary.

The image of the threshold is elaborated more generally as the image of a boundary, real and imagined, between inner and outer, private and public places, and between the warring communities of the film. (For example, a body of water is invariably shown as separating the Indians from the whites.)

The image of the self-enclosing circle (implied by the reversed symmetry of the pair of shots) represents both the fruitless circling of the five-year search and the larger symmetries of narrative and narration which shape the counterstructure of the film.

The Searchers constructs out of these and related image types a complicated system of rhyming and variation.[7] The variations usually signify an important opening up of perspective. The rhyming links disjoint episodes across the duration of the film. The deepest explanatory connections are imbedded in these links. But they will be perceived as explanatory only if they are set against, and understood in terms of, the widest prospect that the film, in the end, divulges.

The dramatically significant questions that a narrative fiction film can raise about its characters are effectively unlimited. The topics of these questions can range from matters of individual psychology to the determinants and consequences of one's socioeconomic position to one's problematic relationship to the Divine. Moreover, there is an extensively diverse range of variables pertaining to sight and sound which can be structured into a focused overview of whatever issues have been broached. This is one of the reasons that something like a rhetorical figure of narrational instruction is found so commonly in complex, interesting films. Some paradigm is needed to ostend those objects, properties, and relations, out of all that appear on screen, that are to have a weighted explanatory function in the film.

As important as these issues of explanatory coherence and opaqueness are, they plainly presuppose the existence of answers to some equally important issues about our more immediate apprehension of the contents of

Narration in Light

a slice of narration. The overall explanatory coherence of a film can hardly be in question unless the smaller stretches of narrative information which are meant to cohere with one another have themselves been rendered perspicuously. But then, problems about the nature of perspicuous narrative exposition in film have seemed, even in their most general aspects, both elusive and perplexing.

In theoretical discussions of classical narrative film, these problems have tended to be raised most often in connection with editing. For, of course, it was very quickly realized that perspicuous exposition (in almost any possible sense) of narrative action has to rely upon the possibility of cutting from shot to shot. At the same time, the transitions between shots, in various forms and styles, constituted discontinuous breaks from one viewpoint on the action to another. As such, these transitions seemed potentially to be unperspicuous interruptions in the viewer's access to the progress of the dramatic events. They were interruptions in viewing unprecedented by anything in normal perceptual experience. How then could a film spectator tolerate and comprehend these abrupt and unnatural intercessions? What are the limits within which the spectator still has an intelligible and satisfying shift in viewpoint? These questions, as we shall see, posed and still pose some searching puzzles about how viewers orient themselves perceptually to complex narrational transactions projected upon the screen. Furthermore, these puzzles include some matters that belong properly to the topic of point of view.

To gain a feeling for some of the relevant concerns, it is useful to examine a famous passage in Karel Reisz's well-known book on the techniques of classical editing.[8] This passage generates, in a certain distinctive form, many of the problems we want before us now. It is a brief elaboration of the proposal that the cuts within a scene should correspond to the natural shifts of attention of a hypothetical, interested spectator who observes, on the spot, the action that we see depicted on the screen. This view, with theoretical roots at least as early as V. I. Pudovkin, was one that, at the time Reisz was writing, had many influential adherents. Indeed, Reisz, like many others, saw the proposal as offering an initally attractive explanation of, and rationale for, the style of "invisible" editing predominantly exemplified in the typical Hollywood film of the period, a style that is extensively expounded in his book. The thesis is that an audience does not consciously notice the fragmentation that is enforced by judiciously invisible editing, because given that their sense of the integrity of space and time is maintained, each new shot supplies the visual information demanded and schematically anticipated by "the normal mental mechanism by which we alter our attention from object to object in real life."[9] Nevertheless, despite the initial attraction of the idea, Reisz rejects it for a simple and decisive reason. He notes, in effect, that many of the instantaneous spatial transitions produced by elementary and standard patterns of editing patently do not correspond to anything that a single fixed or limitedly mobile observer could achieve.

In response to this difficulty, Reisz goes on to suggest the following:

> Instead, the director's aim is to give an ideal picture of the scene, in each case placing his camera in such a position that it records most effectively the particular piece of action or detail which is dramatically significant. He becomes, as it were, a ubiquitous observer, giving the audience at each moment of the action the best possible viewpoint. He selects the images which he considers most telling, irrespective of the fact that no single individual could view a scene in this way in real life.[10]

Although these remarks never receive much clarification, it seems that the model for intrascene editing is the normal operation of engaged attention as it would occur in a "ubiquitous" and "ideal" observer freed from the grosser limitations of actual embodied perception. In this way, the revised account purports to explain the invisibility of classical editing while allowing that cinematic narration constitutes an articulated extension of ordinary perceptual experience.

This explanation has been widely criticized, and a host of questions comes to mind. However, I am more interested in the ways in which this formulation, on a particular reading of it, offers a rather good picture (in something like Wittgenstein's sense) of some main features of the way in which we experience traditional narrative film. It provides a partial but useful description of the viewer's characteristic impression of what it is to see such a film. But, as noted, certain matters need to be elucidated.

For example, is it a part of the idea that members of the audience are supposed to see the series of shots as representing the visual field of Reisz's observer, so that they identify their perception and attention with that of this fictional observer? In other words, do all such films have, in this sense, a visual narrator who mediates the action in a manner that is standardly effaced? Certainly, something like this is a cliché of a lot of writing on film: the camera is or has an eye, and the screen image is understood as its phenomenological product. Reisz's use of the "observer" metaphor is too sketchy to answer even this query with certainty,[11] but an emphasis on certain phrases in the quoted passage suggests a different interpretation. It is the film maker, and not the viewer, who is asked to regard himself as the ideal observer, and his job is to establish "at each moment a *viewpoint" for* the audience. They are to be situated at a fictional point from which a segment of the secondary world of the film is *directly* viewed. Reisz seems to envisage the audience as viewing—that is, sharing the same view—of a scene that is paradoxically felt to be both right in front of them and yet existing in its own impenetrable system of space.

Whatever Reisz's own conception here, the issue is of some importance. It will help us to define a new type of "reliability" that the classical film standardly presupposes. The screen and the imagery that fills it are, as a rule, reflexively represented, in the course of a film or a segment thereof, as having one or another epistemic status. For instance, it is a possible "first-person" mode of representing the contents of the screen to render them more or less explicitly as making up the perceptual field of some observer, human or idealized as the case may be. Or, in related modes of subjectivization, the screen imagery may be represented as the visual effects of a mechanism of dreaming, hallucination, visual memory, and so on. Alternatively, in certain experimental films, the screen is represented, in a reductive manner, as being nothing more than a physical surface that captures the moving shapes of projected light. The "illusions" of photographic depiction are forsworn. Now, it is certainly true that classical film has frequently adopted some of these possibilities. The latter often occurs in the fades, dissolves, and so forth that serve as punctuation in the transitions between scenes. More notably, the modes of subjectivized narration are frequently employed. But this device almost always occurs in segments that have been clearly set off as subjective, and these segments are placed in the wider context of the total film, which is predominantly "objective."

However, it is this "objectivity" in the visual depiction of narrative fiction that we want to understand more clearly. What do we take to be objective about the way in which the screen and its images present the narrative facts? The answer, I believe, is given by a famous analogy. In the objective mode that is primary for classical narration the screen is experienced as a rectangular window or opening that faces onto the movie's secondary world. It is to be, in a new sense, a "picture window" set before locales within that world. The screen is meant to be taken as an almost perfect transparency between the audience and the fictional objects and events they see. The audience is encouraged in every way to accept the make-believe impression of looking into a world that, no matter how stylized and fantastic it might be, exists objectively and autonomously beyond the frame. And it is to be make-believe for them that they see the items of the world directly.[12]

This (standard) mode of viewing films involves something like a suspension of disbelief. It involves, specifically, a suspension of our awareness of, or attention to, the fact that what we are literally looking at is a luminous screen and that what we are, in the first instance, seeing is a series of light-induced images upon this screen. It is a central function of conventional film narration to divert the spectator's active consciousness from the fact that the things seen in the secondary world are seen only *in virtue of* the more immediate perception of the film images themselves. Any disposition to attend to the images qua images is to be suppressed. Analogously, when viewers become immersed in a film story they are distracted from—and indeed permit themselves to be distracted from—their continuing recognition that they are watching a well-known actor portraying a certain character. Their immediate experience is simply *of* the character. Equally, then, their experience is to be for them as though they were seeing the denizens of the fictional world *through* the surface of the screen in much the same way as they really see regions of the actual world through a pair of spectacles or a telescope or through a large and magnifying pane of glass.[13] A fictional world of the cinema is essentially a visible world and that which is presented in the imagery is meant to be the immediate, intersubjective visual appearance of the fictional objects and events as their appearance is manifested to a position within the world's aparently real space. Therefore, these appearances are not construed as the private modifications of an intervening perceptual consciousness. This, then, rules out one role that Reisz's ideal observer might be thought to play.

I am contending that the audience members at a classical film take up a kind of perceptual stance or set in relation to their own viewing of the film, a perceptual set that is provoked and facilitated by the look, style, and format of the narration. In a similar fashion, a range of traditional styles of literary narration aims at engendering in each individual reader the make-believe impression that he or she is being addressed personally by the voice that tells the tale. In both cases, the text does what it can to provide the grounding for the requisite impression, but the audience must actively, although usually unconsciously, play a little game of standing ready to adopt the impression as its own.

Of course, the screen window is remarkably—to use Reisz's word—ubiquitous. The views that are delivered to the audience change frequently, abruptly, and discontinuously, and the changes are felt to be guided by a mind other than their own. A familiar passage by Jean Mitry attempts to describe what this more complex impression is like for the spectator.

> Thanks to the mobility of the camera, to the multiplicity of shots, I am everywhere at once . . . I know that I am in the movie theater, but I feel that I am in the world offered to my gaze, a world that I experience "physically" while identifying myself with one or another of the characters in the drama—with all of them, alternatively. This finally means that at the movies I am both in this action and outside it, in this space and outside this space. Having the gift of ubiquity, I am everywhere and nowhere.[14]

In a related context, André Bazin speaks of the Myth of Total Cinema,[15] but the myth of spectatorship for the classical cinema is perhaps better represented as an elaboration of the older myth of the time machine.

Like Bazin's, that myth expresses a desire to be perceptually present to events of the past, the future, or even the merely possible in such a way that one sees them, so to speak, for oneself. One wants to see these normally irreversible occurrences without the interposition of some human depiction of them and so to be freed from the interpretative assumptions and intentions that all depiction necessarily entails. Thus, the film viewer's impression of his or her epistemic situation in the theater is something such as this. The cinematic time machine is a ghostly one in that it is both invisible and massless in relation to anything it does not contain. The spectator sits in the closed capsule before its large and magnifying window and observes a slice of the secondary world in which the machine is situated. Directed by a prescient intelligence that operates the machine for the passive viewer, the capsule has the capacity to change its position and spatial orientation instantaneously so that its window opens onto a series of wider and narrower prospects, which jointly delineate the action outside. Being massless, the capsule can even occupy the position of a person who is in the world outside and thereby present the precise visual perspective of that person at that time. Taken together, the series of views yields a clear, detailed, and effective narration of the events and processes under scrutiny. This is insured by the work of the intelligence that regulates the machine. (And its activity, not the spectator's, is what Reisz's ideal observer properly undertakes.) But, to repeat, in the present myth the spectator does his own seeing and is aided in this by the analyzing intelligence *only* through the power it has to control the placement of the machine and its magic window. Partially adapting Mitry's formulation, we can say that the spectator *knows* that he is in the theater, but *it is make-believe for him* that he is watching from within the space of the story. Bazin, with his ideas about "photographic realism," sometimes makes it sound as though the Myth of Total Cinema defined an end that actual films can more and less approximately fulfill. This I doubt. In any case, the similar myth of the ghostly time machine is intended as a hypothetical description of a psychological drama of film viewing which audiences enact in responding to the flow of the projected imagery before them.

The success of this adjacent drama by means of which the film spectator assumes a characteristic epistemic position in front of the drama he has come to see depends upon a multitude of factors, most of which are relatively obscure. First, Bazin is probably correct at least in the thought that it is a part of our standard, immediate, and unreflective reaction to raw photographs, still and in motion, to see them in a manner that takes as literal the notion that the photographed object, or a perspectivized slice of its appearance at a time, is captured, fixed, and reexhibited within the infinitesimal crystal sheet of the printed or projected photographic surface. In this regard, we would be more than we suppose like the natives who are said to be frightened by photographs of themselves because they believe that their souls have been captured by the processes of photography.[16] For us, if the hypothesis is right, it is not "souls" but "pure visual appearances" that the camera assimilates and preserves. Given the truth of such a thesis about the *psychology* of our perception of photography, it is not hard to see how this could serve as a basis from which the more complex analogy of screen and movable window might be evolved.

Second, and less controversially, techniques and practices of editing have gradually been developed—the development substantially completed by the end of the silent era—which permit an analytical fracturing of the action that at the same time sustains the viewer's natural sense of spatial and temporal relationships. Closely bound up with this is that in a film world as improbable as Oz or Wonderland happenings that in reality would be causally impossible take place in a network of quite mundane causal processes. Most of what we all believe about the more commonplace inhabitants and operations of the actual world is always shown to have been sufficiently held constant that our basic categories and schemata of objective reference and predication have untroubled application.

Third, the projected screen image contains a vast wealth of diversified visual information within a two-dimensional surface that is apparently "unworked" and relatively untextured. Viewing a comparably realistic painting of the same scene, a viewer's attention tends to oscillate between an inspection of the items pictured and a scrutiny of the handling of the paint upon the canvas. The painting's *facture* is the ever-present mark of the agency that produced it. In the standard photographic image, the visible *facture* is either eliminated or reduced to a minimum. The items photographed appear transparently.

Finally, the famous "invisibility" of classical editing, the self-effacement of the narrating intelligence, reinforces an audience's impression of looking into a solid and autonomous world. It alleviates a temptation to take the film to be (what it is) the segmented construction of an engineer of the visible at work or play. The strategies of this effacement have, in Nick Browne's words," the effect of making the story seem to tell itself by reference not to an outside author but to a continuously visible narrative authority."[17] The problem, at the level of narrative, is to construct a path of activity such that, at each stage as it will be shot, the action seems to call for attention to certain features of the partially anticipated next stage. The visual narration should therefore give the appearance of following out the path. The sequence of plot events sets up a kind of local interest, which an unimplicated observer could be expected to have in its emerging history, and the narration seems then to be merely responding to the product of forces determined jointly by that interest and the unfolding activity upon which it focuses. We have here one partial interpretation of the meaning of Reisz's appeal to "the normal mechanism of attention" within the fuller context of his model. But this is a topic that we shall reconsider later.

My point is not that the opposite of effacement—that is, *self-consciousness* or *self-assertion* of the processes of narration—violates the objectivity of the film world by inducing a subjectivized reading of the visual narration. It is true that there is some disposition to forge this connection and, in some instances (for example, Josef von Sternberg's later works[18]), it may be the right conclusion to draw. However, the link is hardly necessary, and a firm distinction should be made between these kinds of narrational mode. In the deconstructions in Jean-Luc Godard films such as *Two or Three Things I Know about Her* or *Tout Va Bien*, the explicit lesson-giving style of the visual discourse asserts its status as a photographic artifact and positively discourages the thought that the narration is subjective. Strongly marked self-assertion is likely to highlight the use of objects and events in the secondary world as a means of communication, a means through which the audience has been addressed a commentary that the self-assertive figures announce. The salient rhetoric disrupts the spectator's impression that the semantically charged objects and events exist with full autonomy within their supposedly enclosed world.

Let us use the phrase "the transparency of the film image" to refer to this network of mutually implicating representations in virtue of which it becomes make-believe for a viewer that he or she sees through the screen into the fictional world. This is in broad accord with the use of the phrase in current film theory. The basic classical mode that the phrase describes involves a cluster of perceptual, cognitive, and affective responses on the part of the film viewer who subconsciously adopts it. However, there is a specific but quite general implication of transparency for cinematic narration which ought to be noted; that is, the transparent mode ensures a minimal but absolutely fundamental *reliability* in the transmission of visual information about the relevant fictional world. It is a foundational convention of novels told by the traditional "omniscient" narrator that the narrator's fictionally performed act of stating that p makes it the case that in the world of the novel it is a fact that p. Naturally, this constitutive convention has to be qualified by general principles of overall consistency and coherence, and it operates most definitively in the direct telling of a story line and less definitively, for example, in passages of moral judgment.[19] Various significant weakenings of the convention still allow the construction of a coherent novelistic world, but this one facilitates the most straightforward and least ambiguous construction. Analogously, it is an equally central convention, built into the very nature of transparent film narration, that the following obtains: if things are shown directly to have property ϕ (and the showing is not set off as a "quotation" from some character's private experience), then those things, as seen from the camera's position in the fictional world, do objectively have a ϕ-appearance.[20] Of course, this principle has to be understood as constrained by general technical limitations of the tools and materials out of which the film is physically made. If the background in a shot in a thirties film with sharp foreground focus looks dim and blurry, this does not imply that the middle distance in that episode looks or would look dim and blurry to perceivers of that secondary world. We discount for this kind of unavoidable by-product of the film-making apparatus. And yet, the issue is tricky. When the heroine of the same film is presented in luminous soft-focus there is an inclination to suppose that this represents the tender and brilliant aura that surrounds her in the fictional circumstances. But here we are dealing with a technical effect that *has* been selected, one that could have been avoided by a change of light and lens. The most obvious instance of the required qualification is the fact that because a film was shot in black and white does not mean that everything in the depicted world occurs in shades of black, white, and gray. Systematic allowance for the immediate consequences of this choice of film stock is made, taking the black-gray-white range as standing in, somewhat indeterminately, for the normal range of colors in normal experience. In addition, the present convention leaves it open that things may very well be shown which are to be seen as ambiguous or simply obscure. They may be shown in a fashion that is radically misleading about the objects in question if and when they are viewed from other secondary-world perspectives. Nevertheless, it is a given that *these objects* depicted *now* are being presented as they objectively look from the indicated time and place within *this world*. By contrast, when, to take one alternative, the narration is subjective, an actual or potential question always exists about whether an item's appearing ϕ is not just a mental artifact, an imposition of the apprehending consciousness. Transparent narration necessarily forecloses questions of this and kindred kinds and proceeds from this informational base to other questions about the elaboration of narrative. The visual surface of the fictional world is guaranteed to be, in this major respect, secure.

Transparency of the image is something at which classical film narration characteristically aims, and it is an effect that, on the whole, characteristically succeeds. At the same time, this complex and basic effect is constantly threatened by other ends that classical narration is concurrently meant to serve. Furthermore, the same can be said about the objective of explanatory coherence. Both of these bedrock properties of most Hollywood films reside in a state of some tension with other formative properties of classical narrational style and strategy. For example, the transparent narrational modes are meant to portray a fictional world that is to be "a free-standing entity which a spectator, irrelevant to its construction, could only look on from outside."[21] And yet, this attempted portrayal of an autonomous objectivity can be damaged or eclipsed by an audience's conscious or subliminal awareness that the shots that bring the fictional world into existence are consistently being *addressed* to them as "ideal" or, at least, especially perspicuous visual communication. Characters X and Y are situated in such-and-such a relation to each other and to the camera in shot Z precisely because the resulting configuration is meant to make clear to the viewer the nature of their psychological interaction. Their being positioned as they are is dimly felt by the audience to be an incident that has been *designed* for their inspection. The standard resolution of this tension is, as was stated at the outset of this chapter, to mask the more overt signs of the audience-directed communicative intensions without sacrificing the clarity of whatever content is to be conveyed. Much of Reisz's book on editing and many comparable discussions from the same period are devoted to working out the strategies of this resolution—to enunciate the bases of a suitably "invisible" narration.

In chapter 4, we shall examine Alfred Hitchcock's *North by Northwest*. One sort of fascination that this beautifully crafted film exerts is the fashion in which it carefully acknowledges the tension I have just described and makes that tension into a provocatively productive key motif. More specifically, although the filmic narration of *North by Northwest* accedes to the usual conventions of transparency, it simultaneously succeeds, when suitable attention has been paid, in undermining our sense of that transparency. The film replicates our transparent position before its fictional world in the epistemic position, within that world, of the bedeviled protagonist. Once this identification is discerned, it becomes impossible to be aware of the character's delusions without reflecting upon the curious mental set that we, as audience, share with him. I described a class of self-conscious or self-assertive narrational modes and cited some of Godard's films as prime examples. *North by Northwest* is irretrievably a borderline example with respect to such a category. I shall argue that the film embeds many of the requisite self-conscious and self-reflexive concerns without ever breaking its pace to assert those concerns overtly.

Just as transparency is often fragile, the condition of explanatory coherence often amounts to little more than a minimal standard of expository connectedness. It is notorious that in many Hollywood films an explanatory nexus that is postulated to end some plot conflict is neither probable nor internally plausible. Characteristically, it *is* demanded that there be some explanation of why X suffered complete humiliation at the hands of worthless Y, but it is open for X's motivations to be ones that would never animate a sane creature from the planet Earth. But again, it is partly this very slackness of the coherence condition which creates the narrative space within which *The Searchers* can incorporate an opaque level of explanation that does not have to be, improbably and self-defeatingly, at the surface of the plot.

Something like this occurs in many of the best American films, and several illustrations will be developed in later chapters. The utter implausibility of the narrative resolution is a signal that the genuine factors of resolution are to be discovered at less apparent levels or that a certain kind of issue (for example, the psychology of the characters, naturalistically conceived) is not really the dimension with which the film is concerned. This point should not be overstated. Most implausible Hollywood stories are no more than that: the implausibility arises either out of silliness, carelessness, or a desire to keep an escapist audience content. But lax standards in the area of familiar plausibilities help to make possible filmic narration that utilizes the extra degrees of explanatory freedom that result for ends that are more rigorous and of more interest to film theory.

It has become common to draw up a list of broad narrational and narrative properties that are supposed to single out the distinctive forms of classical narrative film. Such a list is likely to include many of the properties examined or mentioned in this chapter; for example, reliability, transparency, invisibility of editing, and explanatory closure. I have granted throughout that these terms can, subject to explication, denote important features that are shared by all or most of the films in question. Still, there is a danger in these lists and also in the ways that they are so often used. Most obviously, there is the danger that, when the terms are employed with only the vaguest meanings, they simultaneously gesture indistinctly at cinematic norms that are of real consequence, and yet, because they impose conditions that are, in general, too strong, they imply much that is false about some of the relevant films.

Furthermore, the lists are commonly offered as if they self-evidently constituted a blueprint for the simple and mechanical operation of "*the* Hollywood narrative product.*" They are supposed to define a kind of filmic storytelling which is thought to be immediately recognizable, obvious in the intentions it satisfies and the functions it serves, and is, therefore, dismissible as an object for serious, nontherapeutic critical contemplation.[22] This is like arguing that, because the art of the fugue is strenuously rule-governed, its individual instances are basically trivial variants of one another and their (putatively negligible) merits are determined, on the whole, at the level of shared form. Admittedly, in the case of film, the job of making better-founded discriminations among individual instances demands a willingness to rethink, sometimes in a fairly radical way, our ideas of what there might be to see in a film or, more specifically, in a film belonging to one or another apparently well-worn genre. Rethinking this fundamental problem makes the question of cinematic point of view a topic that deserves a high priority in any evolving theory of film.

Chapter 4

Alfred Hitchcock's
North by Northwest

The fact is I practice absurdity quite religiously.
Alfred Hitchcock

When Roger Thornhill is abducted from the Oak Bar at the Plaza Hotel, he is planning an evening at the theater. Instead, he finds himself deposited by a pair of menacing thugs in the library of a Glen Cove mansion. Phillip Vandamm enters the room, briefly inspects his frustrated captive, and sweeps shut the floor-to-ceiling curtains that border a large picture window. And then the following exchange takes place.

VANDAMM: Games? . . . Must we?
THORNHILL: Not that I mind a slight case of abduction now and then, but I do have tickets to the theater tonight and it was a show I was looking forward to and I get, well, kind of *unreasonable* about things like that.
VANDAMM: With such expert play-acting, you make this very room a theater.[1]

Vandamm's metaphor is given visual emphasis. Thornhill's agitated protests are framed in a medium shot as he stands positioned exactly before those closed curtains—an appropriate backdrop for a piece of histrionics (see fig. 7).

Here we have the type of characteristic aesthetic reversal which recurs throughout *North by Northwest*. In this instance, it is Thornhill's relation to dramatic representation that has been reversed. Deflected from his intended position as a spectator at a play, he winds up featured in a delirious production that he cannot comprehend. The people he encounters are each playing some designated role or do so until that role is dropped only to be taken up again with a new dramatic wrinkle added. For instance, it is not long after the episode described above that he returns to the Glen Cove mansion to establish the reality of the earlier, extraordinary events and is made to recognize the potency of theatrical expertise. When the ersatz Mrs. Townsend puts on an act that reduces his tale of abduction to shreds, he exclaims in appreciative dismay, "What a performance!" But this is only the first step in his education in these matters. Every shift of setting will reveal an occasion for some novel trick of *mise en scène*. In the world of *North by Northwest*, the hawk is likely to appear as a handsaw or vice versa, and it is notably the ostensible villain, Vandamm, who best articulates the Humpty Dumpty aesthetics of this Hitchcockian world.

Of course, the question of playing a role becomes the crucial issue Thornhill faces. In his well-known discussion of the film, Robin Wood has clearly stated a number of the basic premises.[2] At the outset of the film, Roger Thornhill is presented as a kind of moral and emotional "nothing." The application of this term to Thornhill is his own invention. Meeting Eve Kendall on the Twentieth-Century Limited, he reveals that his initials ("his trademark") are "R.O.T." and that "O" stands for "nothing." He is, on one reading of the pun, "Roger Nothing Thornhill." And the name fits. Cooly cynical and manipulative in connection with matters small and large (from taxi cabs to his occupation), he is introduced as wholly incapable of a serious and sustained human relationship. Thornhill has two failed marriages in his past, and his continuing tie to his mother can hardly count as serious in the relevant sense. Indeed, Thornhill is initially sketched in less as a distinct personality and more as the embodiment of a range of familiar fifties stereotypes. He is the cheerful product of Momism, the Madison Avenue advertising executive who drinks too much, and the Man in the Gray Flannel Suit. In contrast, George Kaplan is a daring and inventive spy. He also happens to be a total fiction—a non-existent being created by the Americans as a false lead for Vandamm and his group. Hence, we should note that the film's absurdist plot rests on a paradox. One "nothing," Thornhill, is accidentally mistaken for another, Kaplan, and it is from this confusion of ciphers that all the dizzy consequences flow. Moreover, a second pradox is built upon the first. As Wood emphasizes, Thornhill, by the end of the film, has moved from "nothingness" to a kind of personhood: he gains a capacity for real emotional commitment (to Eve) and, based on this, the capacity for effective independent moral action. But the condition for this achievement has been that he learn to play the Kaplan role and thereby fill the fictional space into which he inadvertently has fallen. It is wholly appropriate that Hamlet's famous line, from which the film's title seems derived, occurs when Rosencrantz and Guildenstern announce the arrival of the players.

Although I think that Wood is right to call attention to and to delineate the character of Thornhill's moral development, I also believe that he is mistaken in identifying this aspect of the film as constituting its center of gravity. Charming and resourceful as Thornhill may be, Hitchcock and Lehman never really attempt to give him a psychological complexity rich and resonant enough to make his personal transfiguration a matter of great moment or serious concern. Indeed, even at the film's cliff-hanging climax when Thornhill definitively puts behind him his vacuous past by proposing marriage to Eve and when, in this way, the question of the new man he has become is rather explicitly broached, the whole topic seems deliberately underplayed in a casual, if not tongue-in-cheek, manner. (For instance, at this juncture Thornhill tells Eve, and reminds the audience, "A funny thing happened to me on the way to the theater.") It seems that what falls under the heading of "Thornhill's Progress" should be viewed chiefly as a framework upon which more substantive and interesting structures are erected. I have already hinted at the structures I take to be in question. They are the paradoxes of representation, the devious conflations of appearance with reality, and the criss-crossing of identities, and it is these matters that need to be brought to the fore. These are the strands that more deeply and more subtly organize the film's conception. What I shall argue for may be provisionally stated thus: *North by Northwest* presents us with a kind of wry apologia for the sort of illusionistic art—more specifically, for the sort of illusionistic cinema—that Hitchcock, paradigmatically, has always practiced. For this is a film in which the protagonist is both implicated in and thrown up against the fact that the contemporary world is a world that consistently generates and exploits the same varieties of illusionism that are directly characteristic of film itself. In a sense, the spectator's problem of "reading" a film is revealed to be not so very different from any person's problem of reading the world and his own (potentially tenuous) position in it. This audacious suggestion, as it is developed in the context of *North by Northwest*, becomes almost as convincing as it is amusing.

I mentioned earlier that it is Phillip Vandamm who repeatedly comments upon the epistemic duplicities involved in Thornhill's situation. This master spy is much given to making critical and aesthetic assessments of the passing scene. When he confronts Thornhill at the auction, he expresses a dim view of Thornhill's talents as a Thespian:

> VANDAMM: Has anyone ever told you that you overplay your various roles rather severely, Mr. Kaplan? First you're the outraged Madison Avenue man who claims he has been mistaken for someone else. Then you play a fugitive from justice, supposedly trying to clear his name of a crime he knows he didn't commit. And now, you play the peevish lover, stung by

Narration in Light

jealousy and betrayal. Seems to me you fellows could stand a little less training from the F.B.I. and a little more from the Actor's Studio.

However, this commentary is followed by a pair of remarks that carries an irony that neither can anticipate.

> THORNHILL: Apparently the only performance that's going to satisfy *you* is when I play dead.
> VANDAMM: Your very next role. You will be quite convincing, I assure you.

And, of course, Thornhill does convince Vandamm when he plays exactly this role in the cafeteria at Mount Rushmore. Here the involutions of role upon role become too much even for the perceptive Vandamm. For he supposes that Thornhill *is* Kaplan and that Kaplan is preposterously portraying a frustrated advertising man by the name of "Thornhill." In the lines quoted above, he means to imply that "playing dead" will be Kaplan's first and final deviation from the "Thornhill" part. In reality, the death at Mount Rushmore is merely a crucial bit of play acting; stage business that represents Thornhill's adoption of the "Kaplan" character. Because Thornhill is so convincing as the Kaplan corpse, Vandamm is mistakenly reassured about Eve's loyalty to him and so sets in motion his plans to leave the country with the stolen microfilm. This is the beginning of his downfall. Moreover, given that Thornhill, in agreeing to play the death scene, fully accepts, for the first time, the role of Kaplan, there is a sense in which the false shooting *does* constitute the death of Roger Thornhill or, at least, the death of Roger "Nothing" Thornhill (see fig. 8).

With *that* Thornhill dead, Eve and Thornhill-Kaplan are free to come together and acknowledge the genuine bond of affection that exists between them. In the forest scene after the staged shooting, this coming together is underscored by a pair of slow tracking shots, moving as Eve and Thornhill move, which brings them together from the opposite edges of the screen. When they meet on this occasion, Thornhill expresses his new attitude toward his unchosen role:

> EVE: You did it [the shooting scene] rather well, I thought.
> THORNHILL (pleased with himself): Yes—I was quite . . . graceful . . .
> EVE: Considering that it's not really your kind of work . . .
> THORNHILL: I got into it by accident. What's your excuse?

Open acceptance of their respective roles curiously cements a permanent relationship. Vandamm has also acquired reasons for having more respect for a Thornhill performance. Just before Eve pretends to shoot Kaplan, he concedes a high estimation of Thornhill's acting ability:

VANDAMM: By the way, I want to compliment you on your colorful little exit from the auction gallery . . .
THORNHILL: Thank you.
VANDAMM: And now what little drama are we here for today?

As we in effect have seen, this last question represents a failure of Vandamm's critical acumen. The "little drama" in the offing is just the one that he had predicted at the auction, but rasied to a level of artistry he does not quite expect.

Thornhill, in his search for Kaplan, moves through a landscape filled with players, props, and cunningly contrived sets. Everything demands interpretation, but the relevant signs are usually both evanescent and misleading. A cabinet in Townsend's library is filled with booze instead of books until, of course, when the police investigate, the harmless books have reappeared. The Tarascan Warrior statue that Vandamm buys at the auction is actually the enemies' receptacle for stolen microfilm. Eve Kendall's gun is fired point blank on three occasions but the gun, filled with blanks, is not lethal. However, the famous crop-dusting plane that does not really dust crops is lethal as can be. The familiar values associated with familiar places are also distorted or inverted. The elegance and comfort of the Plaza Hotel are more than slightly marred by a successful kidnapping and an attempted murder. And murder actually transpires in a lobby of the UN building. In a film in which international relations are seen as conducted in terms of the blackjack machinations of rival cliques of spies, the usual symbolism of the United Nations appears more than ordinarily bizarre. Similarly, with spies and counterspies crawling desperately across the moonlit proboscises of the great presidents in stone, that symbol of American democracy and leadership exhibits less than its usual dignity. We are again and again reminded that the significance of familiar places and objects is a matter of our contrivance and that the familiarity is easily undone and the significance recontrived.

The opening shot of the film creates a striking illusion of its own. A Manhattan street is reflected in the side of an enormous glass skyscraper, but the girders of the building cut down and across the screen like the bars of a gigantic cage. The cars and people in the street below seem to move within these awesome confines. The series of shots that follows depicts great herds of city dwellers pouring like cattle out of office buildings, up from subway outlets, and so forth. Later in the film, when similar crowds and clumps of people recur (especially in the train stations and at Mount Rushmore), their very anonymity becomes both ambiguous and threatening. In *North by Northwest* we quickly learn that even the legions of the nondescript are pockmarked with secret agents, assassins, and deceptive blondes.

The film picks Thornhill out as a member of these legions, and it is simply a chance misidentification that lifts him, as it were, into the higher orders of art and mayhem. The spies, American and other, who elevate him out of his boring existence tend to hover about murderously under the most banal of covers. It is just this combination of the banality of absolutely everything with the ever-present possibility of disastrous mischance that makes the film's world seem so ludicrously dangerous. Vandamm appears principally in the part of an exporter-importer of *objects d'art* (and of government secrets), but he does a lively turn as a UN diplomat as well. The members of his group pop up and down in various guises, which include the Glen Cove matron and her housekeeper, a gardener, a gentlemen's secretary, and an industrial designer. The spies on the other side play at the same game. The head of the American agents is known as "the Professor" and his ordinary-looking colleagues are identified as "the Cartoonist," "the Stockbroker," "the Housewife," and "the Journalist."[3] Linking the spies with those introductory shots of urban hordes, the contending national powers are presented as conducting a cold war under the cover of the humdrum and the commonplace.

The normal humdrum order of things, however, is depicted as an extraordinarily malleable structure. The manipulation of appearance becomes a trivial exercise when a person's status and even identity may be redefined by the slightest shift in context or circumstance. Vandamm's henchmen mistake Thornhill for Kaplan when Thornhill, attempting to send a message to his mother, appears to be receiving a message for the nonexistent Kaplan. Vandamm is taken by Thornhill to be Lester Townsend because, after all, he is met occupying Townsend's Long Island estate. The police are convinced that no Lester Townsend could have tried to dispose of Thornhill with a bottle and a Mercedes without brakes when Townsend is identified as a UN speaker. Each twist of the plot reveals information about Eve Kendall that effects a complete transformation in Thornhill's view of her. The tension of this ambiguity is reflected in ambivalence. Their early interaction is marked by a chilly combination of attraction and restrained violence as each probes at the other's alluring but unreliable façade:

EVE: How do I know you aren't a murderer?

THORNHILL: (to her neck): You don't.

EVE: Maybe you're planning to murder *me* , right here, tonight.

THORNHILL (working on her ear): Shall I?

EVE: (whispers): Yes . . . please do . . .

And naturally, a few prop belongings and a fixed itinerary are enough to flesh out George Kaplan down to the dandruff. This whole issue of casual metamorphosis is brought into relief when Thornhill interrogates a maid at the Plaza:

THORNHILL: Elsie—do you know who I am?

MAID (giggles): Sure. You're Mr. Kaplan.

THORNHILL: When did we . . . when did you first see me, Elsie?

MAID: Outside the door, out there in the hall, just a couple minutes ago. Don'cha remember?

THORNHILL: You mean that's the first time you ever laid eyes on me?

MAID: Can I help it you're never *around*, Mr. Kaplan?

THORNHILL: How do you know I *am* Mr. Kaplan?

MAID: (puzzled): Huh?

THORNHILL: How do you know I'm Mr. Kaplan?

MAID (giggles): Well, of *course* ya are. This is room seven ninety-six, isn't it? So—you're the gentleman in room seven ninety-six, aren't ya?

THORNHILL: All right, Elsie.

Immediately afterward, the hotel valet delivers an analogous line of circumstantial reasoning, and it is repeated when Vandamm's thugs get through to Thornhill on Kaplan's hotel phone. It is almost as if people were interchangeable as long as they fit into a system of expectations and appearance in the right way.

Thornhill is connected with the exploitation of perceptual experience from two directions. The role this plays in Thornhill's entanglement with the Kaplan fiction is clear enough. But Thornhill is supposed to be an advertising executive. The less attractive implications of this situation are given expression when, at the start of the film, he tells his secretary that "in the world of advertising there is no such thing as a lie, Maggie. There is only the Expedient Exaggeration." Thornhill presumably has in mind the uses of distortion to regulate the tastes and actions of gullible consumers. He fails to envision the larger possibilities of Expedient Exaggeration in the hands of a more powerful Exaggerator. It may be a kind of justice, therefore, that his perspective concerning this topic is forcibly expanded for him all the way from Manhattan to Mount Rushmore. We can assume that Thornhill is aware of the power of the media to fix the image that his

Narration in Light

advertising clients want. But this power is brought to bear upon his personal situation as well.

When, at the United Nations, the real Townsend is murdered, the flabbergasted Thornhill removes the dagger from the dead man's back and supports the fallen body for a moment in his arms. "Look!" he cries to the startled people nearby, and he means, of course, by this, "Look at the terrible thing that has just transpired!" But the look that he here invites, the look that the film audience shares with the passers-by, seems plainly to proclaim that he has just stabbed the crumpling corpse. Furthermore, a newspaperman's serendipitous photograph captures this deceptive, instantaneous look and becomes transmittable visual proof that Thornhill is the UN killer (see fig. 9). Subsequently, this "visual proof" pursues him halfway across the country. Later, when the Professor has arranged the fake shooting in the Mount Rushmore cafeteria, the media are employed to give the event widespread public status. Thornhill listens to the announcement on the radio of his imminent demise, and the Professor, with an air of self-congratulation, tells him that "his condition has acquired the authority of the printed word." The widely shared perception takes the place of truth.

These various interrelated motifs are given a somewhat new dimension in the scene at the auction. All the film's principals are present: Thornhill, Eve, Vandamm, Leonard, and the Professor. Behind the main action, fine furniture and works of art are paraded for display across the auction stage while an auctioneer describes their aesthetic worth and stimulates the bidding. What is particularly interesting, however, is the way that the characters come to be linked with the items up for sale. In the scene's opening shot we see a close-up of Eve Kendall's graceful head and shoulders while Vandamm's hand appreciatively caresses the nape of her neck. On the sound track, we hear the auctioneer's insistent patter. The juxtaposition of sound and image yields the impression that these head and shoulders belong to an exquisite bust whose value Vandamm is assessing (see fig. 10). When Thornhill bursts in upon them a moment later, the impression is echoed in his lines. After remarking that the trio, Vandamm, Eve, and Leonard, make up a picture "only Charlie Addams" could draw, he says to Vandamm of Eve, "I'll bet you paid plenty for this little piece of—sculpture. . . . She's worth every dollar, take it from me." Earlier, when the camera has tracked back from the close-up of Eve's head, it reveals, in a medium shot, the elegant pair, Vandamm and Eve, posed squarely in front of another elegant pair—two damask Louis Seize chairs. Just at the moment that Thornhill enters the auction, the chairs are sold

Fig. 7. Roger Thornhill (Cary Grant) dramatically protests his kidnapping while framed by the closed curtains in Townsend's library.

Fig. 8. Eve (Eva Marie Saint) and Thornhill play act a murder in the cafeteria at Mount Rushmore.

70

Fig. 9. A photographer is about to catch Thornhill in the act of removing the murder weapon from Townsend's back.

Fig. 10. Vandamm (James Mason) seems to be appraising Eve's value at the beginning of the auction scene.

Fig. 11. Duplicitous intimacy on the Twentieth-Century Limited—Eve accepts Thornhill's light.

and removed from the stage. As the camera picks up Thornhill's entrance, the auctioneer initiates the bidding on "a lovely Aubusson settee, in excellent condition." (A witty correlate for 54-year-old Cary Grant, who certainly appears in excellent condition.) Finally, as Leonard starts to play an active role in the scene, an antique French curio cabinet comes up for sale. In a line in the script deleted from the film, Thornhill renders this last person-to-object linkage explicit. "And where do they keep you," he asks Leonard, "in a curio cabinet?" At the conclusion of the sequence, while the police haul Thornhill out of the auction he has reduced to shambles, he picks up the dominant metaphor a last time. He warns them, "Handle me with care, fellahs . . . I'm valuable property."

The image of artifacts, valued for the way they look, presented on a stage, and sold to the highest bidder, aptly stands in for a central aspect of the vision of *North by Northwest*. In particular, the conception of people as having a value defined by the appearances they project and so also by the roles that they are fitted to perform runs as a persistent undercurrent throughout the film. In the reconciliation scene between Thornhill and Eve, she raises the issue rather directly. She explains that when she first met Phillip Vandamm she "saw only the charm" and entered into an affair. At that time the Professor approached her and argued that her at-tractiveness to Vandamm made her "uniquely valuable" to the American side. When Eve completes this explanation, the Professor steps in and uses the same language once more. He rebukes Thornhill's unwillingness to let Eve go: "I needn't tell you how valuable she can be over there." There is never the slightest hint of concern on the Professor's part that Eve's value to him and his side involves the betrayal of one love affair and the complete disruption of another.

This is wholly consistent with the Professor we have met before. When his colleagues learn that Thornhill has been mistaken for Kaplan and is therefore likely to be killed, the Professor simply explains why a live decoy is even better than an imaginary one and summarily dismisses the suggestion that his attitude might be a "little callous." Obviously, this willingness to exploit, to employ the expedient exaggeration, is an exten-sion of attitudes expressed by Thornhill at the beginning of the film. It is also notable that although *North by Northwest* allows for minimal observ-ance of the usual conventions about Us and the Enemy, there is no salient moral distinction drawn between the American and Enemy spies. If anything, Vandamm seems genuinely to care for Eve and, consequently, as the jealous Leonard points out, is a little too willing to trust her. It is true that Vandamm's feeling for Eve, like much else about him, is somewhat too coldly a matter of aesthetic appreciation. But even this sentiment is significantly warmer than anything the Professor ever expresses.

In all of this, there is a systematic displacement of the standard assumption that it is the inner being that defines a person's worth. From the refinements of Vandamm's aestheticism to the stage-managing utilitarianism of the Professor, value seems primarily attached to the outer surfaces of both persons and objects alike. The thug of distinction, the attractive blonde, and the importable foreign spy are the commodities that sell well in the current market. Probably the chief mark of Thornhill's self-reform is that he, through his love of Eve, breaks out of this network of skin-trade valuation. And yet, the irony remains that it is only as the embodiment of the fictional Kaplan that he achieves this breaking out.

Certainly *something* has to change in him, for it is clear that the early model Thornhill is as guilty as Vandamm and the Professor of trafficking exclusively in beguiling surfaces and styles. In his first encounter with Eve, Thornhill is bluntly defined as a connoisseur of the well-wrought exterior form and as a man with a keen eye for the agreeable impression, the prospect that attracts. While they circle seductively around each other in her private compartment, we hear the following:

EVE: I ought to know more about you.

THORNHILL: Oh, what more could you know?

EVE: You're an advertising man, that's all I know. . . . You've got taste in clothes . . . taste in food—

THORNHILL: Taste in women. I like your flavor.

EVE: And you're very clever with words. You can probably make them do anything for you . . . sell people things they don't need . . . make women who don't know you fall in love with you . . .

Related to this is a scene a bit earlier. When he responds to her seemingly candid overtures, he specifies that he desires the maintenance of suitably superficial, protective fictions in his dealings with the opposite sex.

THORNHILL: Oh—you're *that* type.

EVE: What type?

THORNHILL: Honest.

EVE: Not really.

THORNHILL: Good. Honest women frighten me.

EVE: Why?

THORNHILL: I don't know. Somehow they seem to put me at a disadvantage.

EVE: Because *you're* not honest with *them*.

THORNHILL: Exactly.

This exchange is an important one, because it turns out to be the leading problem of their relationship to find a way to meet each other honestly, face to face, without false advertising and design.

Toward the end of the film, Eve explicitly identifies the attitudes of Thornhill's expressed above (which she thinks he shares with men in general) as the ultimate cause of her unhappy position with Vandamm and the predicament that it creates for her.

THORNHILL: Has life been like that?
EVE: Mm hmmm.
THORNHILL: How come.
EVE: Men like you.
THORNHILL: What's wrong with men like me?
EVE: They don't believe in marriage.
THORNHILL: I've been married twice.
EVE: See what I mean?

And yet, by the time these words are uttered, Thornhill has been lucky. He, unlike Vandamm, has discovered the worth of penetrating Eve's web of performance and display to understand what they can be together if he allows her to make an "honest" man of him.

However, the lessons he has had to take in order to achieve this understanding have been neither simple, sweet, nor straight-forward. He must, in the first place, recognize the murderous potential that exists in this woman. It is a part of her nature that she is capable of mortal duplicity toward him. She has it in her to help devise his utter obliteration (see fig. 11). Making love on the train, they toy with sexy threats of mutual harm and danger, but this by-play conceals the genuine threat she is to him and the serious threat he poses for her. Her dangerousness and duplicity are brute facts, which he will have to learn, quite literally, to live with. Eve demonstrably has the will and capacity to destroy him, but then, alongside this, she sees him for what he is and loves him nonetheless. It is this volatile combination that lies hidden behind the compelling façades that she so fetchingly presents to him. So it is, in the second place, his task to discern the love in her that his quite proper sense of jeopardy obscures. I take it to be a general point about their evolving "romance" that to know the other well enough to love him or her involves the knowledge and accept-ance of some menacing truths as well. Besides, her latent power to kill a Thornhill has its more immediately positive side. As I have suggested, she does murder the "Nothing" version of the man, and that stage of his development is well disposed of anyway.

After Thornhill escapes the attempted assassination in the cornfield, he happens to locate Eve in her Chicago hotel room. This encounter, like their last, is charged with libidinal energies and barely suppressed violence. But this time the ambience of violence unquestionably predominates. It is unsurprising but significant that Thornhill's attitudes toward sexual fun and games have had a sharp reversal.

THORNHILL: How did a girl like you ever get to be a girl like you?

EVE: Lucky, I guess.

THORNHILL: Not lucky—wicked . . . naughty . . . up to no good . . . Ever kill anyone? Bet you could tease a man to death without even trying. (He pats her cheek.) So stop trying, hm?

The couple is now as withdrawn and sealed off from each other as the pensive pair of Buddhist statuettes upon Eve's dresser in the room.

Just as Thornhill misread Eve's fake frankness on the train, so here he misses the barely disguised expression of relief and affection with which she greets his totally unexpected arrival. It is our first realization that she cares for him, but, understandably, he picks up only the traces of treachery and intrigue. There is a nicely handled moment in the ensuing auction scene which stresses the exquisite difficulty of their situation at this time. Thornhill remarks to Vandamm, "I wonder what subtle form of manslaughter is next on the program. Am I going to be dropped into a vat of molten steel and become part of some new skyscrapper?" Then, glancing down at the seated Eve, he continues, "or are you going to ask *this* . . . female to kiss me again and poison me to death?" As he is delivering this second question, the camera tracks slightly to the left to show us the face she shows him when she rises involuntarily from her chair to strike at him. The camera then tracks right again and forward to show what registers in Vandamm's face. Grabbing her arm, Thornhill says contemptuously to her, "Who are you kidding? You have no feelings to hurt." This jibe wounds too, but its thrust is absolutely wrong. He takes her angry response to be a sham, but, as Vandamm notices, the trouble is that it is not. Here her feelings for Thornhill rend the role she plays for Vandamm, and he has ready means of terminating the casting altogether. The warmth of the as yet unaffirmed emotional connection disturbs the cold war that surrounds the real lovers on every side and renders them eminently dispensable to all the warriors but themselves.

From this nadir, things improve in the vicinity of Mount Rushmore. Thornhill, having closed the auction down, finally gets his much-needed lecture on Miss Kendall from the Professor. The scene in the cafeteria is

Narration in Light

planned and staged, and its success obtains for the protagonists their meeting in the woods—face to face at last. At the start, they are not too good at openness and directness. They stumble, hesitate, and search for words. Still, this interview is the culmination of the complex issue of honesty between them, and Thornhill, lately murdered, confesses that "he has never felt more alive." But circumstances leave him with one more task, a task the hero of a melodrama should be expected to perform. He must, out of his great love and by his own unconstrained choice, risk his continued existence to bring the heroine down from off the steep cliff face. The enactment of this better fiction frees them from the past.

All of these considerations merely hint at the still more specific connection that exists with the aesthetics of the cinema. A number of commentators, including Hitchcock himself, have remarked that *North by Northwest* is the most self-referential of his films. For example, the Eve-Thornhill-Vandamm triangle derives from *Notorious*, Hitchcock's 1946 spy film. This borrowing is even elaborated into a sly joke. In the earlier film, Ingrid Bergman corresponds to Eva Marie Saint, Cary Grant to Cary Grant, Claude Raines to James Mason, and Alan Sebastian's "masculine" mother to the "feminine" Leonard. Beyond this pivotal appropriation, there are more or less extended references, visual, verbal and thematic, to, for example, *The Thirty-nine Steps, Saboteur, Strangers on a Train, The Wrong Man,* and *Vertigo.* The range of references is so wide that one is left with the bizarre impression that the kidnapping has thrown Thornhill out of a normal businessman's existence and into a weird mélange of Alfred Hitchcock films. This impression should be taken as seriously as the playfulness of its conception permits. The world that *North by Northwest* represents is one in which the problem of ordering experience is precisely a problem in the interpretation of filmic representation.

I have attempted to trace some of the ways in which the general question of the exploitation of appearance is central to the film. Here, in summary, is Thornhill's epistemic situation. Segments of physical reality have been judiciously arranged to generate perceived significance of various, usually misleading, types. The bases of perceptual judgment are controlled through assorted tricks of juxtaposition and elision; these devices play upon the perceiver's habits of expectation and bias. The field of action is filled with a parade of performers who bear a problematic relation to their roles. *This* is the art of the cinema with a vengeance, and the vengeance is wreaked on Roger Thornhill. Once his identity has become inextricably interwined with Kaplan's, his experience is qualitatively indistinguishable from the viewing of a Hitchcock retrospective. Indeed, insofar as Thornhill serves as a surrogate for members of the audience, the ultimate joke may be on the detached viewer of *this* Hitchcock film. For it is wholly unclear how much detachment can be justified when the film itself postulates a radical collapse of the normal division between ordinary perception and cinematic representation.

It is characteristic of Hitchcock that the cause of this collapse occurs at the exact point that the viewer is least likely to expect. I commented in chapter 3 upon the importance of the transparency of the image in the classical cinema and observed that it is a fundamental aspect of classical narration that seeks, in effect, to collapse the distinction between perception of the world and perception of film in its own fashion. For the function of transparency is to induce in the spectators the impression of seeing the given fictional world through the screen as directly as they see the actual world through their front windows. Of course, this impression is a kind of audience illusion based upon their setting out of consciousness that the world on screen *is* being mediated by the screen images. Probably the most familiar way of subverting the transparent mode and its consequent audience impression is by choosing various of the stylistic means that exist for forcing the viewers' attention back upon the ineliminable fact that they are most immediately perceiving a sequence of projected film shots. However, this is not, by and large, the strategy of subversion that is employed in *North by Northwest.* (One exception may be the "God's eye" shot of Thornhill fleeing across the grounds of the UN building. He is ostentatiously reduced, at this brief moment, to a dark, mobile speck, which appears on a flat and Mondrian-like surface within the boundaries of the film frame.) In narrational style, texture, and continuity the film predominantly supports transparency. Rather, it is the extracinematic presuppositions that ground the aesthetic importance of transparency which become the object of Hitchcock's subversion.

The presuppositions are these. We ordinarily suppose that our normal perceptual intercourse with the environment is precisely *not* the result of a duplicitous form of representation which has been designed for our consumption by an agent other than ourselves and then set before our credulous eyes. We believe that the people we meet are not mere characters in some fiction that inscrutable actors and actresses are playing, with us as their intended audience. We believe that the look of things about us has not been devised to support the sinister dramatic performances referred to just above, and we believe that outer appearance is not a veil of deception woven by an evil genius with a taste for filmic trickery. Indeed, we would be crazy if we believed the opposite of these things or so, at any rate, it seems. All of this forms a part of our conception of the "directness" of ordinary perception and grounds the character of our impression when cinematic transparency is put in play. Naturally, we all know the elementary facts about the making of a fiction film and therefore know that what we see in films has these very properties that ordinary perception, by hypothesis, does not. Nevertheless, the mental trick in accepting transparency in film viewing is to suppress our knowledge about the film qua artifact in such a way as to make possible a perceptual relationship to narrative constituents which will be experienced as being as direct as our paradigmatic viewing outside the theater and the movie house. What Hitchcock has accomplished in *North by Northwest* is to construct and show us a version of what is recognizably *our* world, but a version in which the perception of the characters, Thornhill's most especially, has lost most of the qualities that would make it a paradigm of directness. If we were to accept—say, for the course of the film—the notion that *our* experience might really be, more than we suppose, a great deal like Thornhill's, then the effect would be both funny and a little baffling. For there we would be in our seats pretending to ourselves that we were seeing directly through the screen into Thornhill's circumstances, while he, at the same time, is grappling with the gradual discovery that his own direct perception of those circumstances places him in the situation of a disoriented primitive visiting the motion pictures. And on our present assumption that we are sitting there identifying with his epistemic situation, our impression of transparency is likely to seem based upon nothing more than a baffling dream of perceptual access which only the magic of film could have induced in the first place.

Actually, various warning signs have been provided to the audience and to Thornhill from the outset of *North by Northwest*. Immediately prior to his kidnapping, Thornhill meets some business acquaintances at a table in the Oak Bar of the Plaza. As he enters the bar, a few strains of the song "It's a Most Unusual Day" are heard from some unseen string ensemble, which specializes, apparently, in cheerful preludes to disaster. Behind the table where Thornhill joins his fellow executives is a mural, which depicts a man standing before the open door of a parked carriage and, from the right, obscure figures rushing toward the waiting conveyance. This anticipates Thornhill's predicament as he is hustled into the kidnapper's car parked outside the Plaza and is taken to Vandamm. So the crucial kidnapping is directly associated in three ways with a reversal in Thornhill's relation to the aesthetic realm. First, he is accidentally mistaken for a character in a fiction devised by an imaginative board of spies. Second, he is thereby converted suddenly from being a theater-going spectator into a participant in an outlandish international coproduction. Third, he is figuratively abducted into the domain of a mysteriously prescient painting. Of course, the ramifications of this reversal continue throughout the film. When, as in the kidnapping scene, it is so repeatedly and distinctively indicated that the usual presuppositions about what stands within and without the contexts of representation have been abrogated, it seems odd if the film's audience can regard its position "outside the drama" as if it were untouched.

Hitchcock's interest in and comments upon the manipulative possibilities of film are quite well-known. He has largely confined his remarks to the topic of how to elicit suspense in an audience, but it is clear that the relevant concerns run much deeper. *Rear Window* and *Vertigo*, the great films from earlier in the fifties, had already taken up the theme of subjectivity, especially in its more obsessional aspects. Both films have a principal character (James Stewart) who has radically turned in upon himself and who, in doing so, projects his private fears, desires, and fantasies upon the surfaces of a recalcitrant reality. Moreover, in *Rear Window*, these processes of subjective imposition are emphatically linked with the processes of seeing or constructing film. The observer, from his fixed position, reconstructs the meaning of the action that he finds screened for his inspection at a safe remove. Hitchcock's expressed attitude toward film seems characteristically ambivalent. On the one hand, the practice of filmmaking offers an analytic mode in terms of which the possibilities of ordinary perception are refined and extended. It gives us the power to delineate the essentials of patterns of experience which the single, limited observer is bound to miss. Yet on the other hand, like the products of an obsessive consciousness, the analyses that we extract are likely to narrow and distort the fullness of the world and our experience. They yield gross simplifications and even self-made lies constructed in the name of discerning a significant order.

Although the ambivalence remains the same in *North by Northwest*, there is a way in which it constitutes a shift in interest. The suffocating permutations of individual psychology recede to the background and the disorienting impingements of a manipulated reality take their place. There is really too little to a Roger "Nothing" Thornhill to sustain protracted psychological investigation. It is just the point that this particular subjectivity is so fragilely wrought that it threatens simply to disappear when a more vivid creation intersects its path. In Thornhill's case, the sources of the projected fiction are public and impose themselves upon the individual consciousness from outside. The identity of these sources—the malign counterparts of the film director—are only vaguely identified. Governments, advertising, and the media are all invoked, but it seems a part of the conception that these powers, like the director himself, are faceless, anonymous, and covert. Only their handiwork is invisibly visible no matter where one looks.

When interviewed by François Truffaut, Hitchcock asserted: "My best McGuffin, and by that I mean the emptiest, the most non-existent, and the most absurd is the one we used in *North by Northwest* . . . the McGuffin has boiled down to its purest expression: nothing at all."[4] The McGuffin referred to is the collection of microfilmed government secrets buried in the belly of the Tarascan Warrior statue, which Vandamm purchased at the auction. In the climactic sequence on the heights of Mount Rushmore, Leonard clutches the statue to his chest as he grinds Thornhill's hand into the edge of the cliff. From the darkness above, a shot is fired and Leonard, toppling over, drops the statue and it shatters against the rocks. Among the broken shards, the secrets finally stand revealed. Given the layers of aesthetic involution I have described, it seems entirely appropriate that the little Tarascan Warrior should, at the end of the long pursuit, disgorge before us—a strip of film. Here then *is* the ultimate McGuffin. The crucial object at the heart of all this film's hallucinatory action, the goal that locks the opposing forces in loony cold war conflict, is no more and no less than a piece of the stuff that films are made of. In a context such as *North by Northwest*, where films are the stuff that reality is made of, there is nothing else the Tarascan Warrion could contain.

Vandamm, first and last the explicit commentator on the rules of the game, remarks adversely on the way that Leonard has been killed: "Rather unsporting, don't you think . . . using *real* bullets." When one reflects upon it, the likable imposter's objection seems correct. Shooting someone down with real bullets constitutes a shocking failure of imagination and that, in this film, is a failure of the most fundamental kind—almost a loss of the reality principle. It sort of lets the whole show down with a bang. Strictly speaking, the film ends, as it begins, with an outburst of visual illusion. In the course of a slow dissolve, Thornhill lifts Eve up from the precipice and into connubial bliss in an upper berth of the Twentieth-Century Limited. It is as though Hitchcock wanted to conclude this good-humored work with an affirmation of the beneficent powers of filmic prestidigitation. These powers permit the consummation of a marriage whose partners would otherwise remain forever teetering above the void.

Chapter 5

Some Modes of Nonomniscience

Several great, and many more not so great, Hollywood films are informed by a conception of film narration which is, in key respects, a natural extrapolation of a view such as Karel Reisz's about the role of editing in the narration of an individual scene. Throughout his discussion of editing, Reisz presupposes the basic overall reliability of ordinary human perception. He understandably leaves unquestioned the capacity of perception to yield knowledge, at least within the areas that common sense most takes for granted. The edited segment is then explicated as a medium that facilitates the extension and refinement of normal direct vision. This has two interrelated aspects. Shot by shot the temporally extended image track commonly presents things and events and their properties to which we rarely, if ever, have perceptual access. This includes items that are too small to make out and expanses too vast to take in. It also includes the more fleeting qualities of various states and processes, for example, the nuances of expression, glance, and gesture. In a complementary fashion, the edited segment, marshaling these materials into a new unity, constitutes a visual analysis of the dramatic or developmental logic of a complex activity. It joins together a series of perspicuous views whose active interconnection delineates an otherwise elusive pattern in the whirl of change. Theorists such as Béla Balázs and Erwin Panofsky have also made prominent in their writings lines of thought reminiscent of this.[1] Panofsky believes that *the* essential properties of film are its capacities, by means of editing, to "dynamize space" and "spatialize time," for it is these properties that permit the unique articulation of a narrative content in the cinema.

Consider now the following remarks by V. F. Perkins on the general function of narrative in film:

82

In the fiction movie, reality becomes malleable but remains (or continues to seem) solid. The world is shaped by the film-maker to reveal an order beyond chronology, in a system of time and space which is both natural and synthetic. The movie offers its reality in a sequence of privileged moments during which actions achieve a clarity and intensity seldom found in everyday life. Motive and gesture, action and reaction, cause and effect, are brought into a more immediate, dynamic, and revealing relationship. The film-maker fashions a world more concentrated and shaped than that of visual experience.[2]

Actually, this is the application of a fairly traditional theory of narrative function to film. But notice that here also is the same emphasis on the capacity of a film narrative to extend analytically the scope of unaided "visual experience," the capacity to "shape and concentrate upon" an explanatory "order," revealed through a "sequence of privileged moments" in a manner more "immediate" and "dynamic" than would be likely without the intervention of film's formative powers. Moreover, as vague as some of these claims may be, they capture something of the aims and accomplishments of a movie such as *The Searchers*.

This conception, whatever its ultimate merits, is not trivial. Its power, in connection with narrative film, rests upon three assumptions. First, we believe or tend to believe that there is some explanation, no matter how hard it might be to uncover, of why a given interesting event took place. Second, we believe that, as a rule, the signs or evidence of the explanatory terms of that explanation are, in principle, available to perception. An explanatory inference, no matter how complicated it may be, is finally grounded in sensible phenomena. Third, the individual human observer and even human observers as a totality are generally not in an epistemic position over time to witness anything like the full extent of observable facts from which the explanation in question is properly projectable.

For example, to return to a topic touched upon before, we think of much animal and human behavior as an expression of an agent's inner beliefs, desires, intentions, and feelings. We *see* patterns of behavior as having this sort of psychological significance, and this is the significance by means of which the behavior is usually explained. (Merleau-Ponty thought that film was the modern art that would or could recall for us the visibility of the psychological *in* behavior.[3]) Often, however, a complex of expressive behavior includes a finely nuanced action or response that is almost impossible to discriminate. Other psychologically meaningful stretches of activity include items of behavior separated by long durations and occurring in widely distanced locations. For this reason, an observer is not situated to follow the unfolding patterns through their full extent. The embodiment of the mental in human action is something we characteristically perceive only in a scattered, piecemeal, and erratic way. Similarly, we suppose that every event has causal antecedents that stretch back more or less indefinitely through time and causal consequences that stretch forward just as indefinitely. Again, no observer has perceptual access to even most of the primary links in any of these causal chains.

Writers such as Perkins in the above passage stress our ability to construct on film a visual reintegration of explanatory patterns of these and related types. Film gives us the ability to pick out from the complicated and obscuring blur of experience those aspects of phenomena that constitute such a pattern and to reassemble for the screen the latent unity that the limitations of ordinary experience would disguise. This capacity for perceptual analysis and reconstruction derives, first, from the film maker's freedom to build those patterns, bit by bit, as part of a secondary world that he or she stages. Thus, the explanations that filmic fictions contain have the character of, for example, moral or psychological "thought experiments" upon a merely postulated dilemma. But understood as such, they are, it would seem, none the worse for that. When well done, they have both the virtues and the necessary limitations that any thought experiment will have. Second, and more centrally, our extended capacity derives from the clarity and the flexibility of photographic and editing techniques as ways of obtaining a visual record of a fictional course of events. We literally focus on the significant parts and literally splice them together into a significant whole. These then are techniques for an analysis of the visible, techniques that demarcate the sensory bases of our inferences from gross perception to syntheses of meaning and explanation. Narrative film is, according to this account, a form that makes global coherence visually *surveyable*, the subject of a continuous, conscious, and contemplative apprehension. It is in this sense, particularly, that film is thought of as extending the meaningful perceptual experience of human observers.

I mentioned a little earlier that these views have close affinities with well-known older notions of the ends of narrative in other arts, and, this being the case, they inherit almost equally well-known objections. And indeed, the idea that fiction films can ever successfully and honestly realize the purposes just described has been the brunt of a lot of influential "antinarrative" criticism. This is not the place to attempt to sort out and assess the varied and often tangled considerations that figure in this debate. Nevertheless, it should be obvious from our previous discussion

Narration in Light

that the present account of film narrative cannot be adequate as a fully general description of the narrational possibilities of even those fiction films whose surface forms are most conventional. If the account seems to fit *The Searchers* fairly well, it makes no provision at all for the specific kind of unreliability in *You Only Live Once* or the oblique self-consciousness of *North by Northwest*. Indeed, the former instantiates in its doubled structure one of the fundamental doubts that one may feel about the aim of a cinematic extension of perception. Any norm or schema of filmic exposition which purports to select out and analyze significant phenomenal patterns is liable at the same time to exclude other aspects of the phenomena whose inclusion would destroy the seeming significance of the subject under view. Relatedly, the use of analytic film procedures can suggest an interpretation of the depicted situation which derives more from our conventionalized reading of those procedures and less from the facts of the situation itself. And, of course, the implied interpretation may be false. Suppose that a three-shot Kuleshov sequence were edited into a film that purported to show what happened to the actor during a given period of time. The implication that the actor actually underwent the psychological reaction that the audience reads into his facial expression on the basis of the montage would, except by coincidence, be false. Unreliable primary narration continuously inscribes this possibility across the whole surface of the action it portrays.

Failure to allow for unreliable narration is really a symptom of a much broader problem. It represents a general failure to take into account that *epistemic authority* in the cinema is a variable matter and that the variations are important. Both Reisz's account of classical editing and the traditional theory of narrative function to which Perkins appeals strongly suggest a style of film whose *narrational authority is unrestricted*. That is, the narration is authorized to show, shot by shot and scene by scene, whatever is demanded by a predesigned and maximally articulated overview of the narrative action. This means, first, that the camera views may arise from any position within the fictional space and time of the film's story which dramatic effectiveness dictates. These views may change as freely as normal continuity and intelligibility permit from one locale to another and from "bird's eye" perspective shots to the most detailed and intimate close-ups. Second, the camera views are also allowed to vary freely between "objective" shots and "subjective" shots that render the visual field of one or another character. Third, this variation occurs within a framework in which the epistemic position established by the narration is, on the whole, superior to the more limited viewpoints of any of the characters. Fourth, the camera set-ups, editing, and so forth are substantially determined by the analytical requirements of the narrating intelligence that exists outside the secondary world of the film and designs an "ideal" overview of the narrative occurrences. Unrestricted narrational authority in film is thus the approximate counterpart of "omniscient" narration in prose fiction. It is by far the most frequently employed mode of narration in classical fiction film.

Despite the predominance of this mode, however, various restrictions on narrational authority have been tried and other restrictions seem possible. It is a reasonable task for a theory of film to develop some systematic conception of what the *viable* possibilities are. Unfortunately, this is both a large and tricky enterprise, and I shall only attempt to indicate some of the important dimensions in which narrational restriction may operate. A good example of the trickiness of this area is provided by the possibility that is most often cited in discussions of the topic; that is, so-called first-person or, as I prefer, *directly subjective* narration. As a form of restricted narrational authority this is to cover cases in which *every* shot of the film (or of a lengthy segment of the film) represents the field of vision of the central character. This device, one would suppose, should yield an interesting analogue to stream-of-consciousness narration in the novel. On the basis of quite general and superficially plausible reflections about the nature of cinematic presentation there seems no obvious reason why this should not be effective. If one thinks of the screen imagery as the representation of some "ideally ubiquitous" observer's perceptual consciousness or believes that a member of the audience literally identifies his or her current visual field with the manifold of screen content, then the directly subjective narration of some character who takes part in the narrative action ought not raise any overriding problems. Why shouldn't the eye of a character take the place of the disembodied outside observer postulated for the standard forms?

And yet, it is notorious that this has been attempted through the whole of *Lady in the Lake* and in the first third of *Dark Passage*, and the results are spectacularly disastrous. The first of these films gives the impression that there is a camera by the name of "Philip Marlowe" stumbling around Los Angeles and passing itself off as the well-known human being of the same name. The film has a good number of faults, but the basic difficulty appears to be this. We do not and probably cannot see tracking or panning shots as corresponding to the continuous reorientation in space of the visual field of people such as ourselves. Despite what textbooks on editing such as Reisz's often claim or seem to claim, we do not see a straight cut, even within a scene, as representing the phenomenology of a shift in a perceiver's visual attention. For these and, no doubt, other reasons, it may be that it is only in very limited sorts of context and style that a shot is acceptably construed as someone's field of vision. It is a genuinely open question whether the type of extended, direct subjectivization of the image track which occurs in *Lady in the Lake* is a feasible alternative of film narration at all. The idea that it ought to be may be a bitter little object lesson in the limitations of excessively a priori film theory.

However, there are demonstrably more successful possibilities of restricted narrational authority which are intermediate between unrestricted and directly subjective schemes. In Michelangelo Antonioni's *Red Desert* and (more felicitously) in much of Roman Polanski's *Repulsion* and Nicholas Ray's *Bigger than Life* a kind of *indirect* or *reflected subjectivity* has been devised for the narration. A certain central character appears in segments throughout the film, and the action is only partially, if at all, seen from his or her physical point of view. Features of the projected image or the *mise en scène* are used to depict or symbolize or reflect aspects of the way in which the character perceives and responds to his or her immediate environment. The basic idea is to let properties of the way in which the fictional world looks to us on the screen *stand in for* properties of the way in which that world is experienced by the character. *Red Desert* is known for its use of color to reflect the heroine's troubled states of mind, whereas in *Bigger than Life* the emphazied expanses of the space in the Cinemascope images become a correlate of the consciousness-expanding effects of cortisone on the protagonist. We see with him, although not usually through his eyes, the distortions of outlook (in several senses) that the drug induces. Actually, the basic strategy here is used with particular clarity and consistency in a cartoon—in Walt Disney's *Dip Drippy Donald*. The subjectivity reflected belongs to Donald Duck. In a film such as *The Devil Is a Woman*, this relatively simple strategy of reflected subjectivity can, where embedded in additional complications, take on a surprising complexity and resonance.

Perhaps because of the overworked analogy between camera and eye, the various modes of subjectivized narration are likely to dominate an analysis of restricted authority. But there are principles that restrict narration in a less psychologized manner and that are of at least as great interest and importance. The narration of Howard Hawks' *To Have and Have Not* constitutes one kind of paradigmatic example of this. None of the shots in the film is from the visual perspective of Harry Morgan (Humphrey Bogart), and there is no attempt to reflect his subjectivity in the sense explained above. However, the narration *is* conscientiously restricted to what might be called Morgan's *epistemological position*. The audience sees just the situations that he sees but, again, not from the places that he occupies. The information that the audience acquires throughout the film is kept in strict correspondence with the information Morgan acquires through his participation in the action. The camera work and editing are notably spare and functional; every effort has been made to refrain from an outside commentary on Morgan's character, on what he sees, and on how he behaves. These matters are to speak for themselves through the action. The viewer is thus distinctly not invited to take up a position that is superior to his in any way. Most importantly, the viewer is not superior to him in his understanding of the evolving narrative situations.

Harry Morgan is established early in the film to be committed to a quasi-moral code that admits only considerations of self-integrity, basic fairness, and professional responsibility as legitimate claims upon a person. Any further claims that people make are seen by him as "strings" that they want to attach to him and thereby constrain and compromise his rigorous independence. Both Morgan and his code are initially portrayed in an extremely attractive way and the viewer's identification with him is, by these means, encouraged. (The opening episodes in which Johnson is introduced, largely as a foil to Morgan's considerable virtues, serve to cement this allegiance from the start.) The primary movement of the film consists in Morgan's coming to see, through his involvement in two kinds of relationship, that his code is too narrow. He learns, specifically, that other types of human and social claims *can* be accepted without compromising his fundamental ideal of integrity based on self-reliance. At the film's end he has formed a sexual partnership with Slim (Lauren Bacall), in which acknowledged affection is no longer regarded by him as one of the strings that would curtail his freedom. From de Bursac, the resistance fighter who self-admittedly lacks Morgan's courage and abilities, he gains the vision of a larger moral enterprise in which an agent may play a subordinate role, dependent on others, without subordinating his individuality or his values.

The film, in effect, defines two extremes between which Harry Morgan and his attitudes are poised. One pole is exemplified in the line of questioning that Morgan's sidekick, Eddie, administers ("Was you ever bit by a dead bee?" and so forth) to determine whether a stranger can be accepted as "alright"—that is, admissable to the isolated circle that consists solely of himself, Morgan, and the café owner, Frenchy. This is a grotesque and demented projection of the challenges, rituals, and tests to which Morgan repeatedly subjects Slim. Contrastingly, the positive alternative to these exclusionary routines is represented by the spontaneous, good-natured unity of the combo, which produces harmony and humor out of the unconstrained and individualized efforts of its members. When Morgan, Slim, and Eddie bounce out of the hotel together to the band's rhythms, this is a definitive resolution of the narrative's main tensions.[4]

The film's severely effaced but restricted narration enforces a special relation between the audience and the moral and psychological developments of the narrative. By setting up and playing upon the strong identification with Morgan—thus implicating the viewer in the narrowness of his code—and by then holding to a perspective that coincides essentially with Morgan's own knowledge and experience, the film tries to bring the spectator to something like the same discoveries that Morgan makes about himself and by a route similar to the one he follows. If it succeeds, the viewer should experience the upshot of the film more as a personal realization of his or her own temptation to find certain plausible but constrictive ideals attractive and less as the intellectual acceptance of a body of ethical truth that has been asserted through the film.

In all of the films that have been examined in this chapter, the narrational authority is restricted in some relation to a character in the film. These are the cases that are easiest to explicate, but some of the most interesting applications of the concept of "restricted authority" in film involve restrictions that are more general and abstract than any of these. It is not a simple matter, however, to obtain a helpful picture of how the more abstract possibilities are to be conceived. Nevertheless, as so often happens in thinking about cinema, there are remarks by André Bazin which, as I am inclined to read them, point in the right direction.

Included in the summary of his argument in "The Evolution of the Language of Film" is the following famous statement: "In analyzing reality, montage presupposes of its very nature the unity of meaning of the dramatic event. Some other form of analysis is undoubtedly possible but then it would be another film. In short, montage by its very nature rules out ambiguity of expression. Kuleshov's experiment proves this *per absurdum* in giving on each occasion a precise meaning to the expression on a face, the ambiguity of which alone makes the three successively exclusive expressions possible."[5] Bazin's point about the Kuleshov experiment is simple and trenchant. If analytical editing can assign a definite psychological meaning to an essentially ambiguous facial expression, as that experiment was supposed to show, then the same experiment proves that if it is desired to preserve a visual sense of the expression's ambiguity, then analytical editing may be just what should be avoided. The ambiguity of a person's countenance or actions may be the dominant fact about him for an interested observer on the scene. The unresolved possibility of different interpretations all resident in his look or behavior may be what most defines the observer's problematic relation to him. So this precise quality of ambiguity is something that a film maker may want to capture for the screen. If so, certain kinds of interpretative interventions in the editing are necessarily precluded.

This insight is easily generalized and Bazin intends it to be. In the quoted passage, he speaks quite generally about the montage-imposed "unity of meaning of the dramatic event." That there is such a unity in any activity is always a presupposition, justified or not, which is at least open to question and debate. Insofar as film accepts the role of analyzing and extending the possibilities of integrated perceptual experience, it forswears the role of mirroring a number of the restrictions that are imposed by their perceptual capacities on human observers in general; namely, those restrictions that the analytical style attempts to abrogate. In our ordinary experience of the world, nothing outside of us singles out for our attention the most significant aspects of, and patterns in, the space-time slices we perceive. Nothing presents us with the telling close-up or the synoptic long shot, and nothing cuts the moments of perception into a segmented, transparent ribbon that adheres to a "dramatic logic" in the visible action. For this reason, the phenomena we witness often appear to us as puzzling, indeterminate, ambiguous, and without a guiding structure. This is a fundamental truism about our fragile perceptual connection to the world and, as a fact about our universal limitations as perceivers, it is one that has the deepest human consequences. Naturally, it is no part of the conceptions that underlie most traditional narrative film to deny these undeniable propositions, but it is a part to treat these propositions as specifying conditions that it is the function of film narrative and narration to *transcend*. The idea, as discussed before, is to extend our perceptual powers in ways that cut through some of the limitations and unveil the perspectives that they hide. But Bazin's proposal seems to be that there is no reason why these very limitations and their significance for us should not be a major subject of film. Given an appropriate shift in style away from some of the narrational configurations of the unrestricted, analytic mode, the image track can be ordered in such a way that certain of the general conditions of human perception would be implicated in its form. This form would be embedded within cinematic structures that make the nature and effects of these perceptual conditions a part of what the film explores. The alternative style that Bazin envisages would respect the continuity and complexity of the spatio-temporal integration of a field of action while being willing to leave the causal and psychological/teleological integration of the action less articulated. In regard to the appropriate shift in style, he hails the use of greater depth of field and the more frequent occurrence of long takes as its most typical components.

He also cites Jean Renoir as the most important exponent of the kind of film narration that he is trying to describe and names *The Rules of the Game* as one of its leading instances.[6] Certainly, one does have a sense of the narration of that film as struggling under limitations that any embodied observer would face. It represents a continued and intermittently frustrated attempt to keep under surveillance a complex of interlocking activities, which progressively become too irrepressible and impenetrable to be kept effectively in sight. Characters that seem to have been misplaced five minutes before pop up suddenly in deep focus, screened by some action in the foreground, an action that subsequently results in inexplicable tears or evolves into an unexpected piece of farce. These people are likely not so much to enter and exit a scene as to fall by graceful happenstance into the tracking camera's range. When the marquis has laid down the terms of the icy order that reigns at the film's end, every aborted resolution in the previous narrative proclaims that this calm can be no more than an artificial and temporary prelude to chaos, a chaos that, when it comes, no form of vision will adequately survey.

The short scene after the hunt in which Berthelin loans Christine his small field glasses serves as a kind of negative rhetorical figure of narrational instruction. It instructs the audience in the dangers of a too finely focused scrutiny, a method of investigation that the film has renounced. In a point-of-view shot (rare in this film), the film viewer looks with Christine through the field glasses at a squirrel in a nearby tree. Berthelin at the same time announces that the instrument is optically so refined that an observer can live every detail of the squirrel's life with it. But Renoir's squirrel, like Lang's frogs in *You Only Live Once*, appears as a shiny-eyed little creature whose sensibility and cognition are irreducibly alien to our own. The figure of the squirrel is magnified and, in that way, brought closer, but the effect of this is simply to distance any impression that the details of the squirrel's life have thereby been grasped. Shortly afterward, looking again through the field glasses, Christine spies her husband embracing Genevieve. She finally sees what everyone else has long known—that these two have been having an affair. And yet, this sighting also occludes from her view every significant feature of the context—for instance, that this embrace is a gesture of farewell as Robert parts from Genevieve for the sake of Christine and their marriage. It is the central formal problem of the film to discover a style that does not foster illusions of the field glasses variety.

This film must not pretend to reveal what is really inscrutable; it must not superimpose an order on an actual disorder; and it must be as open and responsive as possible to action and context, which constantly shift against all conventional expectations. The action promises, again and again, to assume the outlines of one familiar theatrical form or another, but then it collapses into the equivalent of a cast stampede when someone in the wings cries "Fire!" In the mixture of tragedy and comedy that makes up *The Rules of the Game*, the "god" who arrives on stage from a machine, the pilot André Jurieu, appears at the beginning of the piece, and the problem henceforth is to eliminate the disruption that his intercession provokes. It is characteristic of the film that it is a confused and complicated incident of chance that takes care of the job and so brings down the curtain on a traditional device of plot resolution, the *deus ex machina*, which has been effectively turned inside out. Such pointed reversals of narrative structure are matched by a narration that discards many of the analytical strategies of more conventional contemporary films. This is what Bazin so much admires. Most scenes start up without any sort of standard establishing shot, and many seem to end arbitrarily while the action proceeds without closure. The use of single figure close-ups is quite restrained and, related to this, the normal shot/countershot treatment of two party conversations is strikingly infrequent. And, of course, the narration is marked by its realization of the stylistic principles that Bazin endorses. On either side of the rhetorically separate hunt sequence, the duration of the shots is, on average, unusually long, and the shots are very often taken with the camera in more or less elaborate motion. The conceptual sophistication of the use of depth of field has probably never been surpassed.[7]

Many people, when they see *The Rules of the Game* for the first time, come away with the feeling that its narration is somehow in a state of disarray. The idea is wrong, but it is not an unreasonable first response to a style that is designed to acknowledge the limitations of film or any other finite apparatus of observation set up to watch comprehensively and with comprehension a process as intricate as the breakdown of the lives of these characters. The film assembles the fragments of a spectacle that almost no one in 1939 was prepared to see. The film's governing attitude is *not* a blanket skepticism about human knowledge and perception, and the fragments it assembles tell a great deal. But the narration declares its responsibility to the thesis that any overview of events such as the ones in this film will be slightly off center, in dubious epistemic focus, explanatorily disconnected, and, in various ways, incomplete. The audience sees that these fragments cannot honestly be joined into a well-shaped whole and, in some respects, they see why. In accomplishing this, *The Rules of the Game* discovers a new form for narrative film.

Bazin's position in "The Evolution of the Language of Film" has been construed here as identifying the existence and value of a nonsubjectivized form of restricted narrational authority. According to this interpretation, his insights belong to a part, although an important part, of a theory of point of view in film. It should be admitted, however, that this may not be the interpretation that he intended. As his essay's title suggests and much of its content confirms, Bazin gives the appearance of thinking that he is describing *the* narrational mode that answers properly to the "intrinsic realism" of photographic representation. This is not the place to work through the intriguing but maddening pronouncements, hints, and metaphors by means of which he tries to explicate his concept of the kind of "intrinsically realistic" representation that he takes to be the sign of any true photographic art. Like many others, I find this cluster of suggestions ultimately opaque, but, for present purposes, judgment may remain suspended.

The proposal before us is to hold onto Bazin's insights about the significance of form and technique within a more modest framework. Actually, in a passage on *The Rules of the Game* in his unfinished book on Renoir, Bazin echoes some of the themes of "Evolution," but does so in a context that is much closer to the one I favor. Referring, in the first quoted sentence, to the episode of the field glasses, he asserts:

> Just as it was chance that brought the husband into [Christine's] field of vision, so it is chance that determines to a certain degree what part of the scene the lens will uncover. And, paradoxically, it is this chance which makes the perspicacity and the vigilance of the eye so important. The point of view of the camera is not that of the novelist's omniscient third-person narrator; nor is it a stupid, unthinking subjectivity. Rather it is a way of seeing which, while free of all contingency, is at the same time limited by the concrete qualities of vision: its continuity in time and its vanishing point in space.[8]

This is an excellent short statement of some of the points that I have wished to stress, and they are independent of the stronger views that "Evolution" seems to contain. Bazin has succeeded, I have claimed, in describing a system of film narration that is aimed at reflecting the conditions of human perception more *realistically*. And this may very well be as far as "realism" enters into the matter at all. I also cannot see that the narrational mode that Bazin specifies exemplifies better than other stylistic alternatives "the real language of film." In each instance, I have been arguing throughout, different styles can be employed to give aesthetic shape to different assumptions and questions about either our perceptual relationship to the world in general or to film in particular. There may even be reasons for generally preferring one mode over others (although I doubt it), but they would have nothing to do with the supposed requirements of an underlying grammar or semantics of the cinema.[9] The merit of Bazin's argument is that it sharpened our awareness of a large and important narrational option where one all-embracing conception had seemed to stand before.

An advantage of giving Bazin's theory of film form a reduced scope is that it may help discourage the belief that there is a central and intelligible debate about whether film is or is not a realist medium. Too often writers on film theory seem to imagine that they are obliged to stake out a "realist" or "antirealist" position, no matter how vague and arbitrary that may be, before they are entitled to proceed to another topic. However, the theorist is free to develop Bazin's remarks, considered as a partial account of restricted narrational authority, without deciding for or against the murky proposition that a photographic image "shares its visual being" with its subject. And development of what is surely a very partial account is exactly what is needed—needed, in particular, by a theory of cinematic narration. We patently do not possess satisfactory discriminations between what either restricted or unrestricted narrational modes can achieve. We have nothing like an adequate understanding of the epistemic and aesthetic presuppositions upon which different concrete narrational possibilities have been or might be based. Here as elsewhere more detailed attention to the strategies of instructive individual films is likely to be the theorist's most reliable guide. But much of the needed work is likely to be blocked if the issue of "cinematic realism" continues to have the precedence that it has so long enjoyed.

I have stated several times that traditional theories of film narrative and narration tend to regard film as an instrument through which the range and acuity of human perception is to be extended. Futher, I indicated, more narrowly, that this conception is likely to build upon an acceptance of commonsense assumptions about the kinds of natural significance that are rightly ascribed, through perception, to appropriate segments of empirical reality. From this theoretical orientation, it is by applying these assump-

tions—assumptions that are often constitutive of intelligible experience—
to the novel structures and aspects of a particular film that we come to a
fresh understanding of their depicted contents as bearers of exhibited
meaning and emotional force. However, corresponding to many of these
types of assumption, there is a general form of skepticism about their
soundness or justification. Indeed, most of our more primitive inferences
from the "perceptually given" to this or that fundamental sort of significance have been made the subject of skeptical doubt. I am calling
attention here not to the broad recognition of, and reflection upon, the
limited and conditioned character of human perception, but to more
delimited questions about the assumptions we unthinkingly make in
describing and explaining the world in certain reasonably specific ways. A
good example, with special relevance to the following discussion, is
skepticism abut other minds. I mean this to include not only radical
skepticism about the justifiability of our inferences from behavior to the
mental states and processes it purportedly expresses but also the somewhat
more moderate doubts about whether our mentalistic conceptual inventory
is the most adequate way of describing and explaining human action.
Similarly, at least since Hume, parallel questions have been broached
about the concept of causality, and developments in contemporary science
have sometimes seemed to reinforce its uncertain status. In addition,
although these and similar skepticisms can be framed as problems for pure
philosophical debate, they also may be felt more immediately, if perhaps
less systematically, as troubled hesitations of thought induced by a sense
of the strangeness and unpredictability of the world. Sensible phenomena
sometimes appear to us as more than merely ambiguous or obscure: they
leave us intermittently dubious about the applicability of the ground-level
schemata with which we order and interpret experience.

I have introduced this reminder of well-known epistemological themes,
because it is still another possibility of film to invite its viewers to suspend
and reappraise some of their automatic assumptions about how and where
significance can be discerned in the workings of the world. It can arouse
that uncanny sense of the world as alien to our concepts and demonstrate
the fragility of the categories that visual intelligence unhesitatingly imposes upon the views before our eyes. By the wholesale restructuring of the
expected order of things in one or another dimension it can elicit a "duck to
rabbit" shift in our unrationalized picturing of even the most familiar
objects of perception. That is, a film may attempt a distancing, of greater or
lesser degree, of various normal and primitive assumptions about the
structure and intelligibility of visual experience over time. When this sort

of *epistemic distance* is established by a film, then, in a sense, a kind of restriction on the perceptual access it offers has been imposed. But this is a kind of restriction of a nature quite different from anything considered up to now. For, in these cases, the range of types of facts the narration may portray can be quite unlimited: the restriction here is on the ways in which the viewer is licensed to draw upon commonsense beliefs and normal observational practices to render that narration into overall significance.

Actually, most films, including the most banal, attempt a certain distancing to some extent by imposing an unnatural framework of blatantly communicated meaning upon the surface of the action. We are encouraged to see, for example, the characters as if they were signs or symbols in a universe imbued with predesigned significance. However, one associates more original and radical strategies of distancing with directors such as Carl Dreyer, Robert Bresson, Alain Resnais, and Pier Paolo Pasolini and with some of the work of the avant-garde and experimental film makers from the twenties to the present. Nevertheless, within certain dimensions at least, the use of systematic distancing is exploited in surprising forms that remain, in other ways, closer to the paradigmatic Hollywood norms.

This is a topic that will arise often in the analyses of the following chapters, but a brief example should help to explain the kind of strategy I have in mind. It will also explain the relevance of my previous reference to general skeptical positions. In von Sternberg's *The Scarlet Empress*, the viewer is offered human psychology in a drastically reductionist format. The central characters are simply stripped of any vestige of intellectual, emotional, and spiritual complexity. Their behavior is certainly motivated, but it is motivated in the most mechanical way by greed, lust, insanity, and the will to personal and political power. These highly stylized characters are repeatedly linked visually to recurring mechanical dolls, which mimic their actions and represent the approximate sophistication of their mental life. Intermittently, a character will make some display of a "higher" emotion or attitude, but these are displays merely, delivered in the most ludicrous manner of Hollywood melodrama or farce. In contrast with the clockwork animation of the mechanical dolls is the brooding immobility of the countless elaborate statues with which the characters are constantly intermingled. The stone figures are frozen in postures of grief, despair, extreme suffering, and religious ecstacy. They register, as representations that the human beings have made, all of the deeper emotional responses that the human beings in this film could never undergo. These devices have an especially interesting point. By also repeatedly underscoring, principally by means of stylization of the acting, that these film characters are themselves representations—beings that are outlandishly represented by stars playing their minimal roles—von Sternberg allows us to place our more "natural" view of human beings within his peculiar outlook.

The vaunted richness and subtlety that we ascribe to our own inner lives are portrayed as deceptive features of roles that we project in our dealings with ourselves and others. The inner life itself is held to be largely such a projected role. Behind these roles and providing their usual aim are the cruder forces that are seen to move the schemes and counterschemes of von Sternberg's creations. The actor's relation to a stereotyped role is given as the model for the relation that we assign to the human figure and the complicated private life that is presumed to animate it. The machines of flesh that are seen in the film embody fully the psychological reality that would emerge if most of our actorish pretensions were suddenly to be swept away. Freed by the film from our psychological presuppositions and concerns, we are also to be freed, in particular, from any misconceived interest in issues of motivation and morality in connection with the creatures of this film. Given that the "inner" is shown to be of no particular significance or appeal, we can contemplate, with fresh eyes, the considerable virtues of the "outer." Human beings, like the works of art with which they surround themselves, can be redeemed by their purely physical beauty, grace, and symmetry. The ultimate order of rank, from von Sternberg's amazing, inverted perspective, is generated by an aestheticized form of the erotic.

The existence of a rather extreme stylization in *The Scarlet Empress* is typical of films that involve the kinds of epistemic distancing which are now under discussion. There is a striking and specific resemblance between von Sternberg here and a more obviously metaphysical director such as Bresson. The latter also goes to considerable pains to deflect the viewer's attention from questions that are merely about the individual psychology of his characters, and a severe stylization of the acting is, again, a key device in achieving this result. Unlike von Sternberg, however, Bresson uses deflection in neither a skeptical nor a reductionist way. Rather, his aim in muting the outward tokens of the psychological is to create a charged field, in the faces and figures of his characters, which is more surely open to the signs and marks of the spiritual (as Bresson quite specifically conceives *this*). His characters are made to embody visibly the states and activities of their souls.

This brief comparison between disparate directors can be generalized. Naturally, the elements that are stylized and the character of that stylization differs greatly from one instance of epistemic distancing to another. But, in general, the strategy of distancing involves the blocking out or screening off of certain types of properties and relations which we would normally expect to perceive in the action portrayed. Correspondingly, other qualities and attributes are heightened and brought to the fore which would normally appear recessively at best. In short, a cinematic fictional world is constructed in which certain familiar properties and relations either do not appear at all or only minimally do apear while other properties and relations become unnaturally manifest. On any ordinary inspection, a film that employs such strategies unavoidably appears strongly "unrealistic." Nevertheless, the suggestion that is meant to inform the whole film is that *if* we did see things naturally and directly in the proper way—if our sight were informed by genuine philosophical insight—then the world would appear to us in a manner much more like the way in which it appears in the film in question. The visual surface of the filmic world is systematically distanced from the visual surface (as we know it) of the actual world. But the film is meant to imply that the existence of this gap is to be attributed, either with full seriousness or, as in the case of von Sternberg, with much self-reflecting irony, to the drastically inadequate and misleading nature of our perceptual powers, beliefs, and habits. The "vision" of the film is affirmed to be a metaphysically more accurate moving "picture" of the world.

It can seem incongruous that these more extreme strategies tend to be found, in Hollywood films at least, in some of the more lurid and less respectable genres; for example, suspense and horror films, soap operas and similar melodramas, the more hysterical fringes of the western. And yet, for reasons briefly considered toward the end of chapter 3, this is really not so surprising at all. It is true, on the whole, that the Hollywood production and distribution system was not going to let through easily a film whose form or style was so idiosyncratic as to be disconcertingly distinct from what its expected audience was used to. However, in the wilder instances of the tackier genres, their audiences were already used to a lot that was pretty strange. Crazy plots, wooden and implausible acting, elaborately unlikely settings, and madly exotic lighting are just a few of the items that had probably been swallowed whole a hundred times before by fans of the relevant genre. Whatever pleasures we may still derive in these contrivances of fun and incoherence, they were not products of artistry and thoughtful sensibility. Nevertheless, if one could not have predicted the specific, carefully wrought weirdness of von Sternberg's films (or, say, of

Welles's *Lady from Shanghai* or Ray's *Johnny Guitar*) from their seedier antecedents, the lesser efforts did serve the function of building up a context within which the truly exceptional development did not appear, on the face of things, outrageously *more* absurd than their genre kin. Beyond this, the merely tacky antecedents created opportunities for exploring styles of acting, manipulated *mise en scène*, and unprecedented patterns of drama and editing which could be employed in creations that had a deeper method to their madness. Forms and techniques that subserve a deviant metaphysics or epistemology could be offered to audiences that had already been freed from an undue attachment to popular notions of "dramatic realism." In films such as *The Scarlet Empress* and *The Devil Is a Woman* the difference between an acceptable genre piece and an experiment in surrealism becomes almost vanishingly small.

In chapter 1, I suggested that the kind of account of cinematic point of view I was proposing to develop would achieve a tolerable clarity of outline by the end of the present chapter. I hope, of course, that this suggestion has already proved to be true, but it may be helpful to sketch in summary the outlines that have emerged. I began in chapter 1 with the thesis that point of view in film can be specified in terms of a set of assumptions about how the viewer is epistemically situated in relation to the narrative— assumptions that are implicit in the large scale strategies of the narration. But, following Gerard Genette, we could just as well say that point of view is based upon the various ways in which information about the narrative is *systematically regulated* throughout all of or large segments of the narration.[10] The assumptions that I referred to are then to be understood as assumptions about the nature and function of the regulation of narrative information. Looking at matters in this light, we can draw up a rough classification of the types of regulative *constraints* upon information that we have thus far identified. The categories of point of view we have examined can be defined, at least partially, by the specific constraints of each type which are operative in a given film. In some cases, a category may also depend upon the manner in which and/or the degree to which narration might deviate from one or another (standard) constraint.

In chapter 3, I dealt with the first two items on this list; in this chapter with items 3–5:

1. constraints that establish the usual forms of classical *narrative*, for example, the autonomous reality of the fictional world or the explanatory coherence of the fictional events; and

2. constraints that establish the usual forms of classical *narration* , for example, transparency of the image or the systematic marking out of explanatory coherence;

3. constraints that establish the nature of the perceptual experience or the epistemic position of the film's chief characters;

4. constraints that establish the relations of the narration to certain general conditions of ordinary human perception; and

5. constraints that establish suitable norms of perceptual intelligibility for the narrative constituents.

Inspection of this list reveals that the divisions are not mutually exclusive, but they impose, I hope, a helpful order on the material covered so far. In chapter 7, I go on to investigate whether there are dimensions of film which bear a significant correspondence to what in literature is known as "voice." Is there a being represented or somehow manifested in a film who can be thought of as showing the narrative to the viewer through the specific construction of the narration? And, if so, what epistemic relations can these beings have to the narrations that they actually or fictionally construct? The answer to the first of these questions will be a severely limited affirmative, and this will make possible an addition to the available categories of point of view.

Just as a theory of point of view in literature explores the broader systematic relationships that can hold between an activity of fictional telling and the fictional situations that are told, so a theory of point of view in film should study fictional activities of showing and their relations to the shown. I have assumed, however, that the literary theory should be more than an inventory of strategies; it should explicate the ways in which the different strategies raise different problems about what the activity of narrative comprehension can and cannot achieve. Similarly, I have assumed that different narrational strategies in film differ in their implications for perceptual comprehension in any of a host of ways. Since verbal telling and cinematic showing are such very different narrational procedures, the issues that get raised in each case are not at all identical. Nevertheless, if one compares the range of distinctions drawn here with the set of "point of view" categories in a standard work of pertinent literary theory such as Wayne C. Booth's *Rhetoric of Fiction* or Genette's *Narrative Discourse*, it will be discovered that a network of substantial but limited analogies exists.[11] But then, it was to be expected that many problems about how the narration yields access to the fictional world would be shared between literary and cinematic narration. It is just that the concrete instantiation of these problems will take quite different forms. It would be interesting to investigate the possibility of a restricted but unified theory of point of view which would cover key properties in both domains. But this is not an investigation that is carried out in these pages.

Nevertheless, I shall affirm my belief that the importance of point-of-view considerations in film and literature are much the same. The forms of narration in question substantially help to define the orientation of the viewer or reader in apprehending the fictional world of the work and thereby fix some of the most general attributes that diverse narrative elements are understood to have. Further, it is not only the apprehension of matters within the narrative that can be formed or altered in this way. One's perception of film or literature as mechanisms of narrative portrayal can also be reshaped at the same time. For us, *You Only Live Once* and *North by Northwest* have been the clearest examples of this possibility, but it is a possibility that is to some extent a factor in all of the films analyzed in this volume. I assume that the power of techniques of point of view to transform the reading of a novel or short story are well-known, but the extent and depth of this power in films has not been adequately appreciated.

It has been the enterprise of this chapter and chapter 3 to point out that there are reasonably determinate narrational structures that underlie the kind of global shift of prospect that I have stressed. These structures can be described and discussed in a style that makes plain their relevance to familiar issues about the quirky interplay of human perception and the world.

In chapter 6, we turn to Max Ophuls' most famous American film, *Letter from an Unknown Woman*. In some respects, this film reinforces and illustrates some of the points made in the present chapter. For example, it is a central fact about *Letter* that its narration is restricted in a special way in relation to the viewpoint of its main character. Partly because of this restriction, the nature of the character's peculiar subjectivity is of paramount concern in the film, and the relevant facts about her subjectivity are portrayed in an unusually vivid way. However, in other respects, an adequate analysis of the precise properties of the narrational restriction reveals how some of the point-of-view classifications I have recently proposed are too broad and crude; for example, the distinction between direct and reflected subjectivity does not suffice. One reason is that we have thus far given no place to the idea that aspects of the film maker's sensibility may themselves come to be reflected in a film, not just in a general way, but by means of strategies that acknowledge rather concretely the fashion in which those personal qualities have shaped the form in which the narrative has been shown. But, here as elsewhere, I take the recognition of such incompleteness as an invitation to extend the framework that we have built.

Chapter 6

Max Ophuls'
Letter from an Unknown Woman

*It has been borne upon me this evening
that perfect music has the same effect on
the heart as the presence of the beloved. It
gives, in fact, apparently more intense
pleasure than anything else on earth.*

*The habit of listening to music and the
state of reverie connected with it prepare
you for falling in love.*
Stendhal, *L'Amour*

In the first half of Max Ophuls' *Letter from an Unknown Woman*[1] there occurs a pair of shots, linked across distinct sequences, which seems paradigmatic of the methods and concerns of this strange and delicate film. The first shot takes place when Lisa Berndle, having fled her family's departure for Linz, stands waiting for Stefan Brand at the top of the stairs that lead to his apartment. The camera, panning slowly, comes to occupy a position slightly behind and above her—looking over her shoulder and down the stairway. From this vantage point, we see, along with Lisa, Brand returning for the night accompanied by a beautiful and unidentified young woman. Later in the film, with the camera in exactly the same position, we are shown Lisa ascending the stairs with Brand. It is she who on this occasion will spend the night with him. The obvious irony, of course, is that Lisa has taken her place in what we know to be a procession of women who have climbed the same stairs with this same man. She has simply replaced that other unknown young woman whom she had watched with so much pain. The repetition of camera placement underscores the repetition of action. But there is more suggested than this. In the second shot, given its relation to the first, the visible absence of Lisa as observer of the scene makes salient that she is now merely the subject of *our* perception and is utterly removed from the perspective that earlier she had held. (If the first of these shots had been a subjective shot that directly presented her field of vision and thus excluded her wholly from the frame, then the echoing second shot would not mark as it does her earlier complicity and later lack of complicity with the camera's point of view.) This simple strategy of echoing with a variation yields the sense, almost as an overtone to the second shot, that Lisa at this juncture lacks any consciousness of herself as an element in a mere recurrence of an event that had overwhelmed her consciousness.

I spoke of these shots as constituting a kind of paradigm within *Letter from an Unknown Woman* for the following reasons. First, this device of "echoing with a variation" is repeated frequently throughout the film, often with the effect of showing the past to be interwoven with the present in ways the characters cannot grasp. And this is specifically connected with an issue, raised several times in the film, about the extent to which the characters are acting freely as they pursue their ends. There is a suggestion, made by Lisa, that destiny, chance, or some other outside agency rules her actions and Brand's. Second, it is central to the conception of the film, I shall argue, that Lisa is depicted as a consciousness who is crucially closed off to the significance of her experience and, particularly, her relationship with Brand. Her perception of herself and her situation is filtered through a complex structure of fantasy and desire—an extreme instance of the kind of fevered crystallization that Stendhal so vividly describes.[2] In a way, Lisa is a fairly conventional heroine of a certain type of "woman's picture": the woman who sacrifices everything for an unworthy male. But this film is probably unique in its sharp definition of that sacrifice as the result of a partially willed obsession with an object of love who is largely the product of a passionate imagination. The film is doubly unique in that its disturbing heroine is viewed throughout with tact, sympathy, and serious affection. In *Letter* and in other Ophuls' films, love is held to be based necessarily on illusion, but the capacity for love is valued as a state of quasi-religious detachment from the self and from the world.

Moreover, if Lisa's love for Brand is sustained by an hallucination of the actual man, this is an obverse reflection of the cause of Brand's constricted and loveless character. For he also represents a closure of consciousness, a narcissistic sensibility turned in upon a dream of an "ideal woman," an ideal whom, as it seems to him, he never finds. Both of these characters are oddly bound together and apart by a deluded worship based upon a conception of a perfect love. The issue is raised somewhat obliquely in the opening lines of the letter that frames the film. Lisa writes to Brand that "the course of our love had a reason that lay beyond our [hers and Brand's] poor understanding." Like much of the letter that we hear in voice-over, the sentiments are familiar from popular romance, but tested against what the film itself reveals, they have an edge that gives them an ironic force.

Finally, this hints at the characteristic mode of the specifically cinematic narration. If the central personages are hopelessly blind in different ways to one another, the film, through its construction and its style, continuously affirms the possibility of a wider and more accurate perception of the human affairs that it portrays. Again and again, the film establishes a larger viewpoint which its characters do not attain. For instance, the famous Ophulsian tracking shots not only repeat and thereby emphasize the fixed configurations that the characters trace out, but, at the same time, holding these configurations at a certain distance, they delineate the telling connections and disruptions that the characters have missed.

Further, Lisa and many of the other characters are presented as acting out some internally constructed drama that they, with varying degrees of self-consciousness, try to impose upon the public circumstances in which they move. This is frequently marked in the visual narration by bringing out a certain theatricality in the manner in which they negotiate a confrontation that, as it seems to them, either favors or threatens the desired resolution of their inner dramas. (This obviously complicates the question, mentioned before, about the freedom or lack of it with which these characters act.) However, these last points raise a definite problem. Most of the film is understood to be, in some sense, a visual rendering of the contents of Lisa's letter to Brand. How then can the film yield a perspective significantly wider than her own?

To make a start at answering this in even the most general terms, a still broader problem should be remarked. Whenever a fiction film includes a verbal narration of past events by a character who is supposed to have witnessed them, and the import of this telling is conveyed on the screen in a flashback, there is a potential question about how the flashback is to be construed, a question that is not definitely settled by the ordinary conventions. Is it that the shots in the flashbacks are meant as a sort of "visual translation" of the verbal narrator's assertions? If so, for instance, it should be possible for the images, like the assertions, to grossly misrepresent the facts. Or is it that the flashback depicts, from its own proper perspective, the *actual* occurrences that the narrator then claims to be describing? Of course, in most cases, where the verbal narrator's accuracy is in no way impugned, the present distinction will not really matter. And yet, there is a strong reason for finding the second of these alternatives far more plausible. That is, the shots of the film present far more information than the speaker's statements could convey, and, thus, the presumption that what the audience sees "translates" what the speaker has said, seems, upon reflection, to be absurd. This, I suspect, is the true source of the controversy about the legitimacy of the "false" flashback that Hitchcock uses in *Stage Fright*. The falsity of the flashback forces one, in retrospect, to take it as a strict visual equivalent for the murderer's words but, for the reason just indicated, it is difficult to accept it on these terms.

In *Letter from an Unknown Woman*, the narration conforms generally to the tacit understanding that the events mentioned in Lisa's letter are being visually portrayed. Moreover, there is no question about the correctness of the letter, at least as an account of what events took place. Finally, there are qualities of Lisa's subjectivity which the film rather systematically reflects. Nevertheless, as I implied, there is also a quite striking effort to make it clear that the perspective that the film offers upon this history is *not* to be identified with Lisa's. The narration simultaneously establishes a certain distance from Lisa's outlook even while it mirrors some properties of her subjectivity. Many aspects of what we are shown seem alien to Lisa's point of view and sensibility. The pair of shots on the stairway with which we began illustrates the point nicely. In addition, many of the explanations and interpretations expressed in the parts of the letter that we hear bear a problematic relation to the facts and situations that we see unfold. We have already noted one instance of this. These and similar considerations entail that what I have characterized as the most plausible reading of a flashback is intended here to be definitely in force. But also, this cinematic narration declares itself to be a largely independent re-viewing of her past and insists that it has a coherence and integrity beyond that of her very special vision. Therefore, *Letter* leaves us with the job of defining the function of Lisa's narrating voice in relation to the film maker's narrating eye. However, since I believe that these relations are fairly complex and that they are central to the final force of the film, this job is feasible only after we have arrived at a somewhat detailed sense of the subsidiary structures that inform the film. We turn now to these structures, but with the broader task in mind.

When Lisa makes her disastrous final visit to Brand's apartment, Brand finds her gazing at a small antique bust of a woman. In response to her apparent interest, he explains the meaning that the statue has for him. He asks Lisa if she admires it as much as he does. The Greeks, he continues, once built a statue to a god they did not know but hoped would someday come. In his case, he tells her, the unknown but hoped-for deity has been a

Narration in Light

goddess. Every morning of his life he has awakened with the expectation that, on that day, the goddess would appear. But, of course, he adds, she never has and now he has given up the hope. These lines, I believe, are to be taken more or less at face value. For instance, they are pointedly reminiscent of Lisa's statement much earlier in the film that she has heard in Brand's playing a searching for something he had not found, a suggestion that seems to startle him with its perceptiveness. Presumably, at least part of the import of Brand's remarks about the statue is that, caught up in his fantasy of a perfect and impalpable ideal, he has moved, always dissatisfied, from one real woman to another. The restlessness this fantasy induces leads him, in Lisa's case, to miss the love she offers now and has offered in the past.

But if Lisa's deity is more distinctly embodied in the person of Brand himself, it is hard to ignore the film's insistence that her god is also an elaborate construction of her own. In a moment, we will examine some of the ways in which this fundamental fact is articulated in the film. However, it should be noted that there is a poignant ramification of the psychological kinship that these two people bear to one another. Both Lisa and Brand seem regularly on the verge of breaking through their private idealizations into some form of more vivid awareness of the other. Lisa, on varied occasions, expresses what seems a truer perception of Brand's character, and he repeatedly struggles to achieve a significant memory of her. It is pathetic and absurd that, every time they meet, Brand is troubled by the sense that he has known her sometime before. That he should not actually remember her *is* absurd, but his recurrent clouded impressions of coming close to something important he has lost in the past marks a continuity of feeling that he has for her, a feeling that, repressed as it is, he nonetheless retains. Lisa, of course, forgets nothing of their past together. It is her dream that there is a future for her love of Brand that is so problematic. And, just as he is haunted by shadows of memories of her, she is struck by a queer intermittent prescience about the fate of their relationship. Standing before a fun-fair wax museum, they discuss the probability that he will become so famous that the museum will someday own a statue of him. Jokingly, he asks her if she would come to see him then, and she answers that she would "if [he] would come alive." She sees various wax figures arrayed behind him while she speaks, and her response, made at the outset of their affair, hints at the very real question of whether the actual man can ever "come alive" to her. Shortly afterward, when they are dancing together, he asks her to promise not to vanish and she informs him gently that it is not *she* who will vanish. Later, when he leaves by train, purportedly on a two-week journey, it is obvious that she at least half-realizes that their parting signifies the destruction of their brief involvement. In these and related instances, it is dubious that the full meaning of what she says and feels is clear to her, but that meaning seems constantly to flicker on the borders of her thought. We have, in these examples, an indication of the enormous repressive weight their fantasies impose upon this pair. It leaves him with only the remnants of memory of her, and she sees him through crazy, curving mirrors that intermittently reflect a potent truth.

Much of the subtlety of the film depends upon the way in which it succeeds in revealing from an outside view the "inner process" of Lisa's self-construction of the object of her love. Indeed, the whole long section of the film before she leaves for Linz serves precisely to set out the basis and development of this construction. Thus, again at the beginning of her letter, Lisa asserts that everyone has two birthdays: the date of physical birth and the date of the birth of consciousness. As this line about the birth of consciousness is delivered, the tracking camera follows a younger Lisa as she surveys the profusion of elegant furnishings, musical instruments, and art objects that are being moved into the apartment Brand will henceforth occupy. In a dazed state of wonder, she drifts with the passage of these items up the stairs until she arrives for the first time at Brand's door. "I had never seen such beautiful things," she goes on in the letter, and it is clear that this is the first startling vision of style, culture, and splendor for an adolescent girl living in slightly straitened bourgeois circumstances. This *is* the birth of Lisa's consciousness, which is already focused, through the marvel and mystery of his belongings, upon a man she has not even seen.

Lisa is an isolated and insecure figure as she threads her way through the commotion of the move, and her general state of isolation becomes a major theme of the first part of the film. Most particularly, the great love for Brand is shown to have been conceived at a distance, without significant contact with the man himself. During this formative period, they never really meet. From what we learn, he appears to her briefly, intermittently, and with hardly a word exchanged. When she perceives him, there is almost always some literal barrier interposed between the two. There are repeated shots in this early section of the film in which we watch from behind her as she looks out at him through a windowed view. The first time that she ever sets eyes upon him she gazes shyly through the glass panels in their apartment door while he leaves the building, and this establishes a motif that recurs in several variants. She also catches a glimpse of his

Narration in Light

picture on a concert program and devotes herself to a course of study in reading about music and musicians. And, most of all, she listens by herself, unnoticed, to the passionate romantic music that he plays. Hence, once more her perception is distinctly at a distance. She listens outside while the music pours down from his open apartment window or through a transom she has set ajar. Her letter informs him that these secret, lonely audiences provided "some of the most beautiful moments of [her] life." In all of this, it is as though her love had been conceived for a mobile wax statue with musical talent with whom she is acquainted only as a faithful visitor to his glassed-in case. There is, then, an added irony suggested when later they speculate about what it would be for her to view him in precisely this way.

In one very striking and curious scene, Lisa sits in the apartment house courtyard and listens while Brand practices the piano upstairs. She rocks herself gently in a crude rope swing as she hears the music. Her abstracted reverie is interrupted by the entrance of a girlfriend who rather contemptuously dismisses the music and goes on to relate an incident that she regards as much more thrilling. She has had an exciting encounter with an interested shopboy down the street. Taking a lusty bite from a piece of cake she is holding, the friend exclaims, "I'm going to have to do something about that boy if he doesn't keep his hands to himself. The things he does—right out in the street." The mock reproval in her tone signals her satisfaction at the rough attentions she has received. At this remark, there is an immediate cut to an insert of Brand playing the piano in his room and then to a shot of *his hands* as they powerfully strike the keys. (The shot is from below the level of the keyboard, emphasizing the downward force of the movement of his hands.) Finally, as the music swells to a crescendo, there is another cut back to Lisa in the courtyard, her cheek pressed against one of the swing's rough ropes. She is visibly stirred by the passion of the music. Both the intended comparison and contrast are clear. Just as the girlfriend has been sensually moved by her meeting with the shopboy, Lisa is likewise moved by Brand's playing. But the commonplace character of her friend's reaction is distinguished from the more private, sublimated, and idealized nature of Lisa's feelings. Nevertheless, the feelings in both cases are sexual. The character of the music, Lisa's dreamy state, her easy swinging motions, and, at one point, her abrupt distracted plucking at the swing ropes as if their tactile pressure were too intense to bear, all conspire to define her experience. Both girls undergo the beginnings of sexual responsiveness, but Lisa's response centers on Brand through the mediation of his music and in the absence of real interaction with him. As we will see later, it is through the mediation of Lisa's letter that Brand is awakened to Lisa and to the significance of her love. It is as if, for both Lisa and Brand, some expressive or representational structure, whether in music or in words, is required to generate and give form to the crucial vision of the person loved.

Immediately after this scene, Lisa proclaims in her letter that she "began to prepare [herself] quite consciously" for Brand. In a series of three shots, we are given a synoptic sense of what this solitary preparation comes to. In the first shot, she assiduously attends to the care of her clothes. In the third shot, she visits the music section of the public library to obtain biographies of the great composers. And in the second, the most unusual of these vignettes, Lisa goes to dancing school. The class consists of facing lines of boys and girls who are being put through their paces by a dancing instructor standing to one side. However, these lines of students are visible to us only through the open spaces cut in the top half of a partition that divides the hall. The partition separates the other students (in the rear of the shot) from Lisa (in the foreground). While the paired-off couples execute their steps, Lisa also practices the same movements, but she alone is dancing without a partner. Or, to describe the impression one has more accurately, she seems to be dancing with a partner who is invisible to everyone but her (see fig. 12). Toward the end of this extended shot, Lisa moves around the partition and tries awkwardly and un-successfully to join the other boys and girls. Thus, the imagined presence and actual absence of Lisa's dancing partner is amusingly portrayed, but, in the conclusion of the shot, another important element has been intro-duced. That is, we see the potential in Lisa's isolated commitment to disrupt the more normal course of male and female interaction.

This theme is handled in a similar but much more complex manner in the pair of sequences set in Linz. In the first sequence, Lisa and a promising young lieutenant are introduced by her parents and his father, a distinguished-looking colonel. As the handsome couple strolls leisurely around the town's central square, they carry on a pleasant if desultory conversation about the respective merits of Linz and Vienna. In the course of this exchange, the lieutenant, who is a bit displeased at her fondness for Viennese music, praises the outdoor concerts given on Saturdays in that very square. It seems as though the first stage of a budding and quite proper courtship is smoothly underway. The camera, which has followed them throughout their conversation, now swings back to permit a wider view. With this, we see the good people of Linz, mostly in couples (wives and husbands, parents and children), headed off to services at the

110

cathedral that fronts the square. Lisa and her lieutenant drift easily and naturally into this respectable Sunday crowd.

In the following sequence set in the same square, the musical glories that the lieutenant had praised materialize in the unlikely form of a stolid military band. The camera cranes up slowly from this ungainly group, rising almost as if it were lifted by the bombast of the music that we hear. As it rises, the camera picks up Lisa and the lieutenant headed for an intimate conversation in a garden adjacent to the square. Lisa's parents and the imposing colonel seat themselves at a nearby café in anticipation of an imminent engagement between the young people. In the next shot, with the camera fixed and framing them squarely, the couple take their places somewhat stiffly on a garden bench. The look and sound of the scene suggests a critical dialogue between the hero and heroine of a romantic and ridiculously banal light opera (see fig. 13). The lieutenant plays his part, correctly if a little clumsily, and delivers the inevitable proposal of marriage. But Lisa is the heroine in a plot that involves much more of passion and intrigue. She is, she confesses with appropriate breathlessness and melodrama, engaged to a musician in Vienna. Her parents know nothing of this secret engagement, but, naturally, she regards herself bound by her solemn vow. All of this, of course, is not quite the truth but it answers most acceptably to everything for which she wishes. The lieutenant is suitably shocked by the announcement and hastens to deliver the errant daughter to her parents. It is here that the arch theatricality of the scene is particularly underlined. Just as the flustered couple make their exit from the garden, the bouncing music rolls to a conclusion, and scattered spectators in the gardens, heretofore unseen by us, burst into appreciative applause at the dramatic departure. Moreover, in the following shot, the military band parades in file off the square leading still another procession of citizens of Linz. The wives and husbands, parents and children, who, in the previous scene, converged tranquilly upon the cathedral, now beat a rather clamorous retreat in the face of the folded courtship. The discomfited couple, returning to their dumbfounded parents, barge confusedly through the disappearing throng. This metaphorical disruption of the way that life is lived in Linz parallels the lesser disruption of the lines of dancing adolescents.

These relatively minor disruptions culminate much more explosively when Lisa later renounces her marriage to pursue Stefan Brand a final time. This is a topic to which we shall return later. But here I want to note that the strain of theatricality just described is found throughout the film as various of the characters play out real or fantasized roles. Consider, for

Fig. 12. Lisa (Joan Fontaine) at dancing school—divided from the other students in the background.

Fig. 13. The young lieutenant proposes to Lisa in a public garden in Linz.

Fig. 14. Lisa and Brand (Louis Jourdain) discuss the past in an amusement park railway.

Fig. 15. Lisa, in an outfit reminiscent of a gentleman's attire, purchases a bouquet of white roses for Brand.

113

Fig. 16. Lisa, shown roughly from the point of view of her observing husband, stands before the gate to Brand's apartment house.

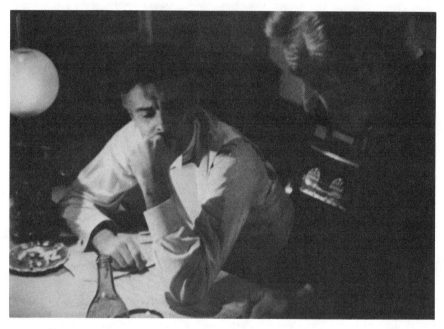

Fig. 17. Brand's manservant, John, writes the name of the "unknown woman" on her letter.

114

instance, the small set performance given by Lisa's mother when she announces her planned remarriage. Or consider Stefan's stagy seducer's manner among the columns outside the opera house. Or Johann Stauffer's stark warning to Lisa delivered beneath the crossed swords and hunting trophies that adorn his walls. Or, going back to the first third of the film, consider the scene in which Lisa trespasses into Brand's apartment. In the opening shot, the screen is initially darkened by what turns out to be a large carpet hung up for beating. The carpet is then pulled away (by Lisa) to display the courtyard and the apartment building where the ensuing action will take place. The effect is that of a curtain being opened with a flourish with the attendant revelation of a theatrical space in which some minor drama will be performed. And this is, indeed, what happens. Lisa, barefoot and dressed in the austere gown of a would-be religious acolyte, steals worshipfully up the back stairs and into Brand's apartment. She has made her way into precincts that are, in her eyes, made sacred both by the man and his music. The relevant connotations of religious service are treated with playfulness and irony in this context, but they come to assume a dimension less theatrical and of greater resonance as the film goes on. This scene constitutes the point at which Lisa first takes positive action to gain some sort of intimate knowledge of Brand and his personal life—to force herself somehow into that life. So, in a sense, it is the opening of the first act of their personal drama together. When Brand, long after their brief affair, reappears to her at the opera house, this renewal of their active relationship is announced at the very beginning of the scene by a voice that cries out "Act II—curtain going up." And so, on the portico of the opera house, it does. A sense of stylization in the acting of *Letter from an Unknown Woman* is partly to be accounted for by the way its characters tend to stylize themselves. It is a kind of measure, within the texture of the film, of the way these characters fail to comprehend their lives.

A number of the themes that have been adumbrated so far are clarified and enriched by the lovely sequence in which Lisa and Brand visit the amusement park. It is a winter evening, the park is almost deserted, and so the lovers' isolation is once again set in relief. What is more, their visit to the park is overtly portrayed as an escape into the sources of fantasy and childhood dreams. The setting, of course, is perfectly appropriate to this, and the implication is repeatedly taken up in the dialogue. When they first enter the snow-swept park, Brand asserts that he has always liked the place best at this time of year, to which Lisa replies, "Perhaps, because you prefer to imagine how it will be in the Spring." A little later, in a discussion of why he continues to climb dangerous mountains, she proposes that he likes to imagine that the next one will be more wonderful than the last. (Presumably, she does feel the particular edge her hypothesis contains.) Driving to the park, Lisa performs the maternal gesture of tucking in his muffler, and Brand muses, "It's been a long time since anyone did that for me." In a similar vein, when Lisa buys a candied apple at a stand, Brand, waiting a few steps back in frank appraisal, says, "Now I see you as a little girl." Finally, having made their first rounds of Europe on the magical fun-fair railway, Brand calls out, "We'll return to the scenes of our youth."

In the part of the simulated train ride that we see, they have returned to the scenes of Lisa's youth—to Lisa "seen as a little girl" (see fig. 14). They talk about her long-departed father, who was, she reveals, a regular champion of imaginary traveling. Although he held the unspectacular position of assistant superintendent of the municipal waterworks, at home he would put on his "traveling coat" to take his little daughter on flights of fancy to the farthest regions of the earth. Apparently, this game caused friction between husband and wife because Lisa reports her mother's claim that he knew the weather everywhere except the place he was. It is obvious that the father is supposed to have passed on his predilection for the realms of the imaginary to his daughter. When Lisa tells Brand that her father had "the nicest eyes," he answers, gazing into hers, that he can see that this is so. What is for him simply a pretty compliment registers the link between Lisa's vision, understood in the broadest sense, and her father's. This scene, above all, makes explicit the character of Lisa's cast of mind and the basis of her appetite for the rare, the exotic, and, especially, the beautiful.

The generally lighthearted ambience of this "magical" journey should be contrasted with the suffering and separation that real journeys on real trains entail, at least within this and other Ophuls' films. Brand, when he deserts her, and Stefan, Jr., before he dies, are taken from Lisa by trains. Brand's desertion seems mysteriously portended, even on his first night with Lisa, by the drawing of a train in a hotel advertisement that appears, rather oddly, in one of his concert programs, which he signs for an admiring countess. Somehow these real journeys in Ophuls' works either never return their passengers to their origin or, when they do, the people and the circumstances that were left behind have become completely transfigured.

The ride on the amusement park train should also be contrasted with a different, more somber nighttime ride that Lisa makes: the carriage ride home from the opera during which she and her husband discuss the consequences of the fact that she and Brand have met again, after many years, at a performance of *The Magic Flute*. This scene is very simply shot, with the camera always stationary and largely at medium range. Lisa and Johann Stauffer sit stiffly in the darkness of the carriage and do not look at each other as they speak. Their respective lines are delivered in a low-key manner, almost without overt expression of emotion, and punctuated by the regular, monotonous hoofbeats of the horses. The content of the lines is stereotyped, but in a fashion that defines the specific melodrama in Lisa's conception of her situation.

JOHANN: What are you going to do?

LISA: I don't know.

JOHANN: Lisa, we have a marriage. Perhaps it is not all you once hoped for, but you have a home and your son and people who care for you.

LISA: Johann, I would do anything to avoid hurting you, but I can't help it.

JOHANN: And your son? You think you can avoid hurting *him?*

This is still another scene in which the conventionally theatrical is evoked with some emphasis. Nevertheless, there are stronger and stranger currents beneath the flow of familiar words. In particular, her assertions of helplessness, while deeply meant, are ambiguously clouded by her dream of who Brand is.

JOHANN: There are such things as decency and honor.

LISA: I have told myself that a hundred times this one evening.

JOHANN: You talk as though it were out of your hands. It's not, Lisa. You have a will. You can do what's right—what's best for you—or you can throw away your life.

LISA: I've had no will but his—ever.

In the full context of the film, this last line—this perfect cliché of fictional romance—sounds absolutely extraordinary. If *Letter* has established any one thing it is the iron will of this woman to pursue the love of Stefan Brand and to possess it on her own terms. (In the letter, commenting on her refusal to identify Brand as the father of her child, she writes, "I wanted to be the one woman you've known that never asked you for anything.") As emerges shortly, she is determined to give up everything to regain this man. In contrast, it is Brand himself who seems to have no will of his own. He is the one who floats aimlessly from one love affair to another and who, it appears, allows his talent to dissipate in rather petty dissatisfaction with himself. When he and Lisa first meet as adults, he admits, "I almost never get to the place where I start off to," and similar thoughts are echoed several times. So the notion that Lisa espouses, that Brand has a will that dominates her, is unquestionably absurd. And yet, when Stauffer coldly dismisses her claims with the words "that's romantic nonsense," he is missing the important truth that lies behind her self-deception here. It may be nonsense that Lisa's will is controlled by Brand's, but it is not at all nonsense that this is exactly the way in which she is bound to perceive the situation. The phenomenon of crystallization is a phenomenon of self-projection, the lover projecting the deepest qualities of herself upon the person loved. It is therefore completely natural that Lisa's will should seem to her a mere reflection of Brand's. It is also not nonsense that her will and actions are apparently determined by the compelling drama that her imagination projects. However, somewhat inadvertently, Stauffer catches the contradiction in her fantasy when he asks the following about Brand.

JOHANN: What about him? Can't he help himself either?
LISA: I know now that he needs me as much as I've always needed him.
JOHANN: Isn't it a little late for him to find that out.

The aspect of theatricality in this scene is certainly not playful. Large issues are at sake for both Lisa and her husband. But Lisa speaks from the very center of her self-constructed illusion, and Stauffer cannot see beyond his codes of reason, honor, and propriety. As a consequence, each speaks stage speeches and cannot comprehend the other.

At the very outset of the opera sequence, Lisa's letter asserts, retrospectively, her powerlessness over her destiny, but this time on rather different grounds. "The course of our lives can be changed by such little things," she writes, " . . . I know now that nothing happens by chance. Every moment is measured, each step is counted." In this case it is Fate that she holds responsible for her reunion with Brand. This is one of the clearest instances of the way in which the familiar romantic rhetoric of the letter is belied by what we are shown. For, in the first place, it *is* apparently by chance that the two discover each other again. And, in the second place, it is she who, having seen Brand on the foyer stairs, subsequently leaves and makes possible their face-to-face meeting outside the hall. When Brand finds her nervously pacing on the opera house steps, he says, "Where there is a pursued, there must be a pursuer." However, his remark is ambiguous, because it is notably unclear which of them is the pursuer and the pursued.

This ambiguity is further heightened when Lisa actually pays her last visit to his apartment. The standard male and female courtship roles seem to have been weirdly reversed, and she is the one who appears in the guise of "a gentleman come calling." The clothes she wears constitute a feminine

Narration in Light

parody of a man's top hat and formal evening dress. Covering terrain over which Brand had once led her on their first evening together, she is forced to seek him out among his old established haunts. She is the one who purchases a bouquet of white roses (a near repetition of his earlier gesture) and bears them to her lover's door (see fig. 15). There is something a little absurd, pitiful, and, at the same time, terrible about this late-night caller with the bunch of white roses, this person in a severe suit of black and white with padded shoulders, standing outside the well-known apartment house gate. And it is this image of her that elicits a surprising piece of film work.

The image track has followed Lisa up to her arrival at the gate. Suddenly, there is a cut from a medium shot of her ringing the bell to an extreme long shot, from down the street, of her standing in the same position, a shot in which she is abruptly presented as distanced for us, diminished, and absolutely alone in acting on her fatal choice (see fig. 16). As soon as this new remote view has been allowed to register, the camera pans rapidly to one side to reveal that we are sharing her husband's perspective on her as he observes her from a carriage halted down the street. We are forcibly pulled back from our natural involvement with Lisa and made, for a moment, to see the figure that he sees. (This is another case in which the cinematic narration rather flamboyantly asserts its independence from the focus of Lisa's point of view.)

Inevitably, Lisa's last interview with Brand collapses into disaster. At this meeting, as before, he is oppressed by a dim sense of having seen or met her on some earlier occasion. But this, aside from his appreciative, predatory interest, is all. He does not remember who she is or what their relationship had been. Moreover, his manner has never seemed so coldly mechanical, so suffused with a glazed charm. While he chatters on, more and more trampling the past as he does, he calls out cheerfully, "You know you are a strange woman, Lisa." To this she has only the power to respond helplessly with the words "Am I?" Although he does not really understand the real force of his remark, Lisa *is*, of course, a very strange woman. It is the depth of this strangeness—the completeness of illusion and the strength of unacknowledged determination—that the film has so carefully laid out. However, the appalling strangeness of their whole relationship is most clearly revealed by the new fashion in which Brand has come to serve as a reflection of Lisa's sensibility. For in this scene, and earlier at the opera house, he enunciates, in his own style, many of the ingredients of her conception of the meaning of her devotion. He tells her, "I followed you upstairs and watched you in your box, but I couldn't place you. And I *had* to speak with you. I know how this sounds. I assure you that in this case it's true. You believe that, don't you?" Or again, "I have a feeling—please don't think I'm mad—I know it sounds strange and I can't explain it—but I feel that you understand what I cannot even say and that you can help. . . . Tonight when I first saw you and later when I watched you in the darkness, it was as though I had found that one face among all others." In his apartment, he continues in the same vein. "I knew last night, didn't you?" he asks her, and, echoing thoughts of hers about the unreality of time for them, "You're here, and, as far as I'm concerned, all the clocks in the world have stopped." Finally, from him to her, the most absurd line of all, "I know you won't believe it, but I couldn't get you out of my mind all day." In the first of the two scenes, we are not quite certain how his words are to be taken. But in the second, our doubts are answered. In his mouth at this time, her notions have become the hollow discourse of the practiced and sophisticated seducer. The convictions that have guided and then shattered her life are played by him like cards to which the infatuated woman should, he supposes, appropriately respond. Two faces of romantic love are captured here. There is the emotion that backs a world transcending commitment, and there is the decorated strategy of a game of sex. The power and emotional complexity of *Letter* depends upon our lively sense of the dialectic between these facets of the claims of love.

In pointing out the distorted reflection of Lisa in the mature Brand, I am not proposing a reading of the film that applies one or another "adverse" judgment to her.[3] It is important to stress this point because, although the movie exploits and undercuts the conventions of its genre to expose, putting it bluntly, a certain craziness in Lisa and her sacrifice, the vision that drives her is significantly a generous and redemptive one. When at last she flees in despair from her last assignation with Brand, she comes upon a drunken soldier in the streets below, a soldier who manages to slur out the baldest and most basic of propositions. The encounter is the final stark reminder to us of the more realistic alternatives to Lisa's impossible idealizations. Here, on one raw extreme, is an offer of the casual and unadorned sexual act. Or, from earlier in the film, there is the economic contrivance of her mother's well-calculated second marriage. Or there is the bland respectability of the life the young lieutenant has implicitly proposed. Lisa's pursuit of Brand is a strict rejection of the convenient, the comfortable, and the ceremonial in personal relations. It is a rejection of all the usual commerce of love. Lisa's work as a dress-shop mannequin is meant to symbolize her potential situation within the transactions of such a commerce. (In voice over: "Madame Spitzer's, where I found work, was the kind of establishment where one learns many things.") From this situation she has turned decisively away.

Nevertheless, the film, with its characteristic moral complexity, does not make it an easy matter simply to endorse her outlook. Certainly, the insistence on the deluded nature of her perception makes this hard enough. But we are also intended to be disturbed, not only by her actions toward her child, but by her desertion of Johann Stauffer. From what we see of him, he is undoubtedly rigid, restrained, and unimaginative, and he holds grimly to fundamental conventions of society that she does not accept. Still, it is clear that he is a man of decency, generosity, and genuine honor. In his reserved way, he loves her and her son sincerely. One is led to recognize that Stauffer is a representative of much that is best in the conventional ordering of things and made to feel the considerable cruelty in her leaving him. In the end, it seems that these tensions in our disposition to make some global judgment about Lisa are deliberately left unresolved. Her impulses toward beauty, perfectability in love, and selfless devotion are held in value as an almost religious aspiration. When Brand, through the words of her letter, discovers at last the spirit of her love for him, he is reclaimed to natural emotion and moral sentiment. The man without a will is redeemed to act again. So the redemptive and destructive sides of Lisa's passion must be balanced against each other and no ultimate assessment emerges.

I believe that this refusal to resolve certain of the larger issues is essential to the narrational assumptions of the film. I spoke of Brand's redemption by Lisa's letter, but there is a question about what precisely happens in this episode. Among the enigmatic shots that end the film, when Brand pauses at the foot of his apartment house steps before entering the carriage that will take him to the duel, a point-of-view shot occurs that shows his memory image of Lisa as she stood, when he first saw her, at the door. The shot is held surprisingly long; held, in fact, until we see the image dissolve away. It is hard to be sure whether it disappears only because he is about to turn and leave *or* because this image of Lisa fades for him now just as his memory of her has always vanished in the past. At least, the slight emphasis on the fading of the image raises the question. Moreover, Brand turns and leaves to fight a duel in which he surely will be killed. The significance of his action, as suicide, seems largely negative. Here, at last, the man takes definitive action, but it is an act of futility and resignation. In the concluding frames, a pair of dark, closed carriages starts heavily off through the rain-soaked morning streets. Hence, the culmination of everything that has gone before remains somewhat opaque.

The upshot of the whole affair, this daybreak journey to a duel, is moving and ghastly at the same time.

One reason for pondering the ambiguity of this scene is that a similar problem arises concerning the state of Lisa's mind at the time of her own death. As the narration of her letter draws to a close, the dominant impression is that Brand's spell over her has finally been broken. The dreadful revelation of their last encounter, the death of her son, the ruin of her marriage have, we assume, opened her eyes to the emptiness of their affair. And this may be so. However, the lines that terminate the letter are striking in this regard. For she says, "If this letter reaches you, believe this: that I love you now as I've always loved you. My life can be measured by the moments I've had with you and with our child. If only you could have shared those moments. If only you could have recognized what was always yours and found what was never lost. If only. . . . " But this is just the perspective she has always occupied: defining her life in relation to his, regretting that something somehow keeps them apart always. Even when the truth is before them both as they face death, it may still be that they are unable to hold onto a drastically altered view of their lives. There are these suggestions that she subsides into her constant fantasy and he into the vivid oblivion of his restless consciousness.

These uncertainties are also connected with the question of the role of human will in the behavior of these characters. Lisa, we know, imagines that romantic forces are unremittingly at work upon their action. But I have argued that it is their private visions or lack of vision that appear to determine their respective choices. The considerations of the previous paragraph hint at another level of complication. That is, it can seem, *if* the characters are substantially unchanged at the end, that there *is* an unidentifiable force, a determinative agency in operation, that binds them repeatedly to the only paths that they are able to perceive, paths that cross for a moment but, on the whole, diverge. This possibility is thus offered by the ending, but is also left as a troubling ambiguity.

That these matters are not closed off and specified assigns a limit to what this film's narration will claim to answer. Since *Letter* is throughout concerned with limits of perception, expression, and representation this should come as no surprise. In this respect, the narrational strategies of the film are deployed with dexterity and precision. At several points in this chapter, we have seen why the narration cannot be read as a mere visual rendering of the contents of Lisa's letter. The interrelationship of sequences and the design of shots and *mise en scène* are used too persistently as a means of commenting upon Lisa and her experience for that. For instance, we noted how the camera is authorized to step out of Lisa's field of knowledge and interest for a moment and how the repeated element of theatricality defines the unconscious self-dramatization that she and others perform. It is impossible to escape the impression of an intelligent and sometimes ironic observer, the implied film maker as it were, who is continuously observing with special insight into the wider patterns that Lisa ostensibly describes. In this light, the letter only fixes the more superficial aspects of narrative sequence and remains subordinate to the visual sensibility that relates it all for us.[4] Indeed, what is essential to the letter, within the framework of the film, is the way that it expresses Lisa's cast of mind and the way it elicits Brand's vision of her while he reads it. On the first point, we have already observed how the statements that we hear from the letter are often played off against the much more complicated facts established in what we come to see. At best, Lisa's words are safely taken to define her own self-conception and her conception of the situations in which she acts. Further, it is just these concepts that the letter conveys to Brand. The letter plays much the same role for him as earlier his music had played for her. It creates a detailed scheme for apprehending her actions and a particular mode for valuing the history that she portrays. In the montage of resurrected memory that Brand experiences after he has read the letter, it is only the most idealized and touching moments that occur. We are given no reason to suppose that the conception of Lisa and of their lives that he forms shares any of the distancing complexity that the film as a whole provides for us. The claims and explanations in the letter invoke a distinctive but somewhat dubious picture of their relations. However, they patently strike home to Brand, conveying just that picture to his eyes. Through the vehicle of the letter, Brand assimilates Lisa's memory of the past—her memories fill that void in him—and comes to see her as the "ideal woman" whom he had not recognized and now has lost irretrievably. This closure is satisfying in that it reverses the situation in which his music creates her vision of an "ideal love" in the future, an ideal that, for other reasons, she was bound to lose.

Implied in these symmetries is a certain ambivalence toward the expressive and representational possibilities of art. In its clarity, affective conviction, and unique beauties, a work of art can touch the intellectual and emotional core of a receptive audience. But, selective of facts, controlled by an interested intelligence, and potentially indulgent to ready emotion, it can simplify and deceive. Film in general and this film in particular does not escape the questions such ambivalence raises. This, of course, was an issue in connection with *You Only Live Once* and, in a different way, with *North by Northwest*. In the case of *Letter*, it was to be expected that it would be widely received with the kind of dreamy romanticism with which Lisa and Brand take in the moving pictures of the fun-fair railway, and there is, perhaps, a quiet warning in this scene to an overly sentimental audience about the film that they are watching. We have one of those episodes in which Ophuls briefly deserts Lisa's viewpoint to open up the context to a wider look around. The dreamers, as we are shown, have to pause in their dreaming to pay the ticket taker for another journey. And this act also sets in motion the ridiculous, clanking machinery that makes their illusory journey possible at all. Nevertheless, romantic escape is only one possible way in which the moving pictures can be viewed. In the fun-fair railway scene we are forced to step back and consider the hidden contrivance behind the images that pass by. By the same token, I have argued that throughout the whole of *Letter* we are also invited, subtly but persistently, to step back and consider the "hidden" contrivance behind its narrative flow. This is one of the main reasons that we are so repeatedly made aware that this film is self-consciously a visual telling by another mind of the tale that Lisa has written. The details of this encompassing narration are to be seen as determining a skeptical but sympathetic perspective that places and elucidates the radical romanticism that Lisa asks Brand and (implicitly) the audience to share.

I have urged that this film refuses to resolve *some* of the chief issues that it poses. This renunciation of judgment and ultimate explanation is fully consonant with what I take the aims of the visual narration to be. There is an affirmation here that film can bring us to see the whole of a complicated pattern with acuity and insight. It is possible to resist the temptations of an engaging but false picturing of the relevant events, to resist simple expression of a sensibility too involved with or too analytically removed from the action. The goal is that these people and their circumstances are to be seen from a variety of angles and thereby with a sort of critical empathy. But this wholeness of perspective does not mean that everything we want to know or judge is knowable and open to judgment. In these lovers' lives, there are truths that they cannot at all discern, which the film reveals to the properly responsive viewer. Nevertheless, there are also mysteries about their lives which this and, probably, any narration will not dispel. It is a part of the affirmation of the possibility of seeing things more openly, broadly, and clearly to acknowledge as well the limits to what we can expect to see in such a case.

In many of Max Ophuls' films (*La Ronde*, *Le Plaisir*, and *Lola Montes*) there is a character who more or less explicitly stands in and speaks for the director. In *Letter*, there would seem to be no one who fills this role. However, upon reflection, there is the puzzling figure of John, Stefan Brand's mute and faithful butler. It is John who first sees Lisa on the stairs and bids her a silent welcome when Brand is moved into the apartment house. He is also the character who gazes after her at the end upon the same stairway when she flees her final interview with Brand. When John first greets her before Brand's door, he is directing the proper disposition of the furnishings and, thereby, in effect, is setting the main dramatic stage of the future romance. And throughout the affair he unobtrusively facilitates the lovers' trysts. Most of all, when Brand has finished reading Lisa's letter and still cannot name its author, John is the person who *does* remember. He writes her name for Brand and, in doing so, implicitly signs the unsigned letter from the unknown woman (see fig. 17). If my recent suggestions about the function of the visual narration are correct, then it is more than appropriate that John should stand, in a sense, as Ophuls' surrogate in this film. He seems to function as an emblem, within the film, of the perfect observer of these painful lives—an observer remaining discreetly at a certain remove, but seeing their respective plights with concern and balance. As such, he matches exactly the leading qualities of the invisible but unfailingly present implied film maker. Although John cannot speak directly either to the characters or to us, and although he does not otherwise intervene in "the course of their love," by registering their history in his perception and memory, he is the ideal servant to the film's enraptured pair.

Chapter 7

On Narrators and Narration in Film

A sure way of obliterating the interest that *Letter from an Unknown Woman* has for a theory of cinematic point of view is to attempt to describe its strategies of narration in terms of an opposition between "subjective" and "objective" or any simple variant thereof. As we saw in chapter 6, most of the movie is a visual exposition of the contents of Lisa's letter, and, because of that alignment with the letter's author, a good deal about her peculiar subjectivity comes to be reflected. However, it is at least equally important that the film's narration establishes, sometimes with special emphasis, a contemplative perspective that stands outside the limits of Lisa's outlook. In accomplishing this, the narration seems to embody a sensibility whose distance from Lisa's vision qualifies and complicates the undoubted sympathy that is shown for her. She is seen, in one sense of the term, with a certain objectivity throughout. It is difficult enough to describe these narrational strategies in a satisfactory fashion, but it is impossible to do so if one has simply opposed subjective film narration to objective, first-person narration to third.

Nevertheless, in the occasional discussions of cinematic point of view which appear in the literature, these are just the distinctions most commonly employed. It often seems to be supposed that the first and most fundamental distinction to be drawn concerning a film's point of view lies in the issue of whether its narration has a first- or third-person perspective. Naturally, the terminology that marks the dichotomy may very somewhat from author to author, and there will be differences about the subcases that are thought to fall under each heading, but versions of the putatively basic division are common in writing on film. It is surprising that this should be the case, because the same dichotomy is not accorded the same primacy in serious literary theory. Indeed, more than this, it has come to be widely recognized that the literary dichotomy often embodies a conflation of different topics. In the light of this, it is perhaps *not* so surprising that there is no consensus and considerable uncertainty about how the concepts of first- and third-person narration apply to film. We shall do well to work our way through some of this uncertainty because, in the course of such an investigation, we shall discover some problems that are crucial to the larger subject of cinematic point of view.

My suspicion is that many of the difficulties that will be confronted are rooted in the following assumption. In analogy with the literary case, it seems as though the very idea of filmic narration must presuppose the existence of visual narrators: if an *activity* of narration is conducted on screen, then there must be a filmic someone who is the *agent* of that activity. It is thought that a fictional figure implicit in the narration must be postulated who *addresses* the audience through the image track and thereby "tells" the film narrative visually. Once this assumption has been made, usually without much attention to the concept of "narrator" it demands, it becomes natural to conclude that some films have a narrator who is suitably placed within the story and many have a narrator who merely renders the story from outside the story's world. This last conclusion is especially natural if one is tempted, consciously or unconsciously, to identify the camera's position with that of a fictional perceiver who looks upon the scenes in which the narrative unfolds. This, of course, would guarantee the existence of some kind of visual narrator in every film.

We have already encountered the most obvious and popular extension of this line of reasoning. First-person narration is equated with film segments whose visual contents are meant to represent a character's visual experiences. Most often, the shots in such a segment portray *what* the relevant character sees of his or her environment and, more or less, *how* he or she is supposed to have seen it.[1] Alternatively, the shots may show certain objects and events as they are remembered, imagined, dreamed, and so forth by that character. Third-person narration then subsumes all film narration that is not tied directly to the subjectivity of a character in these ways. However, as noted in the previous paragraph, the analogized talk of a "third person" in the narration is frequently taken rather seriously and literally. That is, it is suggested that third-person narration presents the perceptual fields of a camera-observer who serves as witness to the action without in any way participating in it. This suggestion allows for a visual narrator who is not a character in the narrative but is a kind of invisible but visual Other whose perceptual consciousness informs the imagery throughout.[2]

In chapter 5, I spoke of film narration that would be first-person in the sense described above as "directly subjective" and granted that it plays important roles in traditional fiction film. I also pointed out that it standardly occurs only in individual shots or relatively brief shot sequences and argued that its importance as a global narrational form is quite doubtful. The question that needs to be broached is not whether this form of first-person narration exists, but whether it is to be conceived, especially in relation to alternatives to it, as a matter of who is or is not assigned the job of visual narration. We also want to understand more clearly the significance of this issue within a wider account of cinematic point of view.

These questions can easily become tangled because first- and third-person narration are not always construed along the lines just sketched. A very different conception of the filmic first-person is adumbrated in the following passage from Susan Sontag:

> Godard proposes a new conception of point of view, thereby staking out the possibility of making films in the first person. . . . Godard, especially in his recent films, has built up a narrative presence, that of the film-maker, who is the central structural element in the cinematic narrative. This first-person film-maker isn't an actual character within the film. That is, he is not to be seen on the screen . . . though he is heard from time to time and one is increasingly aware of his presence just off-camera. But this off-screen person is not a lucid, authorial intelligence, like the detached observer-figure of many novels cast in the first person. The ultimate first person in Godard's movies, his particular version of the film-maker, is the person responsible for the film who stands outside it as a mind beset by more complex, fluctuating concerns than any single film can represent or incarnate.[3]

Without trying to elaborate all that Sontag says and implies in these remarks, it is clear that she is discussing types of film narration which are, in the terminology of chapter 3, self-conscious and self-assertive. She is dealing with self-consciously devised and partially reflexive narrational forms that explicitly call attention to the fact that a film that employs them is an aesthetic artifact constructed by a film maker who wishes to insist upon aspects of its artificial and problematically mimetic status. Hence, to a substantial extent, narration in this mode indirectly dramatizes the film maker: it creates, through its reflexive assertions, a self-dramatized version of the intelligence that constructed the film artifact. Correlatively, it dramatizes for the audience some of the issues and choices that were faced in the process of the film's construction. The concept of a visual narrator, implicit in this use of "first-person," is the concept of the guiding, film-making intelligence insofar as its qualities are made manifest within the film. In first-person films, this intelligence makes effective reference to itself. In third-person films, such overt self-reference is more or less effaced.

This concept of first-person film narration, however it might be filled out, patently develops the analogy to first-person prose narration in a new way. There is no reason to believe that Sontag has confused this type of first-person film narration with narration that is directly subjective. The most that one might question is the use of a label that already had a more familiar sense. But there are seeds of confusion present in the vague but plausible assumption that forms of narration that fall under either concept of "first-person" are notably more *subjective* than other conventional modes.

In an interesting book on narration in film, Bruce Kawin seems to have succumbed to this potential for confusion.[4] He deliberately assimilates both kinds of "subjective" narration into what purports to be a unified category of first-person cinematic exposition. (His word for this inclusive category is "mindscreen.") I suspect that the intuition that leads to this would-be unification is precisely the desire to set off the various "more subjective" forms of film narration from the ostensible objectivity of visual presentation predominant in most traditional cinema.

As far as I can make out, he gives just two explicit reasons for the assimilation. First, he claims that in both cases there is someone, identified and characterized by the movie itself, who, as he puts it, "speaks" the image track or some particular segment thereof.[5] The trouble with this, of course, is that film narration, in the sense relevant, is not literally spoken, and the speech-act metaphor demands an exegesis that Kawin never really provides. However, the possibilities for paraphrasing the metaphor that will fit the context of Kawin's discussion appear as follows. In prose narration, the role of the narrator of a particular work, Y (or of a certain extended segment of Y), is defined roughly in terms of this relation:

1. The sentences of Y are implicitly represented as having been uttered, predominantly with descriptive intent, by a fictional or fictionalized speaker, X.

Thus X will be the narrator of Y. In thinking of directly subjective film narration as "first-person," the relation in (1) is being matched to:

2. The screen imagery is implicitly represented as belonging to the visual experience of a fictional or fictionalized observer, X.

But when self-conscious film narration is said to be first-person, the counterpart to (1) must be something such as

> 3. the screen imagery of Y is reflexively acknowledged to have been constructed by the manifest version X (in Y) of the actual film maker.[6]

Setting the issue out directly in this way, it is hard to see how and why the utterly distinct relations in (2) and (3) are being linked—even by analogy—to the relation in (1). The epistemic and aesthetic dimensions of these filmic relations are so disparate, and the questions, expectations, and types of access that they generate are so remote from one another, that it is hard to grasp the point of yoking them together under the suspect idea of "speaking a film." One might as well stipulate that, in a third way, the apparatus of film projection is always the "speaker" and add still another first-person mode that all films necessarily exemplify. There is as much reason to take this concept to fall with the others into a coherent category as there is to suppose that directly subjective and self-conscious narration belong together in this way.

Kawin's category of "mindscreen" is likely to mask and blur distinctions that we need to keep sharp if talk of first-person film narration is to have any use at all. In discussing literature, Genette has highlighted the observation that many familiar analyses of first-person narration run together a question about whether the narrator addresses the reader in the grammatical first-person with a question about whether the events of the narrative are described as they appeared within the experience of some designated character in the tale.[7] Although there are many narrators who are "first-person" in both possible senses, this is, assuredly, not always the case, and the questions must be asked independently. Kawin's general category of "mindscreen" simply invites a related confusion about film by shifting both who and what is "first-person" in the narration.

Kawin gives a second reason for regarding self-conscious narration as, in effect, first-person. He holds that film narration of this type exhibits the thoughts or—using his own word here—the "mentations" of the film maker.[8] Construed most literally, this might mean that the image tracks of the relevant films are to be read as series of visual images which depict stretches of perceptual thinking on the part of the film maker (in his self-dramatized guise). The film or film segment depicts a visual slice of his cogitating mind. However, nothing that Kawin goes on to say makes it likely that any of the films that he considers are to be construed in this rather bizarre manner.

More plausibly, Kawin might mean that the contents of the screen are presented so that they will be recognized, directly and explicitly, as film material about which the film maker has reflected, judged, and made decisions in the activity, partially on display, of forming that very film. This is a better description of, for example, some of Godard's work, but it once more leaves unexplained why narration of this sort is being linked so closely with directly subjective narration. After all, in most narration in the latter mode, the audience is supposed to apprehend the character's visual experience directly with no specially enforced consciousness about the cinematic construction that presents it to them.

The tensions that are generated by mixing these distinct categories together show up overtly when Kawin feels obliged to ascribe "mentation," not to a film maker, but to the film itself. He asserts that, in certain films of Bergman and Godard, it is the "minded" narration that has, is aware of, and cognitively responds to the images it contains.[9] He grants that these pronouncements employ another metaphor—that is, that the films in question are sentient beings—but for what unjumbled thought this is a metaphor remains a mystery. The jumble is the result of trying to find "mindscreen" in almost any film that systematically dispenses with the usual canons of "objective" narration. If the narration is not objective by these standa ls, the conclusion is reached that the constituent shots must have a sub ective character, and this is interpreted to mean that their visual contents must somehow be the inner product of an intervening mind. But now, when the film in question is not directly subjective and also does not reflexively assert or dramatize the film maker's presence, there is little recourse but to ascribe the mind containing the images to the film itself. This mangled reasoning has as a component the impression, mentioned before, that both self-conscious and directly subjective narration should be classed together as subjective forms. This impression is not so much simply wrong as it is one whose import demands critical reflection. We should remember that the "subjective-objective" dichotomy is commonly used to mark *several* different contrasts. Hence, an impression that a type of narration is, in some sense, subjective should serve only as an invitation to sort out some of the vagaries of our scattered use of the term and to avoid the bewilderment its naïve application is so likely to provoke.[10]

When the phrases "first-person" and "third-person" are used to classify narration, the "person" in question is a narrator, and our brief discussion already illustrates the way in which the concept of filmic narration is likely to give trouble. Moreover, this is one illustration only: the trouble caused by this concept seems pervasive. I asserted earlier that it is easy to suppose that if we experience a film as the telling of a story, then we experience the film as the product of someone who does the telling. And then it seems that there should be a taxonomy of filmic narrators just as there are useful taxonomies of narrators in literary fiction. What we have seen so far in this chapter is some of the difficulty in working out even the first steps of this apparently natural idea. It is time to confront the concept of a filmic narrator more directly.

Let us reconsider more carefully the basic considerations already sketched; that is, the considerations contained in our brief examination of what it might be to "speak" a film. The narrator of a fictional narrative in literature is the fictional or fictionalized *character* who is created, in the first instance, as a direct presuppostion of the conventions in virtue of which the work is understood as if it were a *description* of an evolving, independently existing series of events and situations. The sentences of such a work are read as having the force of statements or, intermittently, of other speech-act types. Taken together, these "mock statements" purport to make up a continuing and coherent account of a partial history of their recurring fictional referents, an account that seems to issue from a unified, personal perspective on the fictional action. Thus, the narrator is just the instantiation of that perspective; he or she is the fictional figure who is presupposed as the progenitor of this total speech-act performance. The narrator is that character, implicitly dramatized in the purported speech acts of the narration, who is understood as describing for the reader a sequence of events about which he or she has some mode of knowledge, whether that mode is specified or not. Of course, the narrating character may or may not be a character *in* the narrative that he or she tells.

This fuller characterization makes it clearer how a suitable concept of a filmic narrator would have to be devised. It would be the concept of a fictional or fictionalized being, presupposed in any viewing of the film narrative, who continuously provides to the audience, from within the general framework of the fiction, the successive views that open onto the action of the film. This is what a suitable concept would require, but I believe that we have no coherent general notion of the function that such a fictional being is supposed to serve. For what could this implicit activity of providing views amount to?

We have several times noticed that the most popular expedient here is to construe the ordered views that constitute a film as being always the personal views of a witness to the depicted action. It is the visual experiences of this fictional witness which are given directly on the screen.

We are now in a position to deal briefly with this conception. It would be harmless but misleading, in instances of directly subjective narration (where there plainly is such a character), to call the focalizing character the visual narrator of the film or film segment. Nevertheless, this possible usage fails to generalize beyond this very special case.

In order to generalize, one has to posit the presence of a "third-person" observer who is, on the one hand, located wholly outside the fictional world of the narrative occurrences and yet, on the other, perceives these occurrences as they take place. It will be the perceptions of this meta-narrative observer which fill the frame when the narration is not directly subjective. But, in earlier reflections, we have, in effect, located at least two decisive objections to this attempt to generalize upon what is but one limited option of point of view. First, the properties and relations of edited imagery in the cinema are generally so far removed from the actual or possible properties and relations instantiated in a single stream of visual awareness that the concept of a being that holds a sequence of the projected manifolds within its experience is one that is essentially empty for us. Our model of such a being's consciousness would be parasitic upon our perception of film and not the other way around. Second, the postulation of an interpolated observer blantantly contradicts the transparency of the image track for the viewer—the viewer's impression of seeing, in the shots of the film, the undistorted, public apearance of the circumstances pictured. I argued in chapter 3 that it is an important aspect of our movie-based perceptual transaction with these circumstances that we regard it as a *direct* connection and not as one that has been filtered through the idiosyncratic mechanisms of another perceiver's field of vision. If this is right, the narrator qua observer must drop out.

All of this still leaves open the possibility that there is some other way of understanding the putative activities of filmic narrators. Perhaps the narrator should be alternatively thought of as an agent, once more an invisible part of the total fictional construct, who now simply directs the audience's attention upon the scenes of the narrative by setting a progression of movie views before them. Considered in this fashion, the narrator is to be a ficitonal figure who, at each moment of the film, *asserts* the existence of certain fictional states of affairs by showing them to the audience demonstratively; that is, by ostending them within and by means of the boundaries of the screen. It is certainly a part of our experience in film viewing that we feel, usually subliminally, a constant guidance and outside direction of our perception toward the range of predetermined fictional facts which we are meant to see. Moreover, there is often widespread agreement that the exact style and manner of this guidance—the fine-grained articulation of the processes of showing—manifest traits of sensibility, intelligence, and character which we attribute to our implicit cinematic guide. The precise way that charcter X, in the extremity of misfortune, has been presented through the camera work and editing is felt to manifest, for example, a sense of cynicism mixed with pity, cynicism and pity that we are inclined to ascribe to whomever contrived to show us that misfortune in that particular way. (Think of the "humanism" that has so often been thought to be expressed in Renoir's visual *style* and of the austerity of temperament frequently discerned in Bresson's.) The originator of the narrational assertions *and*, therefore, the subject of the manifested personal qualities is to be, on this hypothesis, the narrator of the film. This is probably the best way to interpret Kawin's idea that there is always someone who "speaks" the film.

The main objection to the present hypothesis is easy to state, more difficult to explain. The remarks of the last paragraph establish the basis of a concept that has relevance to questions of point of view, but its correlate in literary theory is the concept, not of the narrator, but of the implied author of a work.[11] Moreover, it is one of the more elementary lessons of the rhetoric of literary narration that narrators and implied authors are not to be confused. Naturally, we may often conclude in individual cases that the narrator speaks for the implied author, but the two concepts are distinct. Now, the previous paragraph does offer sound reasons for introducing a concept of "implied film maker(s)" to be applied to films. At the same time, it gives no reason for thinking that the *persona* of the film maker which is expressed through the film has the status of a filmic narrator, and this is a thesis for which argument would have to be supplied.

Our sense of the personal qualities embodied in the point-by-point crafting of a piece of narration, and, based upon that sense, our experience of the piece as a communication to us from someone having those qualities, are both factors that are often very important to the responses that a work elicits from us. We often have a need to say something about our sense of the peculiar sensibility and intelligence that we find manifested in the way the narration has been crafted, and we often wish to describe our impression of how we have been guided, played upon, and moved by a craftsman of the type that we infer. No doubt, we frequently suspect that the flesh-and-blood author or film maker had, in reality, the personal qualities that we find thus manifested, but we are cognizant of the various ways in which these suspicions may be historically false and thus require a terminology that permits us to articulate the character of the relevant impressions and experience without incurring any direct commitment about the artist's psychic biography. I take it that the concept of "implied author"—that is, the concept of an implied version of the author—was designed to contribute to such a terminology, and I believe that a parallel concept of "implied (version of the) film maker" can play a similar role.

In the chapter on *Letter from an Unknown Woman*, I have already made use of a concept of "implied film maker," and that film is an especially clear example of the value this concept can have. I emphasized the distinctness of the perspective that it gives upon Lisa and her life from the perspective that she herself holds. Nevertheless, I also elaborated upon the kind of careful balance which the film's perspective achieves. If we are often asked to observe her actions with skepticism and a sense of irony, we are repeatedly made aware of the grounds that exist for compassionate concern and even a certain qualified admiration. In all of this, we develop a rich impression of being made to attend to Lisa in a certain well-defined and complicated way. But the manner in which we are made to attend to her is, from an opposite angle, precisely the attention that we feel the film maker, in making just this film, has paid to its central character. Further, the qualities of sensibility and intelligence resident in a person capable of giving this kind of human attention to another seem clear and striking. Whether Max Ophuls actually had those traits and whether he meant to diect our attention to Lisa so that we would view her in this special way are different, additional questions. It is nevertheless a part of our deepest experience of *Letter* to feel, throughout its duration, that we are being shown its story through the guidance of a mind with whose strength and sympathy we seem to be acquainted.

These considerations, therefore, support and sustain critical discourse about implied authors *and* implied film makers. To place either of these contructs in a narrator's position is to sow misunderstanding all along the line. In literature, to repeat, a narrator is a fictional character created by the work—a personlike dramatic role the text defines without, in many cases, describing. Within the conventions of the fiction, the words of the narration are necessarily the words of the narrator, and each of us, in reading those words, plays that character role, playing it to ourselves as audience. The personal attributes of the narrating character may be minimal or abundant, but we always have some conception of the person whose "voice" we render when we read. However, it is the major point of the argument I have been developing that there are no grounds for recognizing in narrative film, a being, personlike or not, who fictionally offers our view of narrative events to us. It is important that the implied film maker (like the implied author) is not a character of the given fiction at all. To think otherwise is mysteriously and gratuitously to import irrelevant ghostly surrogates of the actual film makers back into their works. There is a *version*—an implicit projection—of the actual film maker *implied* by the work, but this is not a *character* that the text *depicts* directly or indirectly.

Misapprehension about these topics is likely to disrupt a fruitful taxonomy of cinematic point of view. We have already seen how this can occur when classifications of film in terms of "first-person" and "third-person" are involved, but similar problems arise when other more useful classifications are to be applied. The practice of distinguishing a number of significant varieties of point of view in literary fiction by distinguishing the epistemic situations of narrators makes perfectly good sense. There are narrators who are unreliable in the way they tell their stories, and some narrators exhibit their keen self-consciousness about their task of narration. However, the guiding intelligence manifested in unreliable movie narration (as in *You Only Live Once*) may be experienced, for example, as clever, manipulative, and cynical, but having, even fictionally, made no assertions, this implied film maker is not strictly unreliable. Similarly, the implied film maker of a film whose narration does not contain overt assertions of directorial self-consciousness may be experienced (as in *North by Northwest*) as being just as self-conscious about the crafting of the narration as his more explicitly intrusive counterpart in some modernist film. In the absence of reasons for inserting visual narrators into an account of point of view, we do best to explicate the needed categories in terms of the properties and relations of the narration itself.

Despite my rejection of any general concept of "filmic narrator," it seems that some severely restricted version of the concept *might* have a limited use. Imagine a comedy of sexual manners, roughly on the model of Ernst Lubitsch's *Trouble in Paradise*, in which the camera work and editing seem consistently guided by someone with the sensibility of a prurient voyeur keen to know what is going on behind the closed doors. This voyeur, we may suppose, also appears to hold some conventionally proper code about what ought and ought not be shown and seen. Finally, in our hypothetical comedy as a whole, if becomes clear that this mix of voyeurism and conventional propriety is one of the chief objects of the film's satire. The hypocritical will to watch and decorously look away is exposed for what it is and so is the complicity of spectators who are happily accomplices to that will. Now, *if* we had a clear-cut instance of this kind, then we might have the grounds for a distinction between a voyeuristic filmic narrator and a satirizing implied film maker. In such a case, there would be enough of a personification of the manner in which the action is shown *and* enough of a contrast between the personification and what is implied about the film makers' views of this to motivate the identification of the personified camera-witness as a narrator. Because I think that this theoretical possibility exists, I have not claimed that no concept of a filmic narrator could ever prove serviceable. Nevertheless, in marked contrast with the situation in literature, this potential concept of "narrator," however it might be spelled out, is of passing interest at best. I am doubtful that there exist actual instances of the concept, and even the possible instances seem quite restricted in their range. The strategies of personification I have envisaged are simply too special, and they would tend to divert film narration from a host of important functions which normally it performs. The point still remains that this is an abstract possibility of point of view whose nature and interest we ought to be able to discuss accurately. But if this possibility is subsumed and buried by a muddled idea of what a filmic narrator might be, then no such discussion can take place.

Setting the hypothetical aside, it is even more important that there are point-of-view relationships between implied film makers and various kinds of characters within their films. That is, by recognizing implied film makers and their relations to the films in which they are implied, we are able to extend the *kinds* of point-of-view distinctions we are able to make. For example, there is a question as to whether a given character of a film speaks for and/or somehow stands in for the implied film maker. Included among the possibilities in this context is the case in which there is a voice-over narrator who is not a character in the narrative upon which he or she comments. It is probably the natural assumption here that the assertions of the voice-over narrator are to be taken as truths of the fiction because the epistemic grounding of these opinions will not have been specified and therefore will not be open to skepticism about the warrant of the grounds. In other words, it is the natural assumption that this sort of voice-over narrator does speak for the implied film maker. However, the example of Kubrick's *Barry Lyndon*, cited in chapter 3, is proof that the natural assumption may be wrong. [12]

When there is an on-screen character who also is a voice-over narrator, as Lisa is in *Letter*, the character qua narrator is usually speaking from a point of time which comes after the period of the narrative events. The voice-over narrator therefore speaks with a degree of hindsight and experience which his or her earlier self cannot have commanded. Again, this tends to suggest that the commentary is to be taken at face value. Still, since we know that the results of experience are not always sound, and since we may know much from the narrative which casts doubt upon the retrospective views, we cannot automatically conclude that the spoken narration of the character is to be trusted. Indeed, other characters may provide commentary from within the narrative which implicitly contradicts the narrator's prima facie claim to wisdom and insight.

It follows from this that the more experienced character qua narrator need not speak for the implied film maker. We have had in *Letter* a paradigmatic instance of this point. Moreover, the Ophuls' film also shows the danger of reducing the potential complexity of these relationships to a question of "Who speaks for whom?" It is crucial that in this film the visual narration is conscientiously in the service of the Lisa who writes the letter to Brand; that is, it renders her narrative faithfully, attempting empathy for her and justice to her view of things. The film speaks for her in this way. Despite this constraint, it is also true that Lisa's attitudes and sentiments in her letter diverge from those of the implied film maker—she does not speak for him. The force of this film will be misunderstood if both of these facts are not observed and given suitable weight.

I also proposed that Brand's servant, John, can be seen as a character who stands in for the implied film maker of *Letter*. I claimed that he is meant to mirror, with particular emphasis and purpose, some of the main attributes that the implied film maker is experienced as possessing. Whether this interpretative proposal is accepted or not, it constitutes at least a possible example of a nonnarrating, on-screen character who instructively exemplifies properties of the filmic narration upon which its special quality depends. In my analysis of *The Devil Is a Woman* in the next chapter, a much more elaborate illustration of this same possibility is developed.[13] There is a character in this film who not only reflects aspects of the implied film maker but also signals the reflection by bearing a salient physical resemblance to the actual film maker, von Sternberg. Not only are the facets of the reflection more complex than in *Letter* but it also turns out that this narrational conceit is made to impinge upon the progress of the narrative itself. The character who functions as a surrogate for the implied film maker seems mysteriously to have acquired some of the director's actual powers to shape and move the film's secondary world. The filling out of this example will have to wait until its proper place, but these first hints, taken together with the hypothesis about John in *Letter*, are sufficient to point a moral about the issue at hand. The idea of a character who stands in for an implied film maker is a schematic one: it holds the place for a variety of concrete relationships which can exist between the character and the sensibility and intelligence expressed in the film's construction. When the question of a surrogate relationship surfaces, one is forced to think through, film by film, just what a significant "standing in" relationship might be.

The problems about the concept of a filmic narrator (and about its connections with other dimensions of narrative film) which I have discussed are only a small part of a much larger set of problems about the nature of cinematic narration itself. Indeed, I have claimed that many of the misconceptions about narrators which have been uncovered here derive from related misconceptions about film narration. Beyond this, I believe that there are many more direct questions about film narration which merit at least as much serious and concerted scrutiny. In the remainder of this chapter, I would like to outline *some* of the questions I have in mind and, in some instances, to make some positive suggestions concerning them. However, these are problems of great difficulty, and I have no satisfactory general answers to expound.

It is easy to work with a conception of film narration which hides a number of problems from us. One is likely to begin with the intuitive conviction that there is a fairly clear demarcation between the people, objects, and events that the film has depicted and the material of the sound and image tracks by means of which these fictional items have been depicted. This notion, by itself, seems sufficient to justify at least a rough distinction between a film narrative and the narration that portrays it. It appears, given this first thought about the matter, that film narration can be characterized in terms of the formal properties of the sound and image tracks; explained, that is, as a matter of camera angles and movements, compositions in the frame, editing juxtapositions, and the like. These are, after all, the materials and methods, perceptually present to us, in virtue of which the narrative elements come to be represented on the screen. But, putting other objections to this thought aside, it ignores a fundamental and almost unique fact about the nature of representation in fiction films. For it is both a necessary and elementary fact about fiction films that two types of representation are always simultaneously operative in establishing the minimal narrative content of a work. As often happens, the implications of such a fact are likely to be elusive.

The individual shot is a *photographic representation* of, for example, the actress Marlene Dietrich and of certain actions she actually performed. The idea of film narration in the previous paragraph attends only to properties of this type of representation. But, in addition, Dietrich herself *dramatically represents* a fictional character, and her filmed behavior dramatically represents the same or similar actions of the character.

Moreover, the point is not only that both types of representation must be considered, although that is true and important. It is rather a key part of the point that there is a complex, dynamic interaction between these types of representation which makes it impossible, in analyzing a film, to unfuse the interaction, to treat them as discernibly separate and distinct. In watching a film, we are concerned with the attributes of the performance only insofar as they are captured and exploited in the shots, and it is well known that the manipulation of cinematic imagery, notably though not exclusively through editing, can substantially reconstitute the performance as it appears in the finished product. Conversely, the dramatic interest that resides in the performance normally draws attention away from many of the formal properties of the shots and editing, and the subordination of these properties is aesthetically significant. We saw, for example, that the transparency of classical narration depends importantly on this.

Most film theorists who have attempted to specify *the* medium of film have seized upon the material basis of either photographic or dramatic representation. The medium is found to be either the stream of projected imagery or the physical reality that has been photographed. Despite the elaborate rationales that are given for each choice, both alternatives are bound to be restrictive and arbitrary in focusing upon representation of one type at the expense of the other. In view of the constant interaction between the types of representation, both alternatives are also bound to seem confused. The same reflections apply with equal force to any attempt to treat film narration as if it were confined within one dimension only or to any attempt to divide out two *levels* of narration as if the crucial interaction were a phenomenon to be analytically unwoven. It is only the performance as filtered through the image track which is accessible and relevant to the viewer. Actually, despite the discoveries made by Griffith, Kuleshov, Eisenstein, and others up to the present, it is notorious that there is a great deal about the interaction of performance and filming which is not well understood. But this is to confess an enormous and unsolved set of problems about the topic I have broached, since all our ignorance about this interaction is ignorance about the nature of film narration.

The impact of these considerations can be heightened if we notice some consequences of ignoring them. I have urged that, because the elements and features of performance (including, besides acting, the sets, props, costumes, lighting, and so forth) are parts of the overall apparatus of cinematic representation, they should figure, with the sound and image tracks, as aspects of the way in which films are narrated. And yet, in thinking about self-conscious narration, one thinks first of a cinematic strategy that calls attention to the boundaries of the frame, the recording presence of the camera, or the visual discontinuities the editing imposes. In short, one thinks first of film narration that is self-conscious about the film's form of photographic representation. Nevertheless, it is equally a possibility for the conditions and strategies of dramatic representation to be foregrounded in an assertive way. In von Sternberg's American films with Dietrich a radical stylization of the acting serves this very end. An instance of this in *The Scarlet Empress* was mentioned in chapter 5, and a different but related realization of this possibility in *The Devil Is a Woman* will shortly be examined in detail. In both films, the narration moves back and forth between a focus upon the character Dietrich portrays and an alternative focus on Dietrich herself—the real woman on a sound stage playing with her role. In *North by Northwest*, we discovered a variation on this ploy. A conception of film narration which slights the performance dimension of film narration will also slight distinctions of this kind.

Even if performance is given its due in this regard, our troubles about film narration are compounded by the absence of clear criteria for sorting out what belongs to a film's narrative, on the one hand, and to the narration, on the other. In the King Vidor version of *War and Peace*, Henry Fonda, speaking in his familiar, distinctive midwestern accent, plays the part of Pierre, but this aspect of his performance does not signify that Pierre speaks with such an accent or some Russian analogue to it. This is to be regarded as an incidental by-product of Fonda's acting, irrelevant to the story, and, therefore, not a device of the narration proper. It determines no fact of the narrative. By contrast, in the opening scene of *The Searchers*, Ethan's brother and his family file out of their cabin onto the front porch to await Ethan's imminent arrival. Their movements, as they do so, have an odd, unrealistic, ceremonial character: it is as if they were executing a pattern in a peculiar, solemn dance. Suppose also (as I believe to be the case) that this fact about the manner of their movements occurs purely as a small figure of narrational instruction. The only reason for its occurrence is that it is to be an initial sign or signal from the director that, in this film, movement and spatial relations will have an unusual weight and special significance. (It is also a first element in the network of devices that establishes the nature of that significance.) Correspondingly, the ceremonial manner of the movements of these characters has no place within either the specified or the presumptive explanatory framework of the story. The world in which the action of *The Searchers* takes place is one in which, we may assume, facts and events do have causal or purposive explanations. However, we are not expected to wonder whether there is, in this fictional world, an explanation of why the family's movements are here so formalized. We are not even to suppose that this world potentially contains such an explanation, which the film has just not bothered to provide. The nonnaturalistic features of these movements *are nothing more* than the result of a stylization of the narrative behavior at this particular juncture. On these grounds, it seems wrong or very misleading to view the fact that the characters move in this way as a state of affairs belonging to the narrative of *The Searchers*. It violates the kinds of explanatory coherence upon which the integration of the film's action into a narrative otherwise depends. Nevertheless, I am strongly inclined to hold that the *performers'* movement *is* a fact of the film's narration and to hold this even though we will have here a narrational fact that also does not determine a fact of the narrative.

My inclination, in this last instance, is based upon the point that this stylization supplies a nonnarrative clue to the global aspects under which the narrative developments are to be seen and comprehended. It is meant to help shape the way in which we understand the characters' overall behavior and their circumstances. But, of course, this leads to new questions, and I have cited my disposition to describe the example in the way indicated mostly to bring out the problems that arise. For if a constituent of the narration need not determine a corresponding constituent of narrative, then the relation between film narration and narrative is even more troublesome and obscure. There is the added task of differentiating the genuine components of narrative and narration from elements that are only "incidental by-products" of the movie's construction *and* from elements whose sole function is to define a way of seeing and assessing the narrative. These problems, and others related to them, are extremely perplexing, and I admit to not knowing how they are to be resolved. Futhermore, I am even unsure about the extent to which a general account will turn out to be possible. And yet, these are difficulties that come up again and again in trying to elaborate a close analysis of any film with the complexity and interest of those that I have discussed. Especially when one is working with a film such as *The Devil Is a Woman* or *The Scarlet Empress*, in which so much of the filmic material has been radically and obtrusively stylized, the confident use of terms such as *narrative* and *narration* is likely to be badly shaken. There is much that theoretical reflection can, one hopes, achieve. But certainly, until more *has* been achieved, the concept of "film narration" will remain, at best, a provisional tool of criticism and analysis. However this turns out, the concept remains, despite my reservations, the tool that I have (provisionally) preferred in talking about the distinctions of point of view.

There is one consequence suggested by the last few paragraphs that will surprise and even dismay many, but it is a point that seems unavoidable and correct. It is easy to imagine a film much like *The Searchers*, containing the exact opening sequence I have discussed, which, within the altered scope of the whole film, *would* provide information for a narrative explanation of why the opening movements of the characters have their dancelike aspect. And there could be still another much altered version, beginning in the very same way, where the designated fact would plainly be only a "by-product" of, perhaps, bad acting or inept direction. That neither of these possibilities obtains in the actual film is not determined by the episode's internal properties or by its relations to immediately adjoining contexts. The argument I would offer for viewing the relevant behavior in the actual film as I do would have to be elaborated as part of a comprehensive reading of the complete film. (An outline of some of the pertinent considerations was presented in chapter 3.) That is, the argument would be that my account of the style of that behavior fits best with that comprehensive reading. But this means that it will be impossible in many cases to specify fully the facts of the narrative or the narration without appeal to apparently "higher level" issues about theme, meaning, and underlying cinematic strategy. The determination of narrative and narrational constituents will not, in general, be independent of the deepest and most difficult questions of overall interpretation.[14] And yet, this conclusion violates the commonsense assumption that the plot of a work is a stratum or segment of that work which is given to us much more directly than this—that it is a part that literally appears, in the course of the film, on the screen. The plot's elements and structures and the way they are narrated, given the prevalent conception, are decidable without the contamination of speculative hypotheses. These levels are available to us first, and interpretation proceeds from there.

However natural this protest may sound, it mixes up two different matters. It is a reasonable methodological maxim that interpretation should, where possible, make its start from relatively well agreed upon truths about the work in question. Commonly, many or most of the facts of narrative and narration will answer to this rule of thumb. Nevertheless, it does not follow that we have or could possess generally applicable criteria for narrative or narrational constituency which are not inseparably intertwined with a range of more risky interpretative judgments. Despite the impressions that we concoct for ourselves here, works of narrative fiction do not divide nicely into "levels" or "strata," some of which are open to inspection and others of which the critic finds hidden beneath the rest. The illusion here is obstructive, not only because it affects our general ideas about film narrative and narration adversely but also because it reinforces those prejudices about the accessibility of plot which help to blind us to the oblique counterstructures of many excellent films.

Many authors on film and its history either celebrate or denigrate the fact that the cinema has been predominantly a narrative art. However, both celebrators and denigrators alike have evinced a surprising lack of curiosity about basic facets of the ways in which films accomplish the business of narration. The ready invocation of "visual narrators" is symptomatic of this. There is a widespread notion that film somehow provides the most "direct and immediate" mode of narration, and this supposed directness and immediacy will easily seem to preclude the existence of deep problems about the fundamentals of cinematic narration. If everything is direct and immediate, then there can only be the obvious to state. And yet, as tempting as this notion apparently is, it is very hard to grasp. To believe that film viewers see fictional objects and events directly and immediately is to confuse the aesthetically important impression of transparency with the underlying facts that they know about the *construction* of narration. Even if it were true that viewers see segments of a film performance directly and immediately (in some sense), it would hardly follow that any similar directness and immediacy attaches to their perception of the fictional states of affairs portrayed by that performance. Indeed, we have just discussed a number of reasons why this conclusion has to be false or senseless.

My own conviction, of course, is that the fundamentals of film narration are extremely obscure. I have even allowed that the concept of "narration" in this context may stand in jeopardy. Perhaps my conviction constitutes an exaggeration of the opposite extreme, but my holding it explains why I have devoted so much space to some of the prevalent misconceptions and oversimplifications that plague the subject. Correlatively, the seriousness of many of these confusions offers some justification for the skepticism I feel about our present understanding of what it is to show a story on the screen.

Chapter 8

Josef von Sternberg's
The Devil Is a Woman

In Josef von Sternberg's quirky and sometimes exasperating autobiography, *Fun in a Chinese Laundry*, he sketches a view both of the nature of human beings in general and of actors and actresses in particular. Indeed, these two topics are for him barely distinct. The theories he delineates, especially on the first topic, are never set out in great detail and, as peculiar, in some respects, as these positions are, they are neither original nor especially deep. They seem to derive, fairly directly, from components of the "decadent" aesthetics so influential in Europe at the end of the nineteenth century. Nevertheless, it will be useful to give a brief outline of his thinking on these matters, because this will serve as an orientation to some of the more specific and interesting questions about the narrative and narrational strategies of *The Devil Is a Woman.*[1]

Von Sternberg repeatedly makes a sharp distinction between what he refers to as the "exterior" and "interior" aspects of a person. Basically, these terms are not used in an unusual way in this connection: the first designates, at least roughly, a person's observable physical appearance and behavior; the second denotes a person's inner mental life. In keeping with the standard connotations of the terms, von Sternberg means to convey that, whereas action and demeanor are open to the public gaze, the mental is hidden and closed off behind the accessible "exterior." It is private to the subject and therefore problematic from any outer point of view. The following is a characteristic expression of his ideas:

> The average human being lives behind an impenetrable veil and will disclose his emotions only in a crisis which robs him of control. A crisis does not need a great reason. A human being can explode when least expected, as each one has his own way of building a continuity of his admixture of feelings, and his own formula for controlling it.

> Should a forceful event come along . . . , each human being is forced to behave according to a flood of emotions that may have been stored up until then, *even though previously he did not know them to be there* [italics mine]. As it is difficult to study emotions when they do not appear, it is into the flaws, the faults, and the deficiencies, into the pains and tortures of the human being that one must look in order to study them. The pendulum of emotional response normally swings in a small arc, but now and then it receives quite a jolt, and not always from an outside force.[2]

Von Sternberg extends the problematic character of the interior life, as he conceives it, in two related and well-known ways. Both of these are hinted at in the passage just quoted and are developed, in scattered remarks, throughout his book.

First, he often suggests that the essential features of a person's inner realm (he speaks simply of "a person's essence") are largely cognitively unavailable to the person himself. That is, a great deal of what makes up conscious mental life is understood as little more than superficial epiphenomena generated by those unconscious thoughts, desires, and emotions that constitute, again in his phrase, "the motor of our lives." So each person has very restricted acquaintance with the essence of his or her being, with the deep-seated forces that ultimately direct both conscious mental activity and overt physical behavior.

Second, according to von Sternberg, people tend to be actors and actresses almost all of the time. Whether consciously or unconsciously, they are constantly putting on masks for the inspection of others and dissimulating motives and beliefs that are not theirs at all. What makes these proposals puzzling in von Sternberg's mouth is their apparent incompatibility with his artistic aims. He patently has the ambition of employing the cinema to penetrate to truths, however tentatively endorsed, about the essential interior. But, in doing so, he necessarily makes use of what are for him the opaque, superficial, and distorting exteriors of the human specimens he directs.

The resolution of this conflict that he seems, somewhat obliquely, to envisage depends upon a variant of a well-precedented aesthetic strategy. At least it is a strategy that stands comfortably within the traditions of expressionism and surrealism most influenced by versions of "decadent" aesthetics.[3] The artist, the film maker in this case, does have access to the deliverances of his own perception, imagination, and fantasy. He is directly in touch with his idiosyncratic sense impressions, with his dreams, and with the other forms of imagery that may embody thought and desire. Although, for reasons indicated above, the position does not

146

suppose that these elements of consciousness belong as such to a person's essence, it *is* assumed that they may represent, as sign and symbol, the workings of the crucial underlying mechanisms. The artist, with a postulated special sensitivity and receptiveness, has the power to give form and coherence to the stream of imagery in such a way that the results yield a reflected insight into basic strata of the hidden self. Moreover, when it is also assumed that, in spite of all the obvious differences of outward manifestation, human beings tend to share a reasonably invariant essence, then it follows that the reflected insights should have a wide or even universal applicability. A film conceived along these lines—a von Sternberg film, for example—is thus doubly a personal construct, imbued with its creator through and through. For the film is a visual record of a reconstruction, in the actual world, of a segment of the director's fantasy world. The relevant fantasy is, in the first instance, an immediate construct of the director's mind, and it comes to be realized, however imperfectly, in the material film. In the second instance, the cinematic work is also a construct determined by the director's guiding actions. Or so it is, according to von Sternberg, when his recalcitrant human materials, the cast members, abide within his autocratic rule.

I have opened this chapter with this sketch of von Sternberg's views because it will serve as an introduction to interlocking narrative and narrational strategies that need to be elucidated gradually and brought together only after the strategies have been described. Consider, to begin at what is in this film the most obvious place, the question of the acting. Certainly, there are questions about this subject that need to be asked. All of the central characters are ostentatiously offered as standard "personae" who have been drawn specifically from well-known literary, theatrical, and operatic traditions. Concha is, of course, almost to complete absurdity, the prototype of the *femme fatale*. She is, more narrowly, the fatal woman in the "Spanish" manner of Prosper Merimée, Georges Bizet, and, naturally, Pierre Louys.[4] Don Pasqual is the aging lover who is hopelessly in bondage to her cruel and capricious whims, while Antonio, as the younger and more vigorous rival, threatens the older man's dreams of finally and totally possessing Concha. Don Paquito is paradigmatically inept as the buffoonish Sevillian governor, and so on through the system of lesser luminaries in the film. Furthermore, these characters are presented without the least attempt to inflect them with even a minimal psychological reality. As Concha implicitly suggests at one juncture, these characters have the human substance of figures on a strange set of face cards—figures that have somehow been set into a bizarre and stylized motion of their own.

The actors and actresses do not so much play their roles as have their roles playing around them like a stubborn effect of light they cannot shake. Our most vivid sense is of Marlene Dietrich, Lionel Atwill, and others lending their physical presence on the screen to an outlandish cinematic charade whose ground rules of portrayal they do not quite understand.

The acting, such as it is, runs the gamut from varieties of artful posturing to explosions of enigmatic dance. The import of all this is, at best, translucent. But it is suggestive that parts of the film seem designed to make fun of the very notion that direct, intelligible expression of sentiment and emotion is likely or even possible at all. Most notable in this regard, perhaps, is the scene in which Concha dictates a petulant letter of farewell to Don Pasqual. This declaration of her outraged feelings is dictated to a wizened, thick-spectacled old scrivener, who lifelessly repeats her unfeeling words after her as he scratches them into the nasty missive (see fig. 18). "I am deeply offended," she complains, "I never want to see you again. As I write this my heart is bleeding and my eyes are filled with tears." Pausing on these poignant lines, Concha distractedly adjusts her elaborate coiffure while the sepulchral voice intones the positive nonemotion of her speech. Or later, Concha's dubious "Mother" incoherently pours out a torrent of emotional clichés, a mixture of maternal grievance combined with overwhelmed delight at reunion with a long-lost bosom friend. Don Pasqual, toward whose bosom the hammy outburst is directed, receives it with his usual affectless stoicism. Scenes such as these are contrasted with scenes in which genuine feeling *is* strangely present and yet still is not expressed by the characters who ought to be its subject. The state of affairs concerning emotion generally in this film is like the state of affairs described by the dying Mrs. Gradgrind in *Hard Times* when she says that there seems to be a pain in the room but she cannot positively assert that she has it.[5]

In a similar vein, standardized verbal characterizations of people, their actions, and their situations will often assume a surprisingly independent visual life of their own. This works in two complementary ways: a metaphorical phrase will become visually literalized while a literal phrase will generate a visual metaphor. In this chapter, we will notice a lot of this, but here are some simple examples. Antonio, at one point, adverts to the rumor that many men have "lost their heads" over Concha. Just after this remark, a besotted gentleman in evening clothes wobbles into the room carrying a balloon in the shape of a human head. In his drunken fashion, he is literally "staggered" by the sight of Concha and, when he subsequently turns to depart, she explodes his balloon with her lit cigarette.

So we have "seen" still another man lose his head over her (see fig. 19). Similarly, in his narration to Antonio, Don Pasqual expresses intense frustration about one of the occasions when Mother and Concha abruptly disappear from his ken. But even this bitter complaint takes on the tone of farce when, through a mishap of syntax, he seems to describe the incorrigible pair as "mother and daughter, bag and baggage."[6] Or, when Don Pasqual is first introduced into Concha's domestic circle (complete with a lounge lizard cousin), she bursts into the apartment dangling a glass bowl on a silver chain and exclaims, "Look, Mama, a fish!" Simultaneously, she reels in a rather abashed Don Pasqual on her train. From the rakish street vendor's "conjuring up a woman" for Antonio in the first scene to Antonio's final disappearance in a cloud of smoke and vapor, this sort of foolery goes on throughout the film. It is, of course, the sort of foolery that makes so many of our own dreams so sickeningly funny.

However, similar strategies are displayed with an almost opposite effect. If the instances just given tend to be playful, jokey, and sardonic, there are kindred visual puns used to define a dominant or significant passion that, so to speak, invades the relevant frames. This point introduces a curious qualification of what has up to now been said about the style and texture of the film. Despite the constant short-circuiting and outright parody of the normal psychological expression of emotion, the spectator repeatedly has a sense of an emotion, a mood, a feeling that palpably heats or chills a given shot or scene. This sense has a definite but deflected objective basis in the image track. The simplest and clearest example is provided by the recurrent motif of smoke; the smoke, most often from cigarettes, circles, screens, disturbs, and insults the bemused performers. Although this motif is employed with a host of modulations, the smoke is invariably associated with the "hotter" passions: sexual excitement, jealousy, contempt, and injured pride. In one particularly effective instance, Concha, who is working at the cigarette factory, offers Don Pasqual a pair of cigarettes because, as she explains, they will help to soothe his impatience when he learns that she plans to meet him after work. Although his face retains its characteristic impassiveness, Don Pasqual's movements, as he bends to accept her light, are tense and convulsive. He draws on the cigarette as if to choke down the emotions that he feels at her announcement. The shot slowly dissolves into the telltale smoke that curls around his head, a token of suppressed arousal. The device used here is exemplary in that the character's inner state, which is not overtly manifested, is signified by an element within the immediate setting. In other cases, it is an aspect of decor that does the signifying or it is a confluence of light and darkness, a flurry of unmotivated human motion, or an inflection of the screen image itself. Naturally, the use of such tropes is typical of von Sternberg's work as a whole.[7]

A related example occurs in a later scene. Don Pasqual enters, from out of a heavy rainstorm, into Concha's apartment where he finds her with "the greatest matador in all of Spain." An inset closeup of Atwill's face discloses at most a kind of stunned disbelief at what he sees. But, at the same time, the scattering of raindrops left by the storm upon his features emblemizes the extent of the hurt and grief his countenance does not otherwise reveal. Or again, toward the film's conclusion, Concha hesitates before leaving Don Pasqual's hospital room and looks back, musingly and inscrutably, upon the figure on the bed. She wears, both literally, in virtue of her headgear, *and* figuratively "a veiled expression" on her face. As will be argued later, this "veiled" look is important to the enigma of the film's end. In all these cases it is as if the thoughts and feelings of the characters had been painted on by an outside hand. The characters are made to stand in relation to their own psychologies in much the way the performers are related to their makeup and costumes. There is a queer logic to this, because many of the interior states and processes thus depicted are passions and inclinations that the characters repress, or at least cannot fully bear to face.

Among the properties of these devices that should be noted is that they continually mark and acknowledge the artifice of the film. They insist upon the active presence of an intelligence that plays over the characters and their dilemmas with an alien but revealing touch. By now, we have a first impression of the forms this acknowledgment may take, and other instances in the camera work, the use of sets, the dialogue—the dreamlike atmosphere of the film as a whole—are evident enough. However, the existence of a subjectivity that is reflected throughout the fictional space of *The Devil Is a Woman* impinges still more radically upon the upshot of the dramatic action, determining, in part at least, the ambiguous resolution at the end. A pivotal episode is the following.

Concha and Antonio are together in a private room of what appears to be a gambling casino, the casino mad with revellers from the Carnival. She offers to tell him his fortune from the cards and, as she starts to do so, she sets up a series of card-to-character equations. She equates herself with the Queen of Hearts, Antonio with the Jack of Spades, and Don Paquito with the King of Clubs. But coming to the King of Spades she hesitates. Who, she wonders, as if it should lie at the back of her mind, *is* the King of Spades? However, this last equation is shortly solved. She receives a mysterious letter, delivered by a pig-faced masquerader, which turns out to be a passionate declaration of continuing love from Don Pasqual. When she reads the letter aloud to Antonio, he is incensed at Don Pasqual's earlier duplicity in warning him away from Concha and her destructive ways. This latest revelation frees him from the half-hearted scruples produced in him by Don Pasqual's horrific tale, and he sweeps up Concha in their first, violent embrace. At this the doors of the private chamber fly open and reveal Don Pasqual at the threshhold framed by an enormous painting at his back. In that painting a hapless matador is thrown and gored by a maddened bull. It is as though the realization of the result that he so much dreaded, the coming together of Concha and Antonio, impels Don Pasqual into the scene. (Certainly, the timing of this appearance just on the heels of his own letter is very odd.) But now Concha can complete her last equation: Don Pasqual *is* the King of Spades. In the course of an angry exchange, Don Pasqual first challenges Antonio and then prods him into accepting a duel with pistols. A part of Antonio's resistance to a duel stems from his expressed doubts about the aging Don Pasqual's present prowess with the weapons chosen. In mute reply, Don Pasqual takes up the Queen of Hearts, fixes that card upright in the window across the room, and shoots it—"through the heart." Later, when the card has been retrieved by a passing policeman, Concha contemplates with astonishment the effect of the shot. And well she might, given the events that subsequently transpire.

It emerges in the scenes that follow that she has genuinely fallen in love with Antonio. This woman who has been variously described in the film as having no heart, having a heart of ice, and so on, seems now to have had her heart pierced in a fashion that has heretofore been the fate of the men held in her thrall. Visiting Antonio's hotel room before the duel, she is frightened by the prospective clash. She brings the ruined card, which she now carries over her heart, to demonstrate to Antonio the quality of Don Pasqual's marksmanship. In addition to her strikingly concerned unease, she has become suddenly afflicted with suspicion and jealousy over a girl whom Antonio had known in Paris. Perhaps the changed state of affairs is most distinctly indicated by the new *submissiveness* in the manner in which she accepts Antonio's masterful embrace and kiss. At the duel later, it is Concha's face, as she fears the worst for Antonio, that is flecked with drops of rain, flecked as Don Pasqual's had been earlier when he discovered her with the matador. So why does this sudden transformation in Concha take place? It is as if the shooting of the Queen of Hearts had, by some mysterious causality, wrought the change in her once implacable heart.

There is one way in which this has a perverse intelligibility. From the time the film was released, commentators have remarked upon the startling resemblance of Lionel Atwill as Don Pasqual to Josef von Sternberg, circa 1934. The sad, puffy, clever-looking eyes, the droopy, vaguely Oriental mustache, and the world-weary cast of the military bearing all seem unmistakable. The resemblance has usually suggested to critics that some obscure intention of autobiographical comment is embroidered into the film. This suggestion is probably accurate as far as it goes, but the situation developed in the film is more complicated than this allows. Given the pointed resemblance, the director is able to appear, as it were, within the images of his own film. He is represented quite directly by one of his central characters. (In light of this equivalence, there is an extra ironic barb to the joke when Antonio says to Don Pasqual that it is strange to see *him* giving moral advice to the young.) In particular, the director appears as a character who, in most of the film's first two-thirds, literally serves as its narrator. That is, this long segment depicts the story that he tells Antonio in the club (see fig. 20). Hence, there is a crazy basis for the mysterious causality identified above. For if the director does have an existence within his own visual fiction, it is only to be expected that he should have the power to intervene and change his characters and thereby change the course of the story that he constructs. He therefore has the power to "shoot," in a double sense, the card—more specifically, the image—that has been stipulated to stand in for Concha, and so unmake the icy-hearted creature that he has made in the first place. Recall that Don Pasqual is the King of Spades and thus outranks in power all the rest. The reasons for such an uncanny filmic intervention will be taken up a bit later.

Don Pasqual's efficacious shot also seems to have another strange result. The pistol explosion, rocking the casino, sends the Carnival celebrants scrambling from the scene. The Carnival is effectively brought to a close. Shortly afterward, Don Paquito who has opened the film by querulously opening the Carnival, reappears to preside officially over its demise. He orders that the incarcerated revellers are all to be unmasked, and a huge pile of their grotesque masks is assembled in the prison courtyard. This short scene marks transitions of two types. First, there is the implication that all of the characters have been stripped of their masks in order that the predominant line of action can play itself out without disguise. Second, at the end of the scene, a flustered coachman dolefully reports to Don Paquito that the duel between Antonio and Don Pasqual is about to commence. With this announcement, the very atmosphere has a shift of mood. The coachman's news is instantaneously followed by a titanic cloudburst in which the rain falls, as the phrase has it, "in buckets," from somewhere just above the camera's range. The same absurdly morbid downpour continues through the duel, muffling the combatants and grieving over the predicament. The weather appears to be in unlikely complicity with Don Pasqual's state of mind and fortune.

This is not the first outpouring of meteorological sympathy in the film. The rain falls with a similar unnatural force on the night when Don Pasqual finds Concha in her apartment with the matador. Once again, the deluge seems a sign and symptom of Don Pasqual's mood. Ordered by her to wait in a back room of the café in which she sings, Don Pasqual is miserably restless, frustrated, and keenly suspicious. The rain, beating insistently upon the shingles of the twisted waterfront buildings, produces the nervous staccato of countless synaptic explosions. Overcome at last by his jealous impatience, Don Pasqual races up the stairs, forces his way into the room, and has his worst fears brutally confirmed. It is here that those few emblematic raindrops linger on his face.

And there is more. It is characteristic of the film that the sheer horror of the situation elicits a series of wild puns. "Lie once more, you lie so well!" he shouts at the lately recumbent Concha. Standing in fetching disarray before the entrance to her bedroom, she postures her way outrageously through a tantrum of histrionic anger and strikes back verbally. "What do you mean by bursting in here like an assassin," she cries, "and causing this utterly ridiculous scene?" Given Don Pasqual as Sternbergian surrogate, and given what is presented, with heavy emphasis, as "an utterly ridiculous scene," one hears this as a protest against an egregious directorial intrusion into what, after all, ought to be a paradigmatically private scene. The dialogue continues in this metacinematic vein. Don Pasqual responds with the words, "You've gone too far! You're not going to play with me anymore." (This, by the way, is a thought that von Sternberg had, at the time, several good reasons for believing.)[8] In reply, both Concha and *Dietrich*, protesting in her own right, seem to speak in questioning the relevant authority, "What right have *you* to tell me what to do?" The query is well posed. For, really, who is this morbid intruder upon the set? She points out, "You're not my father. You're not my brother. You're not my lover. I must say you are content with very little." Whereupon the storm intervenes again. Just as Concha delivers this last line and just as Don Pasqual's self-control collapses completely, a wrathful clap of thunder shakes the room. With both persons partially entangled in the adjacent curtains, Don Pasqual shoves Concha backward out of the scene and, presumably, onto her bed. It is precisely at this moment in the "utterly ridiculous scene" that the visible action is, with a surprising discretion, terminated. The camera, in a cut, is pointedly withdrawn to a position outside a shuttered window of Concha's apartment, and it remains there fixed and waiting. Through the sounds of the dwindling rain, the noise of several successive blows is heard. Strangely, the camera holds motionless even after the blows have ended and forces the viewer to listen to the subsequent silence within the room. The empathetic storm, at last, subsides.

The incongruous first shot of the following scene shows, in the immediate foreground of the image, spectral masts and sails of ghostly ships swaying gently within an all-encompassing fog (see fig. 21). The shot is disconcerting because, initially, nothing gives sense or context to the sight. But then a knock at an apartment door announces Concha's arrival, and it is disclosed that the action is taking place in an apartment occupied by Don Pasqual. He stands on the balcony of the apartment staring blankly into the space beyond. Indeed, the fuller delineation of the circumstances establishes that the scene's mysterious opening shot has represented Don Pasqual's field of vision as he stands motionless on the balcony looking out at the harbor. Even when seen from within the room, the view of fogbound ships carries an oppressive immediacy and sense of enclosure. Wholly absent is any impression of perspective in depth, any attempt to set the harbor realistically in the middle distance. (A shot in a later scene indicates that there is at least a city street between the balcony and the water.) It is as if a secondary movie screen had been wrapped around the balcony, closing it off to everything except a projected vision of the gray masts. Don Pasqual does not simply look out but is obviously held in a trancelike state before these ships. When Concha comes into the room and begins her provocative banter, he refuses to stir from his frozen posture even to turn his head toward her. Indeed, when she tries to force his attention upon her by interposing her body between him and his view, their heads dance in a kind of crazy counterpoint. She wants to intercept his gaze and he, avoiding her efforts, repeatedly locks his eyes upon the shrouded scene before him.

These facts need to be conjoined with other aspects of the broader situation. The clear implication of the previous episode has been that Don Pasqual, in his rage, has beaten Concha and thereby achieved some degree of revenge for her treatment of him. She even refers to the beating, in the scene now under consideration, by complaining, although with a surprising cheerfulness, that she is black and blue all over. Actually, this inexplicable flow of vibrancy and high spirits constitutes her dominant tone throughout the scene. The woman who has supposedly been cruelly beaten is unruffled, fresh, and dramatically alive—particularly beautiful

Narration in Light

Fig. 18. Concha (Marlene Dietrich) impassively dictates a "passionate" letter to a withered scrivener.

Fig. 19. Concha uses her cigarette to cause still another admirer to "lose his head," while Antonio (Ceasar Romero) looks on.

Fig. 20. Don Pasqual (Lionel Atwill) plays with a puppet as he warns Antonio of Concha's wiles.

Fig. 21. Don Pasqual stares transfixedly from his apartment window at the spectral ships beyond.

156

Fig. 22. Don Pasqual presses Concha to his breast as she holds a captive goose to hers.

Fig. 23. Concha gives Don Pasqual a "veiled" look as she prepares to leave his hospital room.

in her well-appointed black gown complemented with a bold necklace of dark hearts. By contrast, Don Pasqual, when he finally turns toward the camera, appears drained, broken, and ravaged by an unidentified affliction. It is exactly as if he were the one who had taken a beating at her hands. In short, the morning-after condition of each member of the pair is the reverse of what was to be expected. In a surge of particularly vicious high spirits, Concha says, "I came to see if you were dead. If you really loved me would you have killed yourself last night." Don Pasqual continues to stare at those masts that are obscured by the early morning fog.

It was observed earlier that the first of these two scenes closes with the camera stationed in front of Concha's shuttered window: her rooms are blocked from view and a puzzling stretch of silence falls over the events within. The narration merely keeps track of time while the narrative runs on without witness. The meaning of the scene-ending silence seems to be this. Presumably, Don Pasqual's assault, which begins with blows, evolves after the moment of violence into a bout of lovemaking. Aroused to an irresistable degree by her various provocations, Don Pasqual finally does take possession of the elusive object of his desire. However, consummation for him is bound to be less than a triumph of either passion or revenge. Throughout the film, the idea of possessing Concha, having the *femme fatale* sexually, is connected with violence and, more specifically, with death. In establishing this link, the film is taking up the most familiar associations of the artistic traditions within which it operates. For it is a recognized significance of the fatal woman, a significance with a long lineage, that she is, on the one hand, as vital, as desirable, and as arbitrarily uncontrollable as life itself. On the other hand, to gain possession of such a force of life is intolerably dangerous and destructive. Possession is the ruin of the possessor. It tears him to pieces, depletes him of his lifeblood. One historical strand in the development of the diabolical *femme fatale* is the figure of the female vampire. And Concha is intermittently presented in just this guise, no more so than in the present haunting scene with Don Pasqual. This is the only sequence in which consummation between the two is even obliquely implied, and nowhere else does the graceful ghoulishness of Concha's vividness get so strongly contrasted with the impression of Don Pasqual as utterly dessicated prey.

Nevertheless, there remains the matter of that unearthly harbor view. In several ways, as hinted above, its significance lies in its being, as it were, Don Pasqual's "prospect," his "outlook," his "point of view" of the moment. It was argued earlier that Don Pasqual's sensibility has a privileged position within the film which is rationalized by his surrogate relation to the actual film maker. Just as various elements in the image track and *mise en scène* are used to reflect the state of his soul, so also, although somewhat more directly, does this vision of ships waiting ominously in port. Concha informs him that he should have killed himself and to that remark he offers no reply. But as Don Pasqual stands transfixed before the wraithlike outlines of the masts and sails—stands there looking like a man at the edge of death—it *is* precisely the possibility of his death which he so grimly contemplates.

A little later, he is somewhat revived by Concha's promise to leave with him if she can be freed from her obligations to the café. Don Pasqual goes off to find the one-eyed hag who owns her contract and succeeds in these negotiations. However, when he returns to Concha's apartment with her new-bought freedom, he is forced to watch from the balcony as she deliriously departs, still another time, with her favored matador. This humiliating stroke is familiar in form but unprecedented in its impact. Don Pasqual turns from the balcony on this occasion and walks slowly toward the camera. Only the faintest outlines of the ghostly ships are visible in the darkness behind him. Approaching the camera step by step, he is transformed into a hulking shadow, a two-dimensional plane of darkness that enters the camera's eye while his narration to Antonio draws to a conclusion. An instant later, seen seated at his club once more, he says in summary to Antonio that he has now been told "all that it is necessary for him to know." For Antonio this is not quite the truth, but for the film's audience, alert to the implications of what it sees, the remark is more nearly accurate.

The interrelated themes of possession, violence, enslavement, and death play a recurrent and central role throughout the film. That Don Pasqual is in bondage to Concha is, naturally, a given of the plot. That there is a universality to his condition is conveyed, among other places, in the surrealistic opening shots at the Carnival. There, the celebrants act out in their costumes the sort of elemental bondage in question. A giant rooster heavily pursues a bevy of gaily squealing girls; a clownish matador engages with an ersatz bull decorated with flowers; the police, surrounded by a circle of dancing women, are helplessly bound by the streamers that rain into the square. When Antonio struggles helplessly through the crowd in a vain attempt to follow Concha, a grotesque head upon a phallic neck cranes up and obliterates him from view. Nevertheless, it is important to grasp that the dialectic of enslavement and freedom in this film is developed as having its own more devious ramifications.

At least twice in their acquaintance, Concha accuses Don Pasqual of not really loving her but of wanting her out of vanity. The point here is not that her diagnosis is correct. For one thing, the implied dichotomy tends to break down in this or any other Sternbergian world. Still, there is a kind of insight in her assertions all the same. For there is a specific pattern to Don Pasqual's pursuit of Concha. That is, he repeatedly tries to secure her to his desires by offering, as *he* sees it, to free her from some real or imagined entanglement in which she supposedly is trapped. Furthermore, there is a continuing escalation of the terms that he is prepared to offer in this respect. When they first meet on the snowbound train, he extricates her from a brawl with a gypsy woman and subsequently offers her his protection and assistance. This aid she distinctly declines and disappears. Meeting a second time, he is willing to set up both Concha and Mother on a comfortable financial basis and thus to free Concha from the temptations of the cigarette factory. The irrepressible female pair take the money and disappear again. At their third meeting, Don Pasqual proposes marriage and offers the special honor and protection of his name. This proposal is also turned down with blunt disdain. Finally, he becomes fiercely determined to buy up her contract with the café and, when he accomplishes this, he simply frees her to take off with her sexy matador. In the name of Concha's well-being and independence, Don Pasqual tries again and again to bind her to him, and she refuses each of the doubtful bargains.

It is important that Concha takes up Don Pasqual's position in this pattern when she falls in love with Antonio. Now *she* bargains with him, promising to arrange his release from prison if he will promise to take her with him to Paris. Winning his promise, she goes to Don Paquito for political intervention. This is a key indication of the way in which she has been transfigured by Don Pasqual's amazing shot.

There is an image, occurring when Don Pasqual and Concha meet on the train, that seems a symbol of the ambiguous presumptions of possession. When he has pulled her out of the fight, a medium close-up focuses for an underscored moment upon the way he firmly grips her, pressing her back against his breast. She is startled at first and then amused by the strength of his protective hold. Moreover, she carries, pressed against her breast, a goose locked in a wicker basket. It is a queer line-up, front to back, in this shot, and it is unclear with whom the captive goose connects. The best bet is that each sees the other as potentially that goose (see fig. 22).

It is not surprising that Concha consistently rejects the terms of Don Pasqual's various offers. Throughout the first half of the film she rather plainly indicates the terms that she demands for possession of her. Her terms require his death. Don Pasqual should be willing to give up his life to have her for himself. (The morning scene before the harbor view is one especially clear instance of her claims.) As much as he is willing to up the stakes in terms of money, position, and respectability—*his* instruments of protection—he understandably hesitates before the higher stakes that she calls for. There are at least two factors involved in all this gnomic maneuvering. There is, to repeat, the traditional implication that genuine possession of the *femme fatale* is necessarily tantamount to death. But there is also the strong suggestion that these drastic consequences must be chosen knowingly and willingly if possession is to be granted at all. This corresponds, in turn, to Don Pasqual's tacit condition that possession is something that she must give to him freely. She should choose to come under his ironclad protection.

Here is the reason that the director-lover could not resolve the impasse of her frozen heart by simply changing her heart so that she loves him. That would be only a "fictional" solution in every sense. To have her in this way would be to have a Concha who would be *merely* his creation, a result of his art, and not the independent, spontaneous, coldly capricious creature who so obsesses him. In the nature of the case, a delicate tension exists, for Concha-Dietrich is partly an artifact of his fiction and partly, as we say, "taken from life"—more specifically from von Sternberg's life. A certain tact and balance must be maintained by Don Pasqual if he is to respect the integrity of this halfway being who is incarnate beside him and, at the same time, is a product of his mind and art. So this tension arises at the center of their implacable struggle and is expressed in the following near paradox: each must choose of his or her own volition the particular forms of enslavement and subordination that the other constructs. This is, I suppose, a near paradox that, in its nonaesthetic dimensions, often guides us in our daily lives.

With all of these considerations at last assembled, the enigmatic ending has an explanation, or better, the multiple uncertainties of the ending can be articulated. By "piercing Concha's heart" with his magical shot, Don Pasqual is in position for the perfect, most personal revenge. He places her in the type of bondage to Antonio that for years he has been in to her. Further, by killing Antonio in the duel—apparently his original plan—the revenge would become exquisitely complete, leaving her forever in a state of suspended passion impossible to satisfy. And yet, at the rain-drenched duel, Don Pasqual fires his pistol into the air, spares Antonio, and is himself struck down by his rival's well-aimed shot. Why this? Why this absolutely uncharacteristic act of self-denial on his part, which will, it seems, free Concha for the man she loves? Is Don Pasqual actually moved by her plea for Antonio at the outset of the duel? Or, more plausibly perhaps, is he moved not so much by the plea itself but by the unfamiliar touch of real feeling expressed in her concern for Antonio and marked by the appearance of the raindrops this time upon *her* face? Or, alternatively, is it that Don Pasqual, for a host of private reasons, is now ready to perform that act of ultimate renunciation that she has asked for all along? Or, finally, is it only that he *appears* to have accepted her terms at last? Is it that this apparent free choice of death is still another performance, another deception devised as a supremely baited trap for Concha?

All in all, I take it that these questions have no definite answer. It should not be unexpected, from our present vantage point, that the cinematic narration backs off from answering such narrative-based questions just at the point at which the narrator figure subsides, for the duration of the film, into stony silence. After the duel, Don Pasqual is barely seen and never heard from again. His motives are certainly not divulged. Nevertheless, I also take it that the above questions are among the sorts of questions that Concha poses to herself when she lingers at the door to Don Pasqual's hospital room. In this, his only postduel appearance, he seems so consumed by exhausted bitterness that he is finally freed from her hold. He will not answer her questions and turns his eyes away from her. While she looks back upon the mute, broken man before her, she hesitates briefly and seems, behind her "veiled expression," to *calculate* (see fig. 23). And then she whirls around and leaves.

Presumably, it is this moment of private calculation that determines her last decision of the film—her abandonment of Antonio and return to Don Pasqual. But then *her* motives are not revealed either, and it is only clear that her leaving Antonio is an overwhelmingly painful act of renunciation, self-denial no more characteristic of her than it was of Don Pasqual. Antonio is the man who, by no matter what extranarrative device, she has come to adore. The train starts to pull out with Antonio standing stricken at the coach window and Concha remaining behind on the station platform. Both are obscured and blinded by enormous gusts of smoke and steam that sweep across them. If earlier the swirls of cigarette smoke hinted at burning emotion beneath the exterior, the engulfing cloud from the departing train signals a veritable explosion of passion that has been blocked and frustrated by her action. Concha's slow passage through the station, her weary air as she goes, and her rueful manner with the waiting coachman all manifest, within her style at least, the despair she feels at Antonio's absence. Remembering, it appears, the fires of other days, she tells the coachman, "You know, I used to work in a cigarette factory."

Bowing her head slightly into shadow, she lights the cigarette the coachman has given her and, with this gesture, seems to choke emotion down very much as Don Pasqual had done so many years before.

Her carriage is escorted by a rambling flock of sheep when it begins its slow descent into the becalmed valley that is shown with its peaceful town with its hushed hospital with Don Pasqual lying silent in his bed. Certainly, the impression of his being "down there" where she is going pervades this closing shot. If he is waiting there, we do not know what it is that he is waiting for. It is possible that, through her choice, these lovers will be happily united in the end. Given the total context of the film, this possibility seems remote indeed, but it is a hopeful reading that is offered nonetheless. But then again, if Don Pasqual is really dying in the white room below—if, that is, he has satisfied her strenuous terms at last—then the dark, muffled woman who comes to join him represents his death. And last of all, if Don Pasqual has now merely won the latest battle in their long war of deceit and manipulation, then the splendid pair of adversaries will be face to face again in a war that apparently goes on forever. These possibilities cluster around the receding carriage in the final shot, and the image fades on this.

Don Paquito, Concha told us, is the King of Clubs, and he has limited political dominion over the characters of the tale. He has the power to make arrests, to grant passports, and generally to promote or inhibit people's freedom in these and similar ways. Antonio is and Don Pasqual has been embroiled in politics. Concha is *not* political, at least in this sense, and she expresses contempt for the ultimate importance of the politics that men play at as a determinant in human lives. Don Paquito can prohibit this and facilitate that, but it is demonstrated that her beauty rules over him. And yet, for reasons we have sufficiently explored, it is Don Pasqual, the higher ranking King of Spades, who wields an even more impressive, if still imperfect, power. For this filmic world is his world, and he lays down its law and performs its unexpected miracles. During the recitation of his history to Antonio, he idly picks up a hand puppet and jerks it on its stick. At first glance, the puppet seems identified with him dancing under Concha's erratic guidance. This, after all, is what his narrative describes. With more hindsight, it looks as if Antonio is the puppet moved by the storyteller's guile. This, after all, is what his narrative accomplishes *within* the film. But, why stop at this? There is a much wider audience to Don Pasqual's narrational art, and each of its members sits and watches that puppet jump. Each viewer of *The Devil Is a Woman* watches all of these astonishing creatures on the screen as they jump and fall and jump once more. On final reflection, it would seem that no member of his audience is left untouched by Don Pasqual's effaced but dominating hand.

The Devil Is a Woman may be the film discussed in this book which best demonstrates the need for careful discriminations among the possibilities of cinematic point of view. It is nearly impossible to say anything enlightening about the general *conception* that informs its elliptical and apparently illogical plot, its incredible acting, and its sensuous but "campy" visual style unless one attends sensitively to the question of narrational perspective. Certainly, the relevant considerations in this regard are rather complicated.

We have, in the first place, a prime example of what I have dubbed (in chapter 5) "reflected subjectivity." I have stressed that, in this film, many features of the decor, lighting, and staging are employed to denote a passion, sentiment, or feeling that one or another of the main characters experiences but does not personally express. Thus, the film image becomes a painterly field across which various encoded psychological forces are permitted visibly to play. But then, this strategy is complicated by the constant acknowledgment that these reflections of subjectivity have been "painted onto the scene" by the intelligence and sensibility that made the film. More generally, there exists a constant acknowledgment that what we are seeing is only a construction on film and is not to be simply taken as a transparent windowing onto a familiar, naturalistic world. In other words, the narration of the *The Devil Is a Woman* is, I believe, properly classified as "self-conscious"—narration that calls attention to its own artificial techniques of presentation. That this reflexive affirmation is not made as broadly and explicitly as it is in, for example, some of Godard's later films, does not alter the basic nature of the case.

The chief purpose of the self-consciousness of this narration is significantly different from its purpose in most other films that would fall within the category. I have tried to explicate the point, in connection with *The Devil Is a Woman,* by outlining at the beginning of this chapter some of von Sternberg's views about human experience and about the cinema and by showing, in my analysis of the film, how these views are presupposed in the detailed working out of the exposition of its remarkable action. The whole of the film, shot by shot, can be viewed as the extended expression of a psychic drama that has putatively been played out in the mind or soul of its creator, von Sternberg himself. The work's repeated assertion of its status as a filmic artifact is, by implication, an assertion of the all-encompassing presence of the maker within his product. This is not, of course, a matter of a directly visible presence, but one that surrounds each scene and shapes it to his private fancy. If we wished to extend the meaning of the phrase, we could say that the narration of *The Devil Is a Woman* involves reflected subjectivity of two kinds. It reflects the subjectivity of some of its characters, but, in a different and more fundamental way, it reflects through and through the obliquely depicted subjectivity of its director.

Finally, these formulations are complicated once again by the director's introduction of a central character who is to stand as his embodiment inside the fiction. This means, among other things, that the director has symbolically delegated some of his power over the course of the narrative to a designated member of the secondary world. As a consequence, Don Pasqual, who appears as a narrator whose activity of narration elicits a large segment of the film's imagery, is to be seen, somewhat mysteriously, as a figure who also can control strands in the primary narration of the whole film. We have here a curious and clever solution to a significant structural problem. I claimed in chapter 7 that film, unlike literature, does not generate the role or position of a narrator of a (cinematic) narration. Hence, in general, there is no filmic narrator who can speak for, act for, or even appear for the real or implied "author" of the film. Yet this is just what von Sternberg has formed for himself in the character of Don Pasqual. The film maker has discovered a way of creating a personage who appears as his representative, who, at crucial junctures, can intervene for him in the plot, and who, at one remove, provides him with a voice. This solution is as special as it is ingenious. It depends upon strategies that can operate only in a film, such as this one, whose narration is substantially distanced from common-sense assumptions about experience and exemplifies the thoroughgoing self-consciousness noted above.

However, the odd ingenuity of this solution is not, in one way, surprising. Von Sternberg's unprecedented works teach many amazing lessons about what film narrative and narration can achieve. Or, at any rate, they do if we are alert to the intelligence and sensibility behind the veil of self-irony and formal play that exists in *The Devil Is a Woman* and his other films.

Chapter 9

Nicholas Ray's
Rebel without a Cause

Even more than *You Only Live Once*, *Rebel without a Cause* has the characteristic format of an American social problem film from the classical period.[1] Its narrative surface specifies a familiar social problem, identifies a set of factors out of which the problem is supposed to arise, and suggests a means by which the problem might be solved or ameliorated. Moreover, I shall argue that *Rebel* is like Lang's film in its ultimate rejection of the social message it seems to proclaim so overtly. Nevertheless, the way in which this rejection is registered is quite different in the two films. *You Only Live Once* is rhetorically unreliable and leaves the competing possibilities of closure it invokes utterly suspended. From the film's perspective, they are all equally suspect. *Rebel*, however, belongs with *The Searchers* as a film that *does* establish a favored, explanatory coherence, although that coherence is presented opaquely. And yet, the respective strategies of opacity are distinct.

The question of Ethan's obsession in *The Searchers* is answered by a global pattern whose elements become intelligibly complete only when the crucial action at the conclusion has occurred. At that point, an answer to the key narrative question (albeit a surprising one) is supplied. In *Rebel*, the ending is a final working out of processes whose character and whose bearing on the narrative questions can be understood only after the viewer has learned, through the film, to reframe those original questions in a fundamental way. The social problem of ostensible concern is one that would require the delineation of responsive social action. But *Rebel* depicts a world in which no such response would be possible or relevant. The film affirms that to conceive the dramatized situation in terms of social problems that have social solutions is to hide from ourselves a much deeper truth about the sources and nature of social bonds, a truth that shows the problematic situation to be essentially inevitable. Therefore, the very *issues* that *Rebel genuinely* attempts to explicate are themselves raised opaquely. The viewer must come to give up his or her ideas about what a dramatic and thematic resolution should be in such a case, locating, instead, the perspective that *Rebel* will accept on this.

The difference between *Rebel* and *The Searchers* poses puzzles about some of the key point-of-view distinctions that I drew in chapter 3. For it is unclear that we should not say that Ray's film is, after all, rhetorically unreliable *with respect to* its social problem framework even if it is reliably coherent *with respect to* the questions that are opaquely posed. Either some modification of the relevant categories seems required or rhetorical unreliability and opaque closure may not be, as suggested in chapter 3, mutually exclusive.

I do not intend, however, to pursue the needed refinements. The difficulties can be met in several satisfactory ways, none of which would alter significantly my overall account. More importantly, the open-endedness of the larger taxonomic enterprise that these remarks have been meant to illustrate would still remain, and I prefer that, in the last film analysis of this book, the emphasis should be on the extensive work that is left to be done. Because *You Only Live Once* served as the initial motivation for the kind of theory of cinematic point of view I have developed, it seems fitting that a film of the same genre should remind us that the progress we have made is provisional and incomplete.

The social problem in *Rebel without a Cause* is, of course, juvenile delinquency or, more specifically, the incidence of troubled teenagers among middle-class American families in the fifties. The teenagers in this 1955 film are presented as rebelling against their parents and their way of life, but, as the title suggests, not out of any identifiable cause or counterideology and not out of any generalized dissatisfaction that they can state. The film thus invokes the perception, widespread at the time, that the issue of teenage rebelliousness had an especially enigmatic character. Here were young men and women, popular wisdom declared, who had been provided with "everything" and still were prone to alienation, rejection of authority, and outbursts of violence. Because, by hypothesis, there was nothing that these adolescents could possibly want, their actions could not be motivated by any intelligible desire. Although these notions are called up in the film, the story, at the same time, hastens to dissipate any possible sense of paradox. The problem-defining format purports to lay bare the real sources of teenage disaffection. Moreover, it accomplishes this aim in a way that is designed not to be too provocative in relation to entrenched social values and beliefs. It is overtly postulated that the difficulties that are on display are produced by the individual domestic failures of the parents. The parents have only to act with more sensitivity, insight, and moral decisiveness in order for the tensions with their children to be eased.

The causes of the problem are therefore made out to be extremely well-defined and localized, and, like the film's initial statement of the problem, its genetic analysis conforms broadly to conceptions common in the period. What might appear, on the face of things, to be a somewhat serious reaction to the ongoing social order is revealed to be nothing more than remediable psychological maladjustments within the family. The remedy is to be found in what amounts to a renewed commitment to traditional American family structures and ideals. In this regard, *Rebel without a Cause* seems to operate as a fundamentally reassuring contemporary morality play. The characters, parents and children, act out the semiofficial version of "the youth issue" and, in the course of the plot, come to discover an ideologically acceptable resolution of the conflict. Considered in this light, the following rather standard assessment of the film appears just: "With hindsight, the problem of juvenile delinquency seems naïvely treated, the relationship between parents and children schematically drawn, and the preoccupation with psychological fixation superficial."[2] However, such an assessment ignores so much that is most striking and idiosyncratic in the action, dialogue, and, above all, the narration of *Rebel*, that judgment is best deferred. I shall argue that the patent foregrounding of ideological elements in the film constitutes a misleading temptation to the viewer: a temptation simply to accept those elements without looking for a wider filmic framework within which they are subsumed and qualified. Indeed, of all the films discussed in this book, none better illustrates the dangers of a premature attempt to read a film as symptomatic of an extracinematic "ideology" that is thought of as determining its form and content.

It is an oddity of the passage quoted above that it singles out *Rebel*'s portrayal of the relationships between parents and children as schematic. The objection to be registered is not that this is false, but that it is strange to cite just this aspect when evaluating a film that is crisscrossed with schematic oppositions of a variety of types occurring within a number of narrative and narrational dimensions. For example, if there is an implication that the relations among the teenagers are *not* drawn schematically, then that, for reasons to be explored, is mistaken. Beyond this, the peculiar look and texture of the film are built upon a schematic use of, for example, light and darkness, color, movement and posture, and the pacing of the action. Above all, the variable depiction of space in general and of the individual spaces of the characters' lives underlies the basic narrational schema of the film. The film consistently involves a relatively simplified and diagrammatic rendering of personal relationships, and these renderings are intermixed with, if not subordinated to, a schematization of factors that fall outside the domain of the psychological altogether.

As a result, the film occupies a position of some distance from whatever concrete, detailed individuality its characters might potentially have. Each of the three main teenage characters is introduced primarily as an illustrative sample of the wider social dilemma under anlaysis. Each such sample is specified with a more or less stereotypical explanatory tag. One of the chief functions of the opening scene at the police station is to provide a setting in which the wanted system of labeling can be laid down at the start with minimal artificiality. Jim, Judy, and Plato are brought upon the scene in such a way that it is hinted that they are all somewhat mysteriously linked together even though they are each to be seen as a separate "case study." They are interrogated, one by one, by an "understanding" juvenile officer who, during the interrogation, sketches in the nature of their distinct disturbances. Jim's father is an inadequate masculine role model; Judy, as she matures, is barred from her father's affections; and Plato is the unhappy product of a broken home. We shall discover that the cryptic implied connection between the three kids serves several purposes. But, at this juncture, the linkage that is most prominent is that their different problems generalize under the rubric "conflict with parents."

The stage-setting explanations that are offered in this scene are never contradicted in the film and are to some extent elaborated. Nevertheless, I have already mentioned some of the properties of this intitial treatment of the kids which most demand a satisfactory account. As *Rebel* progressively unfolds, the prelabeled psychological mechanisms are seen to be conditioned and affected by natural laws and forces that are remote from anything the pat psychologizing has put forward. The viewer is therefore faced with the question of placing the explicit psychological explanations within an expanded field of possible explanatory connections. It emerges as a genuine possibility, for example, that the psychological causes that have been explicated by an official voice of authority are not more than very restricted and very distorted manifestations of deeper and more impersonal determinants governing the characters' lives.

It is in this regard that the employment of space and spatial relations in the film assumes its considerable importance, but it will take us a little work to see how this is so. Early in *Rebel*, the teenagers attend a lecture on astronomy at the Griffith Observatory, and there they see, projected on the planetarium's domed ceiling, a vision of the dark infinity of space. The obvious weight that is assigned to this curious and famous scene is hard to grasp on a "straight" viewing of the film. This sweeping perspective of the universe stands in stark, ironic contrast to the views that, up to this scene, we have been given of the characters' environment and daily routines. The cinematic style of the earliest segments of *Rebel* emphasizes the severe constriction and the oppressive clutter of the spaces that these people move within. Although this is a motif that runs through all of the scenes prior to the planetarium episode and through several scenes later on, it defines structures that, once again, the opening scene at the police station is used to diagram.

Specific strategies within the narration depict the adolescents as living lives that are, in Judy's words later, "crushing in upon them." We are shown their confused and explosive energies confined meaninglessly by the narrow, claustrophobic volumes that enclose them. The police station is partitioned into small, glassed-in cubicles that serve as private offices. Judy, Plato, and Jim are taken, in that order, into one or another of these windowed boxes to be examined by a specialist in juvenile misbehavior. During the ensuing exchanges, the kids are pictured as literally "pressed into a corner" with "their backs against the wall" and "trapped" without escape on any side. They are repeatedly shot in medium to full close-ups so that the width of the Cinemascope image encompasses great stretches of the adjacent walls and windows. This device has the effect of flattening out the space that appears in the frame and merging the human figures into the two dimensionality of the plane surfaces behind them. Further, many of the shots in this (and other) interior scene(s) are executed with the camera tilted up from such a low angle that the ceilings of the rooms are visible. Here again, the properties of the Cinemascope image come into play. Its extended horizontal line, combined with the relative verticality of the camera angles of these shots, tends to bring the ceilings down and forward into the frame so that they hover, so to speak, just over the heads of the characters below them. Such stylistic choices help make visible the intense feeling that the kids are being subjected to pressure from everything that surrounds them. The rooms of the station and their furnishings encroach upon their perception and sensibility from every direction. Finally, it is not only the real and apparent constriction of these spaces which generates the unique look of the relevant scenes. There is also the impression that space itself in these regions is an almost palpable medium,

170

which the ensemble of unusual camera setups and abnormally jagged editing has the power to slice and manipulate.

Immersed in this transparent and slightly viscous substance, the adolescents intermittently blow up in rage and frustration. The scene at the police station is one occasion of this. Jim pounds his fists brutally and pointlessly into the side of his interrogator's desk. The incident naturally illustrates the reserves of uncontrollable anger which exist within the boy, and the suffering that is entailed because his anger has no clear-cut object. And yet, perceived from the viewpoint this whole scene has done so much to clarify, it *is* appropriate that Jim should strike out, no matter how fruitlessly, at the nearest of the surfaces that hem him so closely and completely in.

In the subsequent scene, much of the sense of personal space described above is carried over into the depiction of Jim's domestic circumstances. While they nag, squabble, and provoke one another over every incidental, the family members are shown to have packed themselves into the tiny breakfast nook of their modest middle-class home. Jim's much harassed father, in particular, is so squeezed into his place at the table that he barely has room to set his feet upon the floor. Thus, when Jim looks away from all of this through the window and sees Judy outside—young, lovely, dressed in green—this view is for him, as Charles Barr has pointed out,[3] a visual promise of hope, renewal, and release. However, even this image is qualified by a looming environmental presence. The unattractive neighborhood surrounds and constrains her much as the police station had in the scene before. As the couple walk down the narrow alley and converse, they are framed closely by the fences, walls, and garages that rise up everywhere around them. The monotonous and undistinguished houses of the neighborhood are jammed together but sharply divided by the huge fences on every lot. (It is in this conversation that Judy makes her remark about "life crushing in upon her.") Similarly, at Dawson High, as school begins, a jumbled herd of students crowd, push, and jostle one another up the institution's steps and through its doors. It is emblematic that *Rebel* begins with its three protagonists under arrest, because it is a premise of the whole first segment of the film that they experience their normal activities as a senseless imprisonment.

The first planetarium scene is, in one way, a continuation of this theme. The students, bored and inattentive, sit massed together in the auditorium, gaze upward at the astronomy show, and listen, at least occasionally, to the accompanying lecture. However, in this scene, the sense of restrictive enclosure is now subordinate to the invocation of its seeming opposite. The part of the lecture that we hear is about "the immensity of the universe," man's insignificant position within that immensity, and the relatively imminent destruction of the earth and all that pertains to man. While images of the vast blackness of space, dotted with stars and galaxies, are projected upon the auditorium dome, the lecturer speaks the following words:

> For many days before the end of our earth, people will look into the night sky and notice a star increasingly bright and increasingly near. As this star approaches us, the weather will change. The great polar fields of the south will rot and divide, and the seas will turn warm. The last of us search the heavens and stand amazed, for the stars will still be moving to their ancient rhythm. The familiar constellations that illuminate our night will seem as they have always seemed, eternal, unchanged, and little moved by the shortness of time between our planet's birth and demise.

The teenagers are not much interested by this introductory statement, and they turn away to engage in horseplay with one another while the speaker begins to catalogue the constellations and their locations in the sky. But all of the horseplay ends suddenly when they are riveted by a renewed and more forceful description of our world's death, a description that introduces a projected enactment of that future catastrophe. The lecturer goes on: "And while the flash of our beginning has not travelled the light years into distance, has not yet been seen by planets deep within the other galaxies, we will disappear into the blackness of space from which we came—destroyed, as we began, in a burst of fire and gas." As these predictions end, the visual show above portrays the blazing finale that the words foretell. A flashing, whirling, pulsating spiral of gas and fire—the earth-destroying star referred to in the lecture—grows larger and larger, descending upon the rapt audience, engulfing them and causing them to cringe back in their seats. Presented with this apocalyptic imagery, they react with primitive dread and horror. They spontaneously huddle closer to one another as though their binding together could protect them from this vision of total annihilation (see fig. 24). This explosion of light ends the visual show, and, as the kids begin to reassemble their composure, the lecturer concludes: "The heavens are still and cold once more. In all the immensity of our universe and the galaxies beyond, the earth will not be missed. Through the infinite reaches of space, the problems of man seem trivial and naïve indeed. And man, existing alone, seems himself an episode of little consequence." The lights go on, and the students slowly, uncertainly get up to leave.

I shall try to explain how the visually assisted lecture constitutes the major narrational figure of the film, providing the viewer with the context in terms of which the narrative is to be viewed. To anticipate some later results, I shall argue that this scene at the observatory announces *Rebel*'s aim of being a diagrammatic meditation—an essay or itself a kind of lecture—upon what it takes to be the fundamental processes that underlie the epiphenomena of the social issues with which it ostensibly deals. More specifically, there are three related major points that are enunciated in the scene which, for future reference, deserve to be set out. First, the scene introduces the concept of the boundlessness of space in contrast to the sharp impression of the restricted life spaces of the characters. Second, this contrast suggests that the infinity of space should be connected with an ideal of freedom or escape, but the lecture explicitly associates it with oblivion and death—the end of man on earth. What is more, the student viewers seem to be bound still more tightly together in the solidarity of fear. Third, there is a blunt assertion of the mindless, inexorable, and law-governed operations of an indifferent universe and, with this, the insistence, quite odd in a social problem film, upon the triviality of human problems. It is the systematic role of these last two points that need especially to be explored.

It is clear that the scene at the "chickie run" extends and refines all of these points. This is the scene in which Jim and Buzz, the leader of the high-school gang, race cars toward a cliff above the sea in a test of courage. The first to jump to safety will be a "chicken" and this, within the code the teenage males all share, is the worst disgrace that can be incurred. Before the race, the two boys look with awe over the side of the cliff and down at the ocean at its base. Visually, the black waters, marbled with white crests and reflected moonlight, resemble the planetarium depiction of the night sky. While they stand there, contemplating the void in front of them, Buzz states, "This is the edge—this is the end." He means, in the circumstances, that this is the edge of the world, an edge that, if crossed, is the end of life for the person who crosses it. His statement also represents, as things turn out, an unconscious prediction of his fate. For he is accidentally trapped in the car he drives, and he plunges to his death at the foot of the bluff. Indeed, we see the car fall into the ocean, exploding in "a burst of fire and gas" which echoes the image of the earth-destroying star. On the sound track, the music repeats the themes that accompanied the conclusion of the planetarium projection.

The reaction of the teenagers to this new disaster is much the same as their reaction to the earlier vision of final destruction. Peering with

horrified disbelief into the world beyond the cliff, they are clustered
fearfully together in a confused throng, which has been abruptly dispossessed of its leader. But perhaps the most telling shots occur a moment
later. Judy remains frozen at the rim of the bluff longer than the rest,
transfixed by the spectacle that she has witnessed. After a brief hesitation,
Jim carefully reaches out his hand to her, and she, without looking away
from the site of the crash, slowly and, as it seems, without volition raises
her arm until her hand finally meets and clasps his. In the background,
Plato, the paradigmatic outsider, watches these apparently automatic
actions from beyond the field of forces that is guiding them (see fig. 25). It
is the effect of binding or being bound together in the face of death,
isolation, and sheer nothingness which is so central here, and he is wholly
excluded from that effect. This instant at "the edge" seems the instant that
really founds the relationship that Jim and Judy go on to develop. But also,
it is simply the most prominent and important instance of a human response to death which the movie pictures as primitive and universal. Thus,
when, in the film's final scene, Plato is shot down in the fierce lights of the
police cars, Jim, with Judy at his side, is once more taken, somewhat pas-
sively and ambiguously, under the dubious protection and support of his
waiting parents. The ties that he had decisively broken earlier are immediately restored in the wake of Plato's death. We shall return to this later.

However, if unrestricted space is presented as dangerous and threatening, it is also presented, as one would expect in this film, as the terrain of
liberation. The tremendous openness of the space at the chickie run *is* the
positive opposite of the suffocating enclosures of the kids' homes, neigh-
borhoods, and the institutions that process their lives. The first part of the
scene at the cliff gives a dramatic sense of their freedom and exhilaration in
this setting. The teenagers are animated vividly by the speed and power of
the cars, by the incipient confrontation between Jim and Buzz, and even by
the prospective dangers that the confrontation entails. The outpouring of
their unchecked energies is conveyed, of course, by the organized exuberance of their behavior, but it is also matched in the narration by the
camera's new freedom: its freedom to offer panoramic views of the
proceedings over which it presides; its freedom, in extended tracking
shots, to follow the movements of the teenagers; and its freedom, assisted
by the editing, to assemble both detail and summary in an account of the
subtle orderings that thread together the tumultuous range of the group's
activities. Here at last in this film is an expanse of space in which the
camera can dolly and crane, an expanse without the boundaries that the
interior scenes so obtrusively have imposed. Hence, in this sequence,

Narration in Light

escape from the earlier claustrophobia *and* the threat of extinction are shown as two facets of its open space.

I have underscored, if only in passing, the ordering of the teenagers' actions at the cliff because it is patent that the chickie run is an established and predesigned rite of challenge among these kids. Buzz, as I have indicated, is the acknowledged leader of the high-school crowd, and Jim has trespassed into his domain in two ways. The charismatic newcomer has asserted his presence too boldly and too soon after his arrival. Moreover, Judy, who is Buzz's girl, evinces an attraction to Jim, which Buzz detects. In the main hall of the high school, Jim sees a placard promoting Judy for "Queen." Presumably, this is a poster for some school dance or prom, but it assumes an added resonance when we note that the whole ritual of the chickie run is set up as a struggle between the forceful stranger and the already established "King." The ritual concerns, after all, acceptance by the given community, acknowledgment of special honor and courage, and rival claims upon the woman. The trick of exposition, here as in much of the remainder of the film, is to cast a rather distanced and anthropological eye upon the familiar but peculiar practices of contemporary adolescents.

Certainly, the chickie run is governed throughout by rules and known precedents. There are rules about how the trial is to be conducted and about what the consequences of a loss will be. The staging of the action is carefully orchestrated; the positioning of the drivers, the arrangement of their audience, and the starting of the run all have an almost choreographed dimension. Even the drivers' prestart preparations seem to follow a fixed and superstitious procedure. Once the challenge has been accepted, the ordained process sweeps up the teenagers and carries them along. For example, when the time of the test has come, there is no substantial animus between Jim and Buzz. Before the race, they take a friendly walk together to the cliff, shake hands, and share a cigarette. Jim asks, "Why do we do this?" and Buzz replies, "Well, we have to do *something*, don't we?" Jim's intrusion into the group seems to have engaged the gears of a complicated piece of tribal machinery, which has to run though its routine completely even though neither the teenagers nor the film's viewers really grasp its inner workings and its purpose.

It was already a stereotype of the 1950s that adolescents made up a puzzling and troublesome subculture within American society—that their supposedly inscrutable modes of thought and action set them apart as a separate social order. This is another of the popular stereotypes concerning its principal subjects that *Rebel* adopts and, for its special ends, exploits. Throughout the film we are offered examples of codes, ceremonies, ritual gestures, and so forth that the kids seem to employ with some meaning among themselves, but these meanings remain, from the viewer's perspective, cloudy and indistinct.

For example, we learn at the beginning of the film that Plato has been arrested for shooting a litter of puppies. No explanation is ever given of his act, and its significance is left enigmatic. But the shooting seems to have been some sort of perverse and private sacrifice, which, performed on Easter Day, has been conceived as a part of Plato's world of fantasy. More public, less violent, but still undeniably peculiar is the little ceremony that opens the school day at Dawson High. A pair of young men in lettermen's sweaters fire a miniature cannon across the yard, and the firing apparently signals the raising of the flag. This faintly ludicrous procedure starts the students in motion up the school steps, and, as they push their way along, an overhead shot shows that they all rigorously and automatically avoid stepping on the school plaque set in the steps. Jim, who is new to the school, fails to observe the odd taboo and has the proscription stated to him by a brawny athlete while Buzz and his clique look upon the culprit with baleful disapproval. After Buzz has been killed, three of his vengeful lieutenants attempt to call Jim out into another confrontation, and they do so by hanging a live chicken upside down over his front door. The primitive nature of this symbol of humiliation is reinforced by a shot from over Jim's father's shoulder when he opens the door to investigate the disturbance outside. We see, with him, the three boys lounging in the trees and brush on the far side of the lawn, and there they apear like "savages" watching their victim from the veiling foliage. Indeed, the whole pursuit of Jim by the gang's enforcers seems the carrying out of a definite but rather mysterious code of revenge, a restitution called for by their leader's death.

However, along with the chickie run scene, it is the segment that leads up to and includes the knife fight outside the observatory that delineates these considerations most boldly. In this segment, the stylization of the provocation and the ensuing violence is strongly articulated. The interaction between Jim and Buzz's followers is laid out quite formally as a rule-directed pattern of challenge, reply, and counterchallenge, a pattern in which the obscure sense of honor of the antagonists demands, at each stage, a suitably conducted response. Much of the carefully arranged behavior in this scene is rendered with a fracturing abruptness and an insistence upon the strict positionality, within the whole, of each major action. This exposition defines the sequence of action and reaction as a series of moves in a game that occurs down and across a three-dimensional board. Because of Jim's unacceptable intrusion upon the group, its

176

members call upon Buzz, in their phrase, "to bring him down." And this is what literally takes place.

Jim and Plato are standing on one of the planetarium's upper levels when the gang emerges on the drive below them. Its members place themselves in a loose configuration around Jim's car. The girls among them, Judy especially, look up at Jim with ambiguous provocation, both mocking him as a part of the set procedure of challenge and exhibiting a sexual interest in him at the same time. As if he senses and is responding to this unplanned note of sexuality, Buzz intervenes preemptorily by pulling Judy roughly out of the line of Jim's gaze. He then glances up in warning at Jim, and eventually deflates his tire. This is the act that succeeds in bringing Jim down. As indicated before, there is superimposed upon this behavior a mildly disorienting fragmentation of the various acts of looking, provoking, and responding. These looks and movements are frequently depicted in such a truncated way that, for example, the purpose of a movement or the subject of a look is left without full specification. The point of such an action is given no greater weight than the place it occupies in the charged pattern of confrontation that the editing constructs.

The act that finally moves Jim to overt anger is Buzz's calling him a "chicken." We know from earlier in the film that this appellation is for Jim and, presumably, for the other male youths, the keenest possible insult, the worst aspersion of one's honor. Jim whirls around brandishing his tire iron. The gesture is viewed by Buzz and the others with shock and amazement, because, it seems, a threat in this form lies outside the protocol they accept. Buzz's response is to take up the challenge but to insist, with his friends' agreement, that the fight is to have the format of what they call "the blade game." This is one-on-one battle with switch-blades, a "game" whose guidelines are then explained to Jim. During the fight, Buzz points up the ritualized aspect of their combat by comparing it, in his taunts and maneuvers, to a bullfight. Jim is "Toreador," and Buzz will be the bull. The blade game comes to an end when Jim disarms him and, with his knife at Buzz's throat, shoves him back against a guardrail that blocks him, on this occasion, from a fall into the enormous drop beyond. This turn of events, surprising from the gang's point of view, leads directly to the more serious, definitive challenge of the run upon the cliff.

It is in the scenes of violence among the adolescents that the ritualization of their behavior, evident elsewhere, is most pronounced. This observation applies to the episode at "Plato's mansion" when Plato is attacked by Buzz's vengeance-seeking friends. The attack takes place at the bottom of the mansion's emptied swimming pool, where Plato wields a heavy hose, swung over his head and flung out, to ward off the black-clothed enforcers. This fight has the look of a gladitorial combat and thereby hints, as is appropriate to the case, of the persecution of the innocent that this particular struggle involves.

It is possible to summarize the more abstract framework that subsumes many of these narrative and narrational constituents in the following way. The gross stultification of the lives of the middle-class parents—lives that simultaneously are aggravating and moribund—is merely sketched in using the crude lines of diagram and caricature. The assumption is made that the conditions of these lives will be recognized and understood by anyone for whom the film can have real content. And these are the conditions against which the teenagers are in revolt. Further, it is essential that their rebellion has certain distinctive, interrelated properties. First, the rebellion is, in effect, a response of the *community* of adolescents. In ways that I have been recently detailing, they have formed themselves into a clan or tribe, and their activities are deeply regulated by the codes and practices implicit in this social formation. They have, in this fashion, set themselves aside as a unity from their parents' problematic world. Second, the rebellion is predominantly instinctual and unrationalized. This characteristic is partly positive. The rules and forms embedded in their actions permit a much more open and direct expression of sexuality, aggression, fascination with danger, and so forth than do the structures of their parents' repressed and distorted lives. The teenagers have created for themselves a kind of relative freedom, a freedom to release their natural emotions and impulses. Nevertheless, the mindlessness of the rebellion has a more disturbing side. By and large, their revolt against the environment of the adults seems hardly more than an unwilled reaction to the restraint and constriction that they suffer. We are given no evidence that the kids have an articulate sense of the real sources of their frustration and despair. All of them are able, at best, to give half a voice to their grievances against the inadequacies of their individual parents as they perceive them. That the total context of their lives and their parents' lives is impossibly oppressive appears never to be grasped. Equally, there is little or no understanding of the orderings that constitute them as a distinctive culture. They are blind to the powers at work in their dealings with adults *and* among themselves. They are, in short, only blindly in revolt.[4]

One consequence of this is that the rebellion is foundationless and fragile. We are shown that in the face of death and the universal prospect of death and in the forced recognition of their individual isolation and vulnerability, their liberating energy, exuberance, and bravado collapse

Fig. 24. The teenagers react with fear and horror to a vision of the earth's destruction at the planetarium.

Fig. 25. Judy (Natalie Wood) automatically reaches out to Jim (James Dean) just after Buzz's death. Plato (Sal Mineo) stands in the background between them.

Ray's *Rebel without a Cause* 179

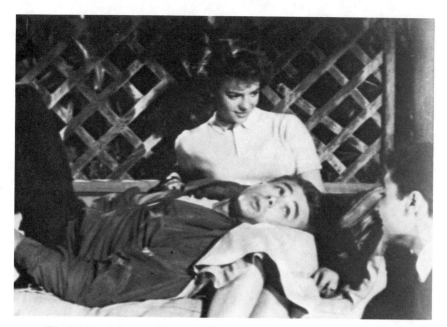

Fig. 26. Jim, Judy, and Plato briefly form a tranquil family unit at the old mansion.

Fig. 27. Before the knife fight outside the planetarium, Judy is startled by something she sees in or beyond her compact mirror.

Fig. 28. Jim confronts his parents. Notice the closure and distortion of the domestic space.

into helpless terror. They cling to one another either for protection from the vision of oblivion or for shared warmth against its chilling effect or simply for obstruction of the view. But this defines a rigidly dialectical process. The spiritual entombment of mass urban society impells the young to seek some release. Yet this release is dangerous and opens more easily upon a prospect of the void. A glimpse of that prospect impells them back into the safety of the baffled herd. Like their parents, they retreat into the shelter of an enclosure without a view of any kind. In *Rebel*, with this ultra-Hobbesian outlook, these are the fundamental processes that underlie both social cohesion and its resulting tensions. They are presented as processes of nature that are fixed and inexorable in their operation. Their emblem in the film is "the ancient rhythm of the stars."[5]

It is in these terms that the day-long destinies of Jim, Judy, and Plato are to be comprehended. For what happens in the course of their day is that the three of them come to form a "family," which then betrays its own "child." (Or, at least, this is the child's perception of the events in question.) Furthermore, the processes that cause this affiliation and its aftereffects are pictured as having the same iron inevitability as the processes beneath the surface of larger social units. I am thinking, of course, of the first part of the sequence at "Plato's mansion." This is the old, spacious, once-elegant but long-abandoned house that Plato has discovered, uses as his asylum from the world, and has, earlier in the day, pointed out to Jim from a balcony at the planetarium. Late that night, Jim and Judy come together to this house, and they are joined shortly thereafter by Plato himself. The mansion, through its association with Plato, is marked as a place of fantasy and nighttime desire, and appropriately, the friends almost immediately start up a game of play-acting. At first, Plato pretends to be a real estate agent who is showing the house to Jim and Judy, who pretend, in turn, to be newlyweds in search of a home. As part of the pretense, they imitate their own parents and parody their attitudes, especially what they take the parental attitude to children to be. This act is continued until they arrive at the area that contains the emptied swimming pool, where, as part of the game, the pool is dubbed "the nursery." Further, the dubbing effects a transformation of the game they play. Entering the "nursery," they suddenly begin to act like very small children cavorting with glee and utter unselfconsciousness in and around the pool. The effortless, completely unreflective transition between the two pretenses marks their actual uncertain and unresolved status between childhood and adult life. After the second game has been played out, they settle down to rest, and it is at this juncture that the formation of the mock family is clearly portrayed. Jim lies with his head in Judy's lap, and they adopt the role of the comfortable, settled couple while Plato sprawls happily and childishly at their feet (see fig. 26). They chat about a number of topics, including Plato's fantasized conceptions of his absent real family until, at last, Plato is lulled to sleep. Wanting to be alone with each other, Jim and Judy decide to go off and explore the huge house. They gently cover Plato up and retreat to a distant room where they express their love, and each declares that the other realizes what he or she has always been searching for. However, their departure exposes Plato to Buzz's friends, who, having broken into the house, find him alone and asleep. When Plato is awakened to the situation, he sees the newly formed couple's desertion of him for their own private, mutual concerns as the characteristic adult betrayal of a child.

At the very center of these occurrences lies that fact that Jim and Judy are now defining themselves as a pair eligible for marriage, which is potentially the nucleus of a family arising, this time around, within their generation. And this is the culmination of processes that are presented as the predetermined upshot of social, psychological, and biological forces. I have already spoken of that crucial moment in which these two, almost as a kind of reflex, clasp hands at the cliff's edge. This is the act that mysteriously ties them so absolutely together that all of the rest of their interaction, including their behavior at "Plato's mansion," seems to be the working out of that moment after Buzz's death. But, if this is the decisive instant of their relationship, it is an instant that has been prepared for by its antecedents. First, it has been mentioned that there is real attraction on both sides from their first sighting of each other. Because Judy is Buzz's girl, her immediate feeling for Jim is initially unwilling and suppressed, but we have observed that even Buzz appears to detect its existence. Second, the complex of parental problems that Jim, Judy, and Plato have anticipates and leads into the roles that each will adopt in relation to the other two. Jim, whose father can give no guidance whatsoever as to what it is to be both strong and protective, is offered this mock family, which unambiguously calls upon him to perform the masculine function that he seeks. Judy has been turned away by a father who cannot express tenderness and affection to a daughter who is on the verge of womanhood, and she finds in Jim a male figure who can replace her father in the needed ways. And Plato is a lost child whose parents have effectively deserted him, so that he is psychologically triggered to create a new pair of parents out of his friends. In other words, their familiar psychological conflicts are, as the film unfolds, reconceived as effects that arise from factors beyond mere psychology *and* as causes of desires that unconsciously guide their actions throughout the symbolic day.

There is a small and rather obscure motif that should be interpreted, I suspect, along related lines. The first time Plato notices Jim, he sees him reflected in a mirror on Plato's locker door beneath which he has placed a photograph of Alan Ladd. I take it that this signifies that Jim, like Ladd (in *Shane?*) is perceived by Plato as an ideal figure, a compelling persona upon which his lonely wishes for a father and a friend can be projected. It is made manifest in Plato's later words and deeds that this is what takes place. Similarly, when Judy sits on Jim's car during the prelude to the blade game, she looks at herself in a pocket mirror, and then, glancing over it, she sees Jim on the observatory balustrade above her. The sight of Jim and of her reflected self causes her to gasp in momentary surprise (see fig. 27). This incident seems to be picked up again when, after Buzz's accident, Jim and Plato take her home. As she gets out of the car, Jim returns a compact of hers he had found earlier at the police station, and he shows her her reflection in its mirror. Once again, she reacts to the reflection with surprise and wonder. It certainly fits well with the present reading of the film that Jim should have the ability to show Judy to herself or, more exactly, to show her what it is she really wants. More generally, it fits well that Jim should serve for his friends as a light-accepting object upon which fantasies are projected and from which the contents of desires are reflected back.

A number of critics who have written on *Rebel without a Cause* have commented upon the artificiality of forcing the story into a period of one day. For example, Jim and Judy seem soon to forget all about Buzz and his death, and this can seem improbable. Nevertheless, this unquestionable artificiality should be connected with the matters lately under scrutiny. The condensed duration of the film's events makes sense as the product of a use of time that is as schematic as the use of space. The day we watch is the day after Easter, and it carries the connotation that *something* is being re-created and renewed. But that something is not the harbinger of a hopeful rebirth or resurrection. Rather, the predominant significance of the restricted duration lies in a metaphorical association of the domesticating revolution that subdues the rebel with the silent, unshakable revolution of the earth in its orbit. The human changes in the narrative transpire with the same mechanistic regularity and irresistibility with which the day passes, and these changes renew what the film posits as the fundamental forms of human social life. Related to this is the "temporal" image of the smallness of such a transformation within the history of an individual's life. In his early discussion with the juvenile officer, Jim asserts that the one thing he most wants not to be is like his own pathetic father. On the other side, his father repeatedly claims that he was once a young man like Jim with the same troubles and that "in ten years' time" these troubles will be as nothing to him. It is tempting to take the father's statement as mere evasion and excuse. However, by the end of the film, when Jim has paired off with Judy and has already failed his temporary "child," and when he has magically reconciled with his parents, who are themselves magically united in their approval of his final acquiescence, it is necessary to reassess the force of his father's trite predictions. In the scene at the mansion, Jim mentions that he, unlike Plato, has never had any memory of the previous day. What memory then of the day depicted is to be expected from such a person after ten years have elapsed? (And this point thematically rationalizes the "unnatural" forgetting of poor Buzz.) Jim also says to the juvenile officer, "Boy, if—if I had *one* day when I didn't have to feel that I was ashamed of everything—if I felt I belonged some place, you know . . . ." The thought is left incomplete and it is doubtful that the boy has a definite conclusion in mind. But the day that is portrayed appears finally to have, in a strange way, satisfied his wish. A place where he is to belong has now been prepared, and he, shattered into a weakness that even his father can suport, should find, as his father demonstrably has, a state of mind in which shame and confusion will be obliterated in a numbed acceptance of his provided space.

In making these claims, I wish to avoid a possible misunderstanding about what I take the tone of the film to be. Despite Jim's blindness to the essence of what is happening to him, and despite the grim resolution of the series of events, neither he nor the other kids is treated with contempt or hostility. On the contrary, the film is, on balance, sympathetic to their youthful sensitivity, vitality, and emotional honesty. The love scenes are typical in this regard. The tenderness, the candid attraction, and the genuinely felt needs are presented with respect. Alone in "Plato's mansion," Judy says, "I love you, Jim. I *really* mean it," and she assuredly does mean what she says. It is less clear, given her immaturity and severely circumscribed vision of the world, just how much, beyond the undoubted feelings of the moment, she has the capacity to mean. It is not that these teenagers are cowards or traitors or liars of some kind. It is simply that they are at the mercy of the hidden causal factors to which the film assigns such crushing weight.

A special sort of sympathy naturally attaches to Plato, who is gunned down on the steps of the observatory. During the attack upon him at the mansion, he has shot one of his attackers and fired at the policemen who arrive upon the scene. He escapes across the wooded hillside to the observatory, hides himself inside the building, and is trapped there by the police. Jim and Judy make their way to him, and he is eventually persuaded by Jim to come back out. But Plato is frightened by the glare of headlights on the planetarium grounds and when, in false alarm, these lights are turned blazingly upon him, he panics, runs, and is shot. Just as Buzz's death was associated with the planetarium images of our globe's destruction by the fiery star, so, in a different way, is Plato's. After Jim enters the planetarium to talk with Plato, he flicks on the switches that start up the visuals for the lecture on astronomy. He even remarks at one point, "Come on, Plato, you've seen this show before." But then, if Jim's action marks the beginning of a projection of that show, Plato's panic on the steps should come roughly at its conclusion. His demise in the overwhelming light should be matched on the domed ceiling inside by the annihilation of the earth in fire and gas. Jim is the new boy in town; but Plato is much more fundamentally a stranger to the world. And thus, it is the unassimilable stranger who is, in the end, eliminated.

Plato's parents have deserted him. He has no friends or social standing at the school. Above all, as his nickname suggests, he is to be seen as a kind of primitive philosopher who lives in thought and dreams. On the one hand, he lives so thoroughly in the imagination that he is clumsily out of touch with immediate circumstances. His loneliness is alleviated only by building fantasies around people such as Jim and movie stars and his real father, to whom he feels some special tie. On the other hand, he is very much in touch with the realities of isolation, emptiness, and death, and these are, in *Rebel*, the basic all-pervading realities of our brief lives. When earlier the lecturer at the planetarium finished his talk, Plato rose from behind the auditorium seats where he had hidden in fear and asked disdainfully, "What does *he* know about 'man alone'?" We are meant to infer that, out of his enigmatic experience, this is what Plato *does* know about, knowing more, perhaps, than the lecture has conveyed.

It is also important that the film hints, as clearly as a fifties Hollywood production could, that Plato's sexual orientation is gay. His being, like Judy, so immediately drawn to Jim presumably has its component of physical attraction too. The importance of this derives primarily from its being still another way in which he is set outside those operations that bring the young couple back into the established structures of family and society. It is because there is no social space for him to occupy that he is eventually destroyed. The mechanisms that assimilate Jim and Judy reject Plato and toss him aside. From this point of view, it is Plato who is, in a sense, the truly intransigent rebel. His rebellion is mostly passive and contemplative, but it is, nonetheless, a rebellion, one that is inevitably struck down at the observatory doors. Jim and Judy, at the mansion, notice and are amused that Plato is wearing one red sock and one of dark navy blue. Color, like space and time, has schematic significance in the film, and, within that scheme, red has its traditional association with rebellion and dark blue with the night sky and all that it has been made, in the movie, to signify. Hence, the pair of mismatched socks symbolizes the schizophrenia of Plato's existence. He is in revolt against the flatness and constriction of "normal life," but his rebellion envisages no worldly change: his eyes are fixed too unswervingly upon the oblivion that surrounds all change of every sort.

In a curious series of shots, occurring after Plato has been killed, Jim and Judy approach his corpse. Jim reaches down and zips up the red jacket that he had given Plato a few moments before, and Judy replaces a shoe that had fallen from Plato's foot. Echoing the earlier images of the temporary "family" the three kids had briefly formed, these actions have the look of an attempt by parents to bundle their child against the cold. The gesture, taken in this way, is pathetic and ironic. Jim's father then bends down and places his jacket on Jim's shoulders. He invites his boy, who is broken by shock and grief, to stand up with him, and he promises, in this context ambiguously, to be "as strong as you [Jim] want me to be." With the red jacket borne away on Plato and with the adult jacket now worn by Jim, an exchange of "uniforms" has been effected. The jacket of rebellion is gone, and, as Jim returns to Judy's side, he wears the token of his new and more acceptable status. As Jim and Judy start to leave together, Jim's parents stare at each other, at first in wonder and then in broad, happy relief. With their arms around each other, they follow the younger man and woman to the waiting police cars.

In the very last shot of the film, the camera cranes slowly up to show the dawn breaking over the observatory. As the assembled crowd disperses and departs, a solitary man (reputedly Nicholas Ray himself) walks up the path toward the planetarium to open it for the new day's work. The standard interpretation of the dawning of another day hardly needs explanation. However, in addition to all the other considerations of this chapter, we should add one terse and wonderfully opaque exchange between Jim and Plato just before the latter is shot. Plato asks, "Jim, do you think that the end of the world will come at nighttime?" and Jim replies simply, "No, at dawn." As far as I can see, Jim's answer does not have an interpretable literal point. What it does is construct an equation between the coming of dawn and the end of the world. And this equation, especially in the context of this film, potentially cancels out the standard, more positive connotations of the dawn that appears in that final shot. Moreover, for the reasons that I have tried to elucidate, this is not only the end of the world for Plato, but it is likely to be the end of access to an open and living world for the young couple who are enclosed in the black cars that we see moving slowly down the drive.

I have placed this discussion last among the analyses of individual films because this treatment of *Rebel without a Cause* suggests some important ways in which our earlier discussion of cinematic point of view, especially in chapter 4, needs to be extended or qualified. For example, within the broad categories of that chapter, this film, like *The Searchers*, satisfies the rough criteria I mentioned for unrestricted narrational authority. For many purposes, this classification of *Rebel* is satisfactory and need not cause confusion. Nevertheless, it is also essential to an understanding of the film that there is a way in which its narration *is* systematically restricted.

It has been argued in the present chapter that the film, in the first planetarium scene particularly, lays down a set of fairly abstract correspondences between various sorts of spatial and temporal properties and global qualities of the lives and actions of the characters. Furthermore, many of the spatial and temporal properties of the film's image track are themselves guided by or, if one likes, restricted in terms of this set of correspondences. To cite two of the simplest instances of this, I have explicated along these lines the relative constriction or openness of the space in certain scenes and the presentation of the narrative events as occurring in a single day. As I have tried to show, the narration is so elaborately restricted in terms of the relevant correspondences that the film seems to have an essaylike or lecturelike character of its own. It is as if simultaneously the viewer was being given an enunciation of a number of quite general principles and a concrete demonstration of their truth was being enacted on the screen. Unfortunately, however, it is not entirely clear how this *type* of restriction is to be described. Many films set up and operate within a system of, for example, symbolic correspondences, but one would not want to count this as a mode or feature of "point of view." What is special about *Rebel* is that (1) the abstract correspondences concern properties or kinds of properties which are actually instantiated in the narration; that is, the narration and its parts have spatial and temporal properties, and (2) the set of correspondences significantly determines the special way in which these formal properties are instantiated within the shots, scenes, and sequences of the film. Both of these conditions have to be satisfied if we are to think of these correspondences as defining a restriction imposed upon the film's *narrational* strategy. At least, these remarks adumbrate the notion that one would like to capture more rigorously so that its significance as a general possibility could be explored.

I mention this case partly because of its independent interest, but also because it potentially complicates some subordinate topics. Once again, the question can be illustrated in terms of *Rebel*. There are many scenes in the film that seem to invite a reading of the narration as reflecting the subjectivity of the teenagers involved in the action portrayed. That invitation is probably most strongly extended in the scene, after the chickie run episode, when Jim returns home, appeals for help from his parents, and winds up lashing out at their weakness and hypocrisy. (This seems to represent a definitive break with the parents: he tries to kill his father and destroy a portrait of his mother as a younger and lovelier woman.) Early in the scene, Jim is sprawled on the sofa with his head hanging over the edge toward the floor, and, as his mother enters the room, there is a point-of-view shot from his position there during which the camera revolves 180 degrees to capture the subjective effect of his getting up to face the situation. In the segment that follows, the claustrophobia, clutter, and distortion of this domestic space is rendered with almost hallucinatory emphasis. Not only is the space again oppressively confined, with furniture, stairs, and railings arising as barriers between the antagonists, but much of the action, most notably that on the stairs, is framed with the camera tilted to one side or the other so that characters artificially rise and fall in the shots in correlation with their attempts to dominate or to retreat from the course of the argument (see fig. 28). Especially with that bizarre shot from Jim's field of vision introducing these events, it is tempting to suppose that the stylistics here are meant to mirror his continuing impressions of the interchange. And, indeed, I am not at all sure that this is incorrect. The problem is that the set of general correspondences operative in the film assigns to many facets of this narration a significance that far outruns anything we can ascribe to Jim's extremely limited perspective. Thus, in this scene, as in others, the use of space may well convey something of the teenager's feeling, but it also bears meaning that he cannot possibly comprehend. Perhaps we can say of this and similar scenes that the subjectivity of a character is reflected *and* it accomplishes more besides. The difficulty with this description is that it is by no means a trivial matter to discriminate the elements that pertain to the subjectivity reflected from the elements that pertain only to the wider conception of the film. Alternatively, "subjective reflection" would have to be redefined to exclude cases with this additional complexity. That task would not prove trivial either.

I have wished to bring out these last considerations without resolving them for the reasons stated at the beginning of this chapter. They are typical of the refinement, qualification, and reformulation any vaguely adequate theory of cinematic point of view will, in the long run, have to provide. This suggestion that there is considerable complication lurking just beyond the scope of the discussion in this book may be discouraging. And yet, the subtlety and complexity of a film such as *Rebel* gives promise that suitable attention to more fine-grained distinctions will yield a satisfactory reward in our heightened appreciation of what the "classical" narrative film can, almost invisibly, achieve.

Chapter 10

Morals for Method

In all of the films discussed in this book, there are central characters whose perception and comprehension of their personal circumstances are shown to be dim, distorted, and severely restricted in relation to their need to see and understand the situations in which they act. The film viewer, from a position outside the relevant fictional world, sees how these characters' ways of apprehending the depicted action collide against the facts that their outlooks have failed to encompass. Thus, the audience is given object lessons in the faltering dynamics of perception over a period of time. However, it is equally the case, and equally important, that the films I have discussed raise questions about the actual and potential illusions of spectatorship at the cinema. The morals that have been taught about perceptual malfunction and misalignment *within* the boundaries of the film have effectively been doubled back upon the viewers themselves. Naturally, the illusions of the film spectator tend to differ from those to which the various film characters succumb, but the revelations about viewer vulnerability are enough to undermine the apparent security of what has probably seemed to be a superior style of judiciously distanced observation. Object lessons about the "privileged" and "innocent" activity of film-mediated perception are therefore offered up as well.

I open this chapter with this observation in part because it contradicts a major motif in much structuralist and poststructuralist writing on film. It is often maintained, roughly, that the strategies, forms, and techniques of classical narrative cinema lock members of an audience into an epistemic position that makes it impossible for them to criticize either their own habits of perception in film viewing or the modes of perceptual intelligibility that the films themselves display. (We shall look more carefully at a version of this "prison house of movies" thesis in a moment.) Now, here is one site at which the more limited enterprise of understanding point of view in film can impinge forcefully upon what purports to be a much larger and more basic claim of a general theory of film. For it seems that the plausibility that has been attributed to the claim I have mentioned is almost wholly a function of the grand obscurity with which it is normally formulated combined with a wholesale failure to think through even the limited implications of a minimally adequate account of cinematic point of view. In any case, this is a thesis I wish to develop, and doing so in some detail will provide an opportunity to draw together and summarize a range of material from earlier chapters.

Because it is impossible to examine all of the formulations of the view in question, I shall concentrate upon the version that figures centrally in a well-known and influential essay by Colin McCabe.[1] McCabe's argument turns upon his explication of a concept of "a classic realist text," a concept that he takes to be exemplified both in the standard nineteenth-century novel and in classical narrative films. The basic conventions of the latter are, according to McCabe, the descendants of conventions of the former. He states that "a classic realist text may be defined as one in which there is a hierarchy amongst the discourses which compose the text and this hierarchy is defined in terms of an empirical notion of truth" (153). Fortunately, this "definition" is partially amplified in connection with literary fiction as follows: "In the classical realist novel the narrative prose functions as a metalanguage that can state all of the truths in the object language—those words held in inverted commas [quotations of the characters' speech]—and can also explain the relation of this object language to the real. The metalanguage can thereby explain the relation of the object language to the world and the strange methods by which the object languages attempt to express truths which are straightforwardly conveyed in the metalanguage" (153).

The misuse of the "metalanguage/object language" distinction in this passage leaves the purported amplification murky, but McCabe pretty clearly has in mind as "the metalanguage" the sentences of a novel which represent the speech acts of the narrator. (It will include everything except the quoted inner and outer speech of the characters.) Furthermore, what makes a literary text one that is "classic realist" is that its narrator has certain general characteristics. First, it seems that the narrator must be relatively omniscient, having the authority to bring together, reliably and without identification of a source of knowledge, the diverse kinds of material needed to explain the behavior, thoughts, and speech acts (the "discourses") of the characters. Second, because we are told that "the narrative discourse simply allows reality to appear and denies its own status as articulation" (154), the classic realist narrator must be substantially undramatized and unselfconscious about the activity of narration. In other words, when the pseudo-logical and pseudo-metaphysical jargon is cleared away, it turns out that McCabe is traveling on the more familiar terrain of literary point of view.

Leaving aside all questions about the adequacy of McCabe's conception of the traditions of the nineteenth-century novel, his presentation of this conception is used to set the conditions that a classic realist text in film must meet. He asks, "does this definition carry over into films where it is certainly less evident where to locate the dominant discourse?" Unsurprisingly, his answer is affirmative.

> It seems to me that it does. . . . The narrative prose achieves its position of dominance because it is in the position of knowledge and this function of knowledge is taken up in the cinema by the *narration* [italics mine] of events. Through the knowledge we gain from the narrative we can split the discourses of the various characters from their situations and compare what is said in these discourses with what has been revealed to us through narration. The camera shows us what happens—it tells the truth against which we can measure discourses. (155)

Consolidating his view, McCabe adds that "the narrative of events—the knowledge which film provides of how things are—is the metalanguage in which we talk of the various characters in film" (156).

Therefore, the "dominant discourse" of classical film is supposed to be a form of visual narration such that:

> 1. it yields a form of epistemic access that is superior to the vantage points of the characters,

and

> 2. it fulfills expected standards of explanatory coherence (explains "how things are" in relation to the characters).

Further, the original stipulation that the dominant narration is defined by "an empirical notion of truth" hints at the idea that

> 3. it is meant to establish a level of objective truth about the characters and their situations which the viewer is able to discern through ordinary perception and commonsense forms of inference.

That McCabe envisages something such as condition (3) is supported by the last part of the following remark: "The narrative discourse cannot be mistaken in its identifications because the narrative discourse is not present as discourse—as articulation. The unquestioned nature of the narrative discourse entails that the only problem that reality poses is to go and look and see what *Things* there *are*" (157). Moreover, the earlier part of this quotation (and similar claims in McCabe's essay) suggest that film narration is classic realist only if:

4. the film does not acknowledge its status as an intentional construction whose function is to depict a world of fiction,

and, related to this,

5. its image track is presented as overall transparent.

Finally, given the necessary existence of the properties described in (1) through (5) in the classic realist film text, it follows for McCabe that films with these properties "cannot deal with the real as contradictory" and, in addition, they "ensure the position of the subject in a relation of dominant specularity" (157). What these charges amount to is not easy to make out, but the imputed consequences unquestionably sound pernicious.

Throughout his discussion, McCabe presupposes that all classical narrative films are classic realist texts in the usage he wishes to establish. Indeed, the technical concept is introduced as a means of capturing the essential form and nature of traditional films. This presupposition, combined with his dark allegations about their putative limitations, is the basis of his demand for radically alternative, nonnarrative forms. Nevertheless, what we have already discovered in the course of this book is that none of the five conditions listed above—with one possible exception—is uniformly exemplified even in Hollywood genre films. Let us briefly take up each of these conditions in the stated order.

About condition (1). It is true that most classical films adopt an essentially unrestricted narrational authority and do so in the service of an ideally objective overview of the narratives they portray. However, the predominance of this mode coexists with the option of film narration which operates, in a systematic and principled manner, under one or another global restriction upon what it is authorized to show and, through the editing, to juxtapose. In the first part of chapter 5, this option of restriction was explored, and I delineated the need for a theory of point of view capable of accommodating everything from an extended, directly subjective rendering of a character's field of vision to a wholly unpsychologized schema of selection which mirrors some of the limitations governing human observation universally. Between these two extremes is a range of intermediate "nonomniscient" possibilities, each of which is notably distinct in its effects and implications from the others. Any framework of restricted narrational authority which has been conscientiously worked out determines the angle at which the viewer's experience of the film intersects the experience of the film's characters. It therefore helps to define the degree to which the viewer is entitled to assume that the film-mediated information is or is not mediated in turn by a reflected subjectivity or is otherwise conditioned by constraints on access which the characters may or may not share. Whenever such issues of mediation or constraint occur, the epistemic superiority of the viewer's position is not assured. We have seen how subtle and complex these issues can be, but McCabe writes as if this kind of consideration can never seriously arise.

I have also allowed that most classical films satisfy the second condition of explanatory coherence. They have been designed to provide answers to the chief dramatic questions raised by the assorted dilemmas faced by the characters and to accomplish this in a manner that makes the resolutions of these questions definitive and clearly marked as such. And yet, we have discovered that a classically styled movie (such as *You Only Live Once*) may appear on the surface to answer its highlighted questions fully and adequately while, at the same time, revealing in more muted ways that these surface answers ought to be suspect and that a more stable closure is difficult, if not impossible, to supply. When this acknowledgment of explanatory incompleteness is a key factor organizing the film's narration, I have spoken of that narration as being "rhetorically unreliable." The existence of this possibility already violates condition (2). But, alternatively, even when a film does contain the basis of a coherent resolution, it may be that the material that constitutes that basis has not been marked so as to signal overtly the explanatory force it bears. Usually, such a film will offer at least the outlines of a superficial closure, which the implicit explanatory counterstructure is intended to outweigh. In one good sense, this sort of narration is also unreliable, because its more overt gestures of resolution are likely to mislead; its true explanatory coherence will be opaque. It does not matter whether we count this explanatory opacity as violating condition (2) or not. It patently represents a sophisticated epistemic possibility that McCabe's analysis certainly does not envisage.

The precise import of condition (3) is hard to pin down. McCabe actually says that the classic realist text "fixes the subject in a point of view from which everything becomes obvious" (161), but, taken literally, this is absurdly too strong. I have supposed, in stating (3), that he means to maintain that whatever significance a classical film presents or expresses is knowable by "obvious" methods of observation and inference. This at least allows that the actual deployment of those methods may be indefinitely complicated. All that is required is that any such method is to be more or less familiar from commonsense practices of belief formation. It does not matter that this condition continues to be extremely vague, because any further specification will still be contravened by films that are epistemically distanced from *any* commonsense picture of the world that we hold. I have argued that a film may force us to discover new patterns of perceptual intelligibility in the narrative action it depicts if we are to locate a unifying order and meaning in that action as it nonstandardly unfolds. When we have been distanced from our habitual styles of visual comprehension, it may take a deviant metaphysics or epistemology to yield a satisfactory configuration of sense within the film. Von Sternberg's *The Scarlet Empress* and *The Devil Is a Woman* were our most sharply etched examples of this strategy.

We really do not need new grounds for rejecting the universal applicability of condition (4). It has already been noted that a film may tacitly acknowledge the inadequacy of some of its surface forms and structures. However, the end of chapter 7 contains a discussion of the fact that there are films that have characters who stand in some privileged relation to the film narration. Several possibilities of this kind were examined there, but one among them is especially important for the topic of cinematic self-reference and self-acknowledgment. That is, a film may contain a character who embodies certain of the leading epistemic qualities of the narration and, thereby, of the implied film maker as well (for example, *Letter from an Unknown Woman*). Or, beyond this, such a character may assume a metacinematic power to which the narrative events appear to respond (*The Devil Is a Woman*). No doubt there are other, similar relationships of characters to film narration to be exploited, but it is difficult to survey the range in a perspicuous way. In any case, it is plain that the presence of a character who is seen as standing in for an implied film maker not only acknowledges the cinematic artifact but permits an elaborate articulation of the nature of that acknowledgment. Condition (4) can seem an invariant of classical narrative film because the relatively effaced narrational styles of these films and the limitations upon theme and subject matter which they typically observe tend to force self-consciousness in and of the narration to appear recessively behind the foregrounded mechanisms of plot. This concession, however, makes it no less a mistake to ignore the striking ways in which self-consciousness can and does occur.

A film whose narration is directly subjective throughout (such as *The Lady in the Lake*) is a counterexample to the last condition of overall transparency of the image track. Still, I have granted that this sort of counterexample is of marginal interest and that transparency of the image comes closest of the five conditions to being a genuine norm of the traditional cinema. I have understood "transparency" to mean that the individual shots of a film are designed to license viewers to take up the impression of having direct perceptual access to the visual appearance of items and events in the fictional world. Naturally, most films that exemplify overall transparency contain shots that do not meet this description, but then these departures from the norm will be suitably flagged and rationalized for what they are. For example, point-of-view shots from a character's perspective are fairly common, but, within a context of overall transparency, they are presented as direct *quotations*, provided by the narration, of a slice of the character's visual experience. Transparency assures the audience of an extensive base of information, guaranteed to be reliable, about the ways in which the fictional world and its constituents look and sound. Nevertheless, as extensive and important as this reliable foundation generally is, it is, in another way, a quite minimal base of information. Transparency, by itself, does not guarantee that the ambiguities, uncertainties, and outright contradictions that a manifold of appearances may generate over time will be resolved or otherwise explained away. For this reason, transparency potentially leaves open almost all of the issues about what kinds of consistency and intelligibility the appearances given in a film may have. Thus, if transparency is nearly an exceptionless condition of classical narrative film, it is largely because the condition is, in effect, so weak. It is, of course, a feature of many nonclassical, nonnarrative films as well. This relative weakness is often unintentionally obscured in film theory because "transparency" is also used to cover many or all of the first four conditions, but then its proper application is sizably reduced. For instance, transparency seems thus inflated in McCabe's essay where phrases such as "the empirical notion of truth" merely blot out the relevant distinctions.

I have tried to show, by this review of considerations developed in previous chapters, how badly McCabe's idea of a classic realist text distorts and impoverishes the possibilities available in traditional films. Like many other authors, he systematically supposes that the customary surface forms and strategies of these films define the limits of their possible concerns and accomplishments. Indeed, because we have recapitulated the degrees of freedom which the surface constraints permit, it is easy to deal rather briefly with the fundamental and supposedly congenital limitations that McCabe imputes to the normal narrative structures. First, he asserts, as I mentioned in passing, that classical film "cannot deal with the real as contradictory." Once again, one is left to guess at the content of this complaint, but it seems to mean that, because he believes that a classical film always purports to establish an objective and intersubjectively available truth about its fictional history, this aim, he infers, precludes the possibility of exhibiting ways in which that very same history might be perceived from different, deeply conflicting perspectives—perspectives whose differences may be ultimately unresolvable. To this objection, my response is simple: its falsity is demonstrated by every film discussed at length in this book. In certain ways, *You Only Live Once* has been our purest counterexample, but, in every instance there exists a standard, plot-oriented viewing that contradicts at many crucial points the richer and more challenging viewing I set forth.

At bottom, McCabe and others of a similar persuasion are just confused about the nature and extent of the "objectivity" to which the classical forms are typically committed. Transparency, narrowly understood, is a weak commitment, and the superficial requirements of closure and effacement can be satisfied *only* superficially. Actually, I am tempted to assert a contrary of McCabe's objection. It is in classical narrative film alone that a more or less determinate fictional history is portrayed by visual narration, which can simultaneously sustain both a salient, standard perspective and a distinct, oblique perspective, both of which may be equally and continuously coherent. Be this as it may, the range of possibilities which McCabe mistakenly denies is central to what the narrative cinema can mean to us. Presumably, the lessons of alternative perspectives in these films are not unrelated to the ways in which we see and comprehend ourselves when we attempt to make a connected narrative out of segments of our own lives and the lives of others.

McCabe's associated indictment of traditional films is that they "ensure the position of the subject [that is, the viewer] in a relation of dominant specularity." When one first comes across this charge, one feels immediately that dominant specularity is not a position that one, as a sensitive filmgoer, would want to be in. The phrase invokes the picture of a brutish viewer who aggressively glares his films into submission. However, McCabe's conception is rather the opposite. It is the conception of passive film spectators who, immersed in transparency, allow their perception and understanding of the screen events to be wholly the products of the narrative apparatus. It denotes the relation to film of viewers seduced from the critical use of their perception and understanding by the regimenting dictates of classical narrative and narration. This is the chief target of McCabe's attack on the classic realist film text, and this passiveness is a phenomenon that merits his rightful, if somewhat overstated, concern. It is not to be denied that normal film viewing is too often intellectually passive and only superficially critical of its object. Far too often conventional films strongly encourage this stolidity and offer few rewards to alertness and analytical reflection. These complaints have over many years acquired the status of truisms, but they are, nonetheless, still true. What is distinctive about the position that McCabe and other recent theorists occupy is the contention that the forms and strategies of classical film render this situation inevitable—render the practice of that cinema a prison house for the perceptually inert. It is supposed to be in the nature of the forms in question that they forego the possibility of eliciting a radical transformation of vision and a recognition of the vast contingency of the manner in which we ordinarily function as observers of the world. Once again, I can merely repeat that the films that we have here examined are testimonies that these "essentialist" theses are false.

Much poststructuralist writing on film speculates on how it is that subjects are fixed in the position of dominant specularity and on the historical development and ideological consequences of this positioning. Setting aside reservations about how this speculation is usually conducted, I do not question that the specific seductions of the familiar dramatic cinema provide issues to be studied. What I do reject is any theory that makes these seductions a necessary consequence of the forms of classical film and ignores the scattered but triumphant instances that show that this is not the case. If we need a better account of the ideological suasion built into so much commercial film-making, we need just as badly a better account of the flexibility of those forms that make the classical triumphs into concrete, realized possibilities.

Late in his article, McCabe proposes that "the method of representation (the language: verbal and cinematic) determines in its structural activity . . . both the places where the object 'appears' and the point from which the object is seen. It is this point which is exactly the place allotted to the reading subject" (160). Here, first of all, is yet another endorsement of the odd, unargued brand of formalist determinism to which I have objected repeatedly. More important, however, is the the explicitness with which it is maintained in this passage that a source of that determinism is the view that the fictional objects and events in a film and the ways in which they appear to a viewer are the results of the "*structural activity*" of the *languagelike elements* that are said to make up a film's narration. Of course, this is an established motif in much film theory of a vaguely structuralist orientation, but sheer repetition has hardly made its import less elusive.

This is not the place to examine the long and unhappy history of the notion of a language of film. Its manifestations are too numerous and too diverse; its confusions are too deeply entangled. Nevertheless, I think it is possible to say enough to shake the conviction that any sort of formalist determinism is supported by the methodological premise that representation in film is fundamentally a function of structural determinants of a quasi-linguistic kind. This conviction and its would-be basis set an agenda for theory of film which excludes the sorts of film criticism and approaches to theory which I have attempted in this volume to promote.

It will be helpful, in this context, to turn to a theorist who is more self-conscious about his assumptions and arguments and who is less tendentious in his aims than McCabe. Brian Henderson, in his book *A Critique of Film Theory*, offers a revealing summary statement of what he counts as the domain of film theory. The reader is told that it encompasses questions about "the relations between film and reality, the relations between film and narrative, and the question whether film is a language and, if so, what kind of language. Related to these questions is *the even more fundamental one of determining the basic units of film (and of film analysis) and the rules governing the combination of these units*" [italics mine].[2] Subsequently, long sections of *A Critique* are devoted to criticism of Christian Metz's attempts, in his early work,[3] to identify "basic units of film" and their "rules of combination." Throughout his book, Henderson's own seemingly a priori commitment to this type of implausible analytical atomism never waivers. His most extreme expression of this Democritean enthusiasm is found in the following passage: "Each [film theory] should provide a comprehensive model of cinematic units at all levels and of the modes of combination and interaction at each level. In short, a film theory should provide concepts, terms, and dynamic models of interaction for the analysis of cinematic parts and wholes of all kinds."[4] This reads, at first, like an invigoratingly ambitious prolegomena to a new, more objective, more scientific theory of film, until one pauses to wonder what scientific discipline could conceivably aim at such an enterprise. We would not even have the theory of the simple pendulum if physicists, in considering, for example, the grandfather clock, had demanded of themselves "dynamic models" of its various "components" at every "level" of (possible?) analysis. We probably would not have grandfather clocks. Finding fruitful and manageable questions in a given area of thought is usually at least as hard as finding answers to those questions. Symptomatically, one is hard-pressed to locate in Henderson's book a set of specific phenomena *derived from real films* which film theory is supposed to explain. Rather, it is flatly assumed from first to last that a general and largely unconstrained inquiry after "units," "rules," and "models" is well-conceived and valuable.

Naturally, the difficulty here is not that there is a lack of parts and wholes in film; everything in a film is a part and a whole of some kind for some analytical purpose. The difficulty, at least in the first instance, is that we are never informed what the cinematic units are units *of* or what general types of rules or laws of combination are supposedly at stake. Presumably, if these units and rules are to play a role within a systematic account of cinematic content (and, after all, this seems the goal), then the units are to be units of meaning (in some sense appropriate to film) and the rules are to be projective rules that determine the meaning of a "combination" from the meanings of its constituent units and the structural relations that the combination embodies. Admittedly, it is hard to be certain of even this much, because we are never given a single example of the hypothesized units or the associated rules, and we are never given any evidence that film narration comes in honest units that generate larger narrational complexes in accordance with determinate projective rules. Still, as noted, at least this construal of Henderson's remarks offers his conception a kind of theoretical role to play while making some sense of the repeated appeals and analogies to linguistics which he and McCabe and a host of kindred spirits so often deploy. Indeed, *if* the resulting conception had some substance, it might give a basis to that formalist determinism that McCabe has been seen to favor. Limits to the expressive power of the putative film "language"—the "language" of classical film perhaps—would presumably set the limit to what such film can show. This, I think, is the idea that McCabe has accepted.

With just this much set out, let us bypass the whole question of locating a conception of cinematic meaning which has promise of being subject to the type of theory envisaged, and let us not concern ourselves about the form that the projective laws or rules might have. (Needless to say, I believe that we are simply bypassing a hopeless morass in each case.) Rather, I want to focus upon a pair of more general assumptions which are engendered here and do their work in tandem. The first is that it *is* possible to segment a film (at least at a given "level") into visual and aural "units" whose "interaction" gives structure and content to the film as a whole. The second is that such a segmentation is epistemically prior to interpretation and forms the core of the evidential basis for whatever interpretation may ensue. It is this second assumption that provides the principal rationale for supposing that the truth of the first assumption would offer a useful foundation for film analysis and theory. Certainly, from the two assumptions together, it follows that it is essential to an adequate theory of film that it provide an account of admissible modes of segmentation. Taken together, these assumptions define a kind of formalist foundationalism with respect to meaning in films. Other less "linguistic" versions are doubtlessly possible, but the present formulation encapsulates a conception that many, consciously or subliminally, have found compelling. It yields, in any case, an explicit statement of a methological view with which much of my previous discussion has been at odds. The explicit statement permits a direct marshaling of the main grounds for repudiating this view and others of its ilk.

In previous chapters, these grounds have already been produced, but without adequate focus on and development of the pertinent implications. For example, in chapter 7, I argued that it is implausible to suppose that narrative, plot, or basic story line can be construed as a "level" where these assumptions fit. This point leaves open the possibility that films can be sliced along other dimensions that would yield a simple level more amenable to the project of segmentation. However, even this vague possibility seems foreclosed by suitable reflection on the example with which I opened the first chapter, the striking series of three shots from *The Lady from Shanghai*. (By way of a quick reminder, the shots were these: a truck pulls out in front of a car containing two men; a woman's hand presses a button; the car crashes into the truck.) I pointed out that, in viewing this segment, one has the impression that the pressing of the button causes the crash. We attribute, immediately and without conscious inference, a causal connection between the two events. If we think about segmenting this three-shot progression two very broad possibilities arise: (1) The onset and culmination of the accident constitute an independent segment crosscut with an unrelated segment showing the woman's action. The impression of causality is to be discounted as inadvertant and irrelevant to the content of the film. (2) The whole series is a unified segment showing the button pressing to be a cause of the crash. If a shot of a cannon firing were followed by a shot of an explosion, we would view this pair of shots as showing cause and effect: the cannon's hitting a target would be an *event* in the film. In our present example, it is merely that the apparent causal connection is a good deal less familiar.

Now, how might one reach a decision between (1) and (2)? Surely, nothing in the three shots themselves—no interaction of units into which this series might be analyzed—will settle the matter. It is just this fact that initially makes (1) and (2) genuine alternatives. At the same time, this does not mean that there is no way in which the choice can be settled at all. I would contend that (2) is correct by showing how the attribution of strange causal powers to the woman is systematically integrated with her peculiar role in the surrealistic context of this unusual film. Obviously, this contention would depend upon a careful and detailed interpretation of *The Lady from Shanghai*, and it does not matter for present purposes whether the argument would be sound. The moral is that it is impossible to resolve a question of segmentation as elementary as the choice between (1) and (2) independently of a thorough analytical viewing of the total film. In this extreme but instructive case, we cannot even identify the *simpler fictional occurrences* in the film without an appeal to the widest framework that contains the problematic three shots. If this is so, then it must be a mistake to believe or hope that segmentation can be treated as prior to, and foundational for, interpretation. In general, the way in which we will be inclined to divide a stretch of film into "interacting levels and units" will rest on large problems about how narrative, narration, and associated aspects of structure are to be construed. The analytical atomism conveyed by the description of film theory given by Henderson ought to be replaced by a lively, reiterated sense of the holistic character of all interpretative work.

The considerations that underlie the general force of this example are these. In everyday perception, we often judge directly that one observed event has caused another, but the immediate perceptual data that elicit that judgment from us are substantially inadequate to give it conclusive grounds. Furthermore, we do not, upon reflection, believe otherwise: we readily grant that, in making the judgment, we have drawn upon a large and somewhat indeterminate mass of background belief about the world. The same is true when we judge that we have seen one and the same physical object at distinct times or that we have observed different stages of a single, continuous movement through space. In short, we do not imagine in any of these cases that such rudimentary and basic judgments are derived from our immediate visual experiences by means of projective rules that take features of that experience as their input. Indeed, it is implausible to suppose otherwise.

But then, why should the situation be essentially altered when what we have been "given" is a series of shots showing events that appear to be causally linked or a series that appears to show the same object or the same temporally extended movement photographed from different times and places? Here also, it is certain that the direct connections and re-identifications that we make are heavily conditioned by our preestablished beliefs about the film world, the actual world, and standing relations between the two. As in ordinary perception, these judgments about the content of the film will normally not be the rule-governed upshot of features depicted within the shots. Finally, if these considerations are correct—if even our rock-bottom judgments about the *identity of objects and events* within a film fail to satisfy the model of units and structural laws—then it is hard to grasp how more sophisticated judgments about filmic content and significance can reasonably be expected to satisfy the model either. One can easily trace out the interpretative arguments propounded in earlier chapters and confirm that the dreamed-of model is useless there. The example from *The Lady from Shanghai* is useful because of the intuitive simplicity of the content in question. It thereby illustrates the hopelessness of finding some more fundamental "level" where the projective account might finally take purchase on the film. That is, this example demonstrates clearly and decisively that basic narrative events cannot, in general, be units *or* functions of units in the sense required, and once this is made salient no "level" still more simple appears on the remote horizon.

The objection that I have been sketching reflects the existence of a deep division about the relations between theory of film and film criticism, a division that is too deep, no doubt, to be settled by these brief remarks. In a passage that Henderson repeats twice in his book, he says, "film theory is, after all, a metacriticism or philosophy of criticism. It is pursued to improve film criticism through the determination of basic film categories and the identification of those assumptions about film on which any criticism is based. . . . [F]ilm theory itself is the continued improvement and clarification of the principles and assumptions of film criticism."[5] It is instructive to set these assertions alongside a passage from Stanley Cavell's *The World Viewed:*

> The aesthetic possibilities of a medium are not givens. You can no more tell what will give significance to the unique and specific aesthetic possibilities of projecting photographic images by thinking about them or seeing some, than you can tell what will give significance to the possibilities of paint by thinking about paint or by looking some over. You have to think about painting, and paintings; you have to think about motion pictures. What does this "thinking about them" consist in? Whatever the useful criticism of an art consists in.[6]

Clearly, I am sympathetic to much of what Cavell here suggests. In particular, I am inclined to see theory of film not as providing the foundations for criticism, but as more or less continuous with that which is most searching, articulate, explicit, and self-reflective *within* criticism. Moreover, these alternatives are not to be represented, as they often are, as a choice between rigorous methodology and impressionistic dabbling. Rigor, in any reasonable sense, and impressionism occur on both sides. For example, we have seen something in this chapter of the speciousness of the claims to rigor made in the name of various "structural" hypotheses. The antifoundationalist sentiments I have expressed are not meant to be justified definitively by the present discussion, but I hope to have issued effective warning that the pretensions of first philosophy are as tempting and dangerous in the study of film as they have been in other fields of thought.

If the modest theoretical apparatus I have suggested—the set of point-of-view distinctions developed before—has a principal recommendation, it is because the distinctions genuinely help to capture the rationale behind the works of film makers as diverse as Ford and von Sternberg, Lang and Ophuls, Renoir and Nicholas Ray. There may be other ways of stating the same or similar observations about the relevant films, but, at a minimum, it is established that these categories are not merely idling in the realm of the a priori: they accomplish straightforward and needed tasks. Also, even in their restricted generality, they serve to open up and enhance our sense of the epistemic possibilities of classical film. This can be a mixed blessing, because the implications that a broadened sense uncovers tend to lack theoretical tidiness and elegance and make the grander ambitions of theory more difficult to satisfy. Still, this situation is preferable to one in which an ambitious but too simple theory, such as McCabe's, has swept the less predictable and more interesting possibilities out of sight from the beginning.

However, if assorted film theories have sinned in their treatment or lack of treatment of epistemic matters in film, more intuitive approaches have hardly fared better. A lot of film criticism and analysis whose theoretical concerns are negligible have been more than ready to make use of general epistemological concepts and dichotomies, impressing them in an ad hoc fashion on the films they scrutinize. It is, for instance, a cliché of film criticism to announce that a certain work deals with matters of "appearance and reality." No doubt this assessment is often enough correct, but the formula is simultaneously too weighty and too slight to characterize the questions about perception and knowledge which a reasonably sophisticated film propounds. The formula fails utterly to discriminate between the bleak investigations of cinematic manipulation in *You Only Live Once* and the more light-hearted self-consciousness about cinematic transparency in *North by Northwest*. It does nothing to help conceptualize the difference between Ophuls' delicate and distanced portrayal of Lisa's private world of fantasy in *Letter from an Unknown Woman* and von Sternberg's rendering of a public world in *The Devil Is a Woman*, whose very substance seems made of the most private fantasies of the film maker. The stereotyped characters and conclusion of *Rebel without a Cause* are likely to be dismissed as the illusions of a simplifying social cinema unless it is noticed that the film's true closure is the expression of a cultural determinism that mocks our bland "reading" of stereotypes our social order presses upon us. The rhetorical strategies that inform these films and guide our experience of them are nuanced and complex, and an analysis of any one of them in terms of "appearance and reality" could only blunt an effort to describe the methods and issues at stake.

This stricture is or ought to be obvious, but it has apparently been less obvious that other very broad distinctions have been equally inflated and correspondingly impoverished. We have already canvassed some of the reasons why talk of "first-person" and "third-person" film narration invites recurrent confusion, and the related pair, "subjective" and "objective," fares no better. It should also be clear that an *opposition* between "the transparency of classical narration" and "the reflexivity of modernist narration" is seriously misconceived, and that divisions of film narration into "omniscient" and "perspectival," "closed" and "open," "personal" and "impersonal," and so forth are bound to be grossly inadequate to the distinctions that fruitful film analysis requires. Admittedly, no taxonomy of point of view in film will yield a set of categories which cleanly carves up the domain of individual films, assigning to each its perfectly apt classification. Nevertheless, it is fair to expect that a minimally satisfactory account will contain categories that are enlightening when we set out to think through a film of at least moderate intricacy. This requirement entails that any such taxonomy will have to be derived from an examination of the variety of epistemic factors which comes into play when film narration provides a determinate form of perceptual access to a connected series of narrative events. These factors, taken singly and in combination, can be realized in many ways, and it is the most central of these possibilities which the classifications of point of view I have introduced are intended to designate. I am sure that these categories need to be extended and, in some cases, revised, but the objective has been to offer a perspicuous setting for the process of reconsideration to begin.

To my mind, the chief advantage of looking at the concept of cinematic point of view along the lines reviewed in this chapter is that this approach places that concept in immediate conjunction with undeniably interesting questions about what we see and how we comprehend when we watch narratives in film. As I have attempted to show throughout the book, many of these questions about how we operate in apprehending film stories have, quite naturally, interested most of the best film makers as well. Their work constitutes a heritage of reflection on film which has been registered in film, and it is important to retain that heritage and value it properly. There is, I believe, no art other than the cinema which has a comparable capacity to reconstruct analytically and thereby explicate the possible modes of perceiving a localized slice of human history as an evolving field of visible significance. Classical narrative film, in particular, engenders and investigates possible modes of seeing a pattern in the events of such a history—a pattern that yields, either genuinely or speciously, "the sense of an ending." It models, in this way, our search for closure and coherence in our long-term view of things. A theory of point of view in film, as I conceive it, is a theory of these reconstructed forms of being witness to the world.

Notes

Chapter 1: Film, Perception, and Point of View

1. While writing this book, I knew of no sustained and sophisticated treatment of the concept of "cinematic point of view." I was aware of several suggestive, short discussions and of numerous helpful remarks on the topic (some of which are cited later), but no systematic analysis seemed to me to mark both the importance and the complexity of the concept. However, as my book was going to press, I discovered Edward R. Brannigan's *Point of View in the Cinema: A Theory of Narration and Subjectivity in Classical Film* (Amsterdam: Mouton Publishers, 1984), and this admirable book does much to fill the lacuna mentioned above. Although there is much in Brannigan's general framework and in his detailed remarks with which I do not agree, there is no question but that his volume is an important contribution to the topic. Unfortunately, it would take at least another chapter in the present book to survey adequately the areas of agreement and disagreement between us. (For example, our conceptions of the central notion of "point of view" overlap but do not coincide.) I have decided, therefore, not to attempt a comparison here, but, for anyone interested in the issues discussed in these pages, Brannigan's book is to be highly recommended.

2. V. F. Perkins, *Film as Film* (Baltimore: Penguin Books, 1972), pp. 119–20.

3. Ibid., pp. 122–24.

4. For remarks on this phenomenon, see Rudolf Arnheim, *Art and Visual Illusion: The New Version* (Berkeley and Los Angeles: University of California Press, 1974), p. 287.

5. This is a slight variant of an analogy that a number of poststructuralists have employed. They have emphasized the way in which the vanishing point in standard perspective determines the position that the viewer will take up in viewing the painting, and they have likened this to various ways in which the practices of traditional narrative film "fix" the spectator in a limited and limiting relation to the possibilities of the cinema. See, for example, Stephen Heath, "Narrative Space," in *Questions of Cinema* (Bloomington: Indiana University Press, 1981), pp. 19–75. However, I want to insist upon a point that they seem to suppress: the

viewer can be moved. Learning to look at the painting with lateral focus in a new way, a person can achieve new satisfactions by shifting back to a centered position before it. The same is true of film goers whose focus has been too narrowly constrained along the path of the narrative. I take the traditional view that it is a key role of criticism and analysis to enable viewers (readers) to learn to shift for themselves. For a good deal more on the idea that classical film inexorably fixes its audiences into certain epistemic modes, see chapter 10.

6. Although I use the phrase "classical narrative film" here and later, I do not mean to suggest that it designates a well-defined species. The phrase is, for me, a convenient label for the major studio fiction films made in the period between the middle thirties and the late fifties. One sometimes feels that there are certain strong similarities among the films of this time and place, but, when one actually looks at cases, it is extremely hard to define interesting shared properties. (If one restricts oneself to a very limited period, say, the middle forties *and* to a particular studio, the job becomes easier but still not trivial.) In chapter 3, I develop my version of some of the chief properties that have been thought definitive of classical narrative film. This will help some to restrict my usage, but not much.

Chapter 2: Fritz Lang's You Only Live Once

1. In speaking, as I do, of Fritz Lang's *You Only Live Once* and of Alfred Hitchcock's *North by Northwest*, and so forth I mean to indicate my belief that the directors' contributions to the overall conceptions of the films discussed in this book have been decisive. I hope that the analyses presented make it clear why I assume this to be the case. However, I do not mean for this claim to suggest that the contributions of the cast and other collaborators are not of great importance. In particular, as the analyses should also make clear, I think that in each of these instances the screenplay constitutes a marvelous framework or foundation for all the rest that is built upon it. In this respect, they are all paradigms of writing for the screen. It is probable, and in some cases certain, that the relevant directors played a significant role in shaping the final versions of the screenplays in question, but this is not to detract from the achievement of the credited writers. The rich and suggestive screenplay of *You Only Live Once* is by Gene Towne and Graham Baker.

2. Lotte H. Eisner, *Fritz Lang* (New York: Oxford University Press, 1977), p. 177.

3. For example, Bonnie says, "You're not helping Jo by trying to keep this case alive. You know as well as I do that Eddie Taylor's been pounding on the door of the execution chamber since he was born." Later the warden's wife will express similar views.

4. Eisner, *Fritz Lang*, p. 177.

5. This note is sounded, as it were, within the film when Joan accidentally strikes a jarring chord as she rises from her seat before a piano to prepare for the suicide she plans to commit.

1. Seymour Chatman, *Story and Discourse: Narrative Structure in Fiction and Film* (Ithaca: Cornell University Press, 1978), pp. 235–37.

2. Mark Crispin Miller, *"Barry Lyndon* Reconsidered," *Georgia Review* 30 (1976): 827–53.

3. By "primary visual narration," I mean to designate the totality of visual information presented in the course of the film. Thus, as indicated in the text, the primary visual narration may include quite extended segments that narrate information that is (fictionally) being conveyed by a character or by a voice-over narrator within the film. Such narration is "secondary" in that it has been "placed," in relation to some special narrational source, within the larger context of the filmic presentation. It is useful to have *some* terms in this connection.

4. Gerald Mast, "Kracauer's Two Tendencies and the Early History of Film Narrative," in *The Language of Images*, ed. W. J. T. Mitchell (Chicago: University of Chicago Press, 1974), pp. 129–50. Mast brings out some of the surprising difficulties with continuity which very early film makers faced.

5. In chapter 5, I say something more about skeptical views of the world and how they might bear on the idea of what there is to see in a film.

6. William Luhr and Peter Lehman, *Authorship and Narrative in the Cinema* (New York: G. P. Putnam's Sons, 1977), pp. 85–136. This chapter on *The Searchers* was written solely by Lehman. Although I am broadly in agreement with Lehman's analysis, a comparison of my discussion with his essay will reveal some substantial differences in general conception.

7. It is worth observing just how minutely these motifs are worked into the film. When Marty and Ethan return to the Jorgenson farm and discover that Charlie McCory is on the verge of marrying Laurie, Marty challenges Charlie to a fistfight. They leave the house, and Charlie lays down a log between them, challenging Marty to spit across it. When Marty does so, the two men stalk each other, moving in *circles* around the artificial *boundary* that Charlie has devised. Eventually they plunge into a ridiculous, uncontrolled, and dirty brawl. The fight, of course, is over who is to possess the woman as a bride. In short, a number of the wider, essentially tragic patterns of the film are reproduced in this scene, on a smaller scale, in the context of broad farce. The suggestion is, I believe, that the larger forces that rend the two great opposing cultures are at work *within* the cultures as well.

8. Karel Reisz and Gavin Millar, *The Technique of Film Editing*, 2d ed. (New York: Hastings House, 1968). The material I discuss was written solely by Reisz.

9. Ibid., p. 215.

10. Ibid.

11. We shall return to this issue in chapter 7.

12. Although I have intended that the term *make-believe* is to be understood in its ordinary, nontechnical sense, I have also meant to invoke Kendall Walton's more special use of "it is make-believe that" as it has been developed in a number of important articles. See especially "Pictures and Make-Believe," *Philosphical Review* 82 (1973): 283–319, and "Fearing Fictions," *Journal of Philosophy* 75

(1978): 5–27. In the second of these articles, Walton provides an account of "audience" emotions (for example, feeling fear of or sadness for a fictional being in the course of reading or viewing a fiction), which is framed, in part, in terms of his notion of "something's being make-believe for an audience." I believe that the conceptual apparatus that is worked out in these articles can be adapted to elucidate the audience impression of transparency as I have described it in the text. However, an adequate treatment of the fairly complicated issues that arise would take us too far afield in the present setting.

13. Kendall Walton argues that if X is an actual photographed item appearing in a certain photograph or film shot, then it is a natural and justified extension of our present usage to say that we *directly* see X *through* or *with the aid of* the relevant photograph or shot. I am dubious about Walton's interesting thesis, and I am not sure that I grasp its import fully. In any event, I am concerned in the text with cases in which X is a fictional item of the film narrative, and Walton explicitly denies that his claim applies to such fictional subjects. Also, whether Walton's main thesis is correct or not, what is of importance here, in relation to cinema, is the audience's make-believe *impression* of seeing the fictional contents of a film directly. See "Transparent Pictures," *Critical Inquiry* 2, no. 2 (1984): 246–77.

14. Jean Mitry, *Esthétique et psychologie du cinéma. I. Les structures* (Paris: Editions Universitaires, 1963), p. 179. This passage is cited and translated in Charles Affron's *Cinema and Sentiment* (Chicago: University of Chicago Press, 1982), p. 7. I have employed Affron's translation.

15. André Bazin, "The Myth of Total Cinema," in *What Is Cinema?*, vol. 1, ed. and trans. Hugh Gray (Berkeley and Los Angeles: University of California Press, 1967), pp. 17–23.

16. For a classical exposition of Bazin's views on this subject see his "The Ontology of the Photographic Image" in *What Is Cinema?*, pp. 9–16. On the whole, Bazin seems to defend a metaphysical thesis of the "intrinsic realism" of photography; that is, the idea that a photograph somehow "shares its being" with the items of which it is a photograph. Yet he sometimes writes as though he were describing the "impression" that he thinks we have in seeing objects in (many) photographs. Therefore, he may be merely defending a counterpart to the suggestion in my text that it is part of our immediate and primitive reaction to photographs that we see them as extracting and capturing the real, unmediated physical appearance of photographed subjects. Thus, we may be more moved by a fuzzy snapshot of Aunt Edith than by her portrait over the mantel because we feel, however dimly, that the former gives us directly the way she really looked at the time or, as we revealingly say, the way she must have looked. If something like this is true, then these psychological facts are crucial to an explanation of the aesthetic force and significance that photography has for us and to an analysis of the artistic elaborations that this force and significance make possible. That we may not retrospectively accept an explicit statement of the belief that underlies our response is beside the point. Even if the "objectivity," the "intrinsic realism" of photography is an illusion, as long as someone is in its grip the photographic image seems to offer privileged and almost magical access to the visual character of the world. Whatever Bazin meant, it is, of course, the "psychological" version of his views that I find more plausible.

17. Nick Browne, "The Spectator-in-the-Text: The Rhetoric of *Stagecoach*," *Film Quarterly* 29 (1975–76): 36.

18. For an elaboration of this suggestion, see the analysis of his *The Devil Is a Woman* in chapter 8.

19. An adequate statement of the relevant principle would require, as the text barely hints, a major qualification to cover *irony* on the part of the narrator. This would not be a trivial task, and it might force adjustments in the basic terms with which the principle has here been stated. It may be that a sharpening of my (too brief) reference to conditions of overall coherence and consistency could be made to handle the problem, but that this is so is not clear to me. Be this as it may, I think that the formulation in the text is satisfactory for purposes of bringing out the type of analogy I have wanted to suggest.

20. It is patent that this notion of "objective appearance," if pressed closely, gives rise to a number of difficulties and perplexities. I do believe that we have some such rough concept as evidenced by our thinking of physical objects as, for example, having colors that they possess whether or not the objects ever appear to anyone as having the colors in question. It is possible that the concept that I am invoking could be spelled out along conventional lines with reference to how things would appear to a normal observer in normal circumstances. However, there are well-known difficulties with this approach. I suspect that quite different accounts are possible, but this is a matter that I shall have to leave, without resolution, to our somewhat confusing intuitions about the status of sensible qualities.

21. Browne, "The Spectator-in-the-Text," p. 37.

22. An example of the sort of overblown and simplistic conception of the relations of film to ideology to which I am here objecting is provided by Bill Nichols' *Ideology and the Image* (Bloomington: University of Indiana Press, 1981). This book contains some useful material, and, in discussions of Hitchcock's *The Birds* and von Sternberg's *Blonde Venus*, it allows that some Hollywood films do go beyond ideologically determined content. However, I believe that these concessions do little to counteract the dominant and very misleading implications of the book. Also, Peter Biskind's *Seeing Is Believing* (New York: Pantheon, 1983) purports to reveal the "ideological messages" imbedded in the American films of the fifties he discusses. Dealing with various poor to mediocre films, he can be insightful and revealing, but when the same strategies are applied to *The Searchers* and *Rebel without a Cause* the blindness induced by his condescending convictions is embarrassing. For more on ideology and film content, see chapter 10.

Chapter 4: Alfred Hitchcock's North by Northwest

Epigraph: Alfred Hitchcock's comment is from François Truffaut (with Helen G. Scott), *Hitchcock* (New York: Simon and Schuster, 1967), p. 194.

1. This and all other quotations from the script are taken from Ernest Lehman, *North by Northwest* (New York: Viking Press, 1972).

I wish to emphasize Lehman's contribution to *North by Northwest*. Not only is the script, as is generally recognized, a marvelous "light thriller" construction, but, as will be seen in this chapter, it plays an important role in setting up the structures I want to outline. Of course, it is well-known that the Hitchcock-Lehman scripts are the result of close collaboration.

2. Robin Wood's essay is found in his *Hitchcock's Films* (New York: A. S. Barnes, 1969), pp. 98–111.

3. These characters are given these identifications only in the screenplay, but is clear enough in viewing the film that they are supposed to be (and look like) ordinary citizen types.

4. Truffaut, *Hitchcock*, p. 99.

Chapter 5: Some Modes of Nonomniscience

1. For the views of Béla Balázs that are relevant here, see the selections "The Close-up" and "The Faces of Man" from his *Theory of the Film*, in *Film Theory and Criticism*, 2d ed., ed. Gerald Mast and Marshall Cohen (New York: Oxford University Press, 1979), pp. 288–98. Erwin Panofsky's "Style and Medium in the Motion Pictures" is also reprinted in this anthology on pp. 243–63.

2. V. F. Perkins, *Film as Film* (Baltimore: Penguin Books, 1972), p. 69.

3. Maurice Merleau-Ponty, "The Film and the New Psychology," in *Sense and Nonsense*, ed. and trans. Hubert L. Dreyfus and Patricia Allen Dreyfus (Evanston: Northwestern University Press, 1970), pp. 48–59.

4. A part of the spareness of the style of *To Have and Have Not* lies in its infrequent use of the moving camera. But there is a tracking shot that I take to be central to the film's vision as discussed in the text. The piano player in the small combo at the bar strikes up, by himself, the beginning of a tune. The relevant tracking shot shows the combo's drummer lay down his paper and pick up the beat, and, as the shot continues, the rest of the group, one by one, fall in with the music. This is the film's chief image of the kind of spontaneous, good-natured cooperation, cooperation that produces a larger harmony, which is, in the end, endorsed by the film as an ideal of human activity.

5. André Bazin, "Evolution of the Language of Film," in *What Is Cinema?*, vol. 1, ed. and trans. Hugh Gray (Berkeley and Los Angeles: University of California Press, 1967), p. 36.

6. *The Rules of the Game* is, of course, the one non-American film that I have singled out for some discussion. I have done so because it is useful, for reasons that will become clearer as we proceed, to work with one of Bazin's favorite examples of his views. I also know of no single American film that illustrates as clearly the points that I, with Bazin's help, wish to make in this connection.

7. Alexander Sesonske, *Jean Renoir: The French Films, 1924–1939* (Cambridge, Mass.: Harvard University Press, 1980), pp. 437–38.

8. André Bazin, *Jean Renoir* (New York: Simon and Schuster, 1973), p. 88.

9. For a sketch of some of my grounds for deep skepticism about the idea that there is a "language" of film, see my review of Christian Metz's *Film Language: A Semiotics of the Cinema* in *Modern Language Notes* 89 (1974): 1068–72.

10. Gerard Genette, *Narrative Discourse*, trans. Jane E. Lewin (Ithaca: Cornell University Press, 1980), p. 162.

11. Wayne C. Booth, *The Rhetoric of Fiction*, 2d ed. (Chicago: University of Chicago Press, 1983). See also chapters 4 and 5 of Genette's *Narrative Discourse*, and chapters 4 and 5 of Seymour Chatman's *Story and Discourse: Narrative Structure in Fiction and Film* (Ithaca: Cornell University Press, 1978). Genette's and Chatman's discussions, like most on this topic, are substantially influenced by Booth.

Chapter 6: Max Ophuls' Letter from an Unknown Woman

1. Although I speak of *Letter* as being a Max Ophuls film, I want to acknowledge the way in which Howard Koch's exquisite screenplay provides a foundation for the film.

2. Stendhal is reputed to have been Ophuls' favorite novelist and, when one thinks about the director's concerns and attitudes as expressed in his films, reflection on the writer's great novels is interesting and instructive. But, more particularly, the views on love and related matters in *L'Amour* are directly and immensely suggestive in relation to *Letter* and other Ophuls' films. I have not attempted in this chapter to analyze the rich connections that exist. However, beyond the words of the epigraph, a further quotation suggests itself: "No matter whether it be in the forest of Arden or at a Coulon ball, you can only enjoy idealizing your beloved if she *appears* perfect in the first place. Absolute perfection is not essential, but every perceived quality must be perfect. Only after several days of the second crystallization will the beloved appear perfect in all respects. It's quite simple; you only need to think of a perfection to perceive it at once in your beloved." The epigraph and this quotation are from *Love*, trans. Gilbert Sale and Susanne Sale (Hammondsworth, Middlesex: Penguin Books, 1975). The former is on p. 65, and the latter on pp. 57–58.

3. In his essay on *Letter*, Robin Wood states: "Yet the more times one sees the film, the more one has the sense—it is a mark of its greatness—of the possibility of a film *against* Lisa: it would require only a shift of emphasis for this other film to emerge." Wood's claim makes it sound as if the film, basically structured around a strongly positive view of Lisa, contains strands, more or less unassimilated, of a darker viewpoint toward her. I am arguing that *Letter* develops a much more complex structure than Wood suggests, a structure that coherently incorporates both the more and less sympathetic aspects of Lisa's character. To repeat, I am *not* trying to provide a "shift of emphasis" that yields a reading of the film as "against Lisa." Despite my disagreement with Wood, his essay is generally sensible and helpful. In particular, his discussion of the use of echoing elements in the film constitutes a good overview of the matter. The quote above is on pp. 129–30 of "Ewig hin der Liebe Gluck," in *Personal Views: Explorations in Film* (London: Gordon Fraser Gallery, 1976).

4. For some discussion of the use of a character to stand in for the film maker see my remarks on the concluding pages of chapter 7.

1. It is easy to overstate what is typically conveyed in a point-of-view shot. Often such shots are easily recognized as not being very precisely from the character's visual perspective—they are a little off. What is important in such cases is simply the information that such-and-such a character saw *this*. Even in instances where the camera closely matches the character's perspective only the above information is usually registered. There is no intention to render phenomenological facts about the character's field of vision. Nevertheless, it *is* an important and familiar possibility of the point-of-view shot to show us something about *how* the relevant objects and events are being perceived.

2. I have intended the faintly Lacanian echo in this formulation because it seems that many of the original, chief proponents of the doctrine of the "suture" presuppose, in their statements of the doctrine, that screen imagery in classical film *is* always the product of a camera observer. Consider, for example, the following passages from Daniel Dayan's "The Tutor-Code of Classical Cinema": "He [the viewer] feels dispossessed of what he is prevented from seeing. He discovers that he is only authorized to see what happens to be in the axis of the glance of another spectator, who is ghostly or absent. This ghost, who rules over the frame . . . Oudart proposes to call 'the absent-one' *(l'absent)*" (p. 448). And, "For the spectator who becomes frame-conscious, the visual field *means* the presence of the absent-one as the owner of the glance that constitutes the image" (p. 449). These brief samples are easily multiplied. The presupposition expressed here is never argued for, and, of course, I believe it is false. Whether the doctrine of the suture can be formulated without this presupposition I shall not venture to guess, having little idea what the doctrine comes to anyway. However, this shows that the temptation to think of a film view as the personal view of some perceiver is recurrent even in the headiest heights of theoretical speculation. See *Movies and Methods*, ed. Bill Nichols (Berkeley and Los Angeles: University of California Press, 1976).

3. Susan Sontag, *Styles of Radical Will* (New York: Dell, n.d.), p. 170.

4. Bruce Kawin, *Mindscreen: Bergman, Godard, and First-Person Film* (Princeton: Princeton University Press, 1978).

5. See, for example, ibid, p. 19.

6. The concepts of "narrator" which are or might be based upon these relations will be discussed more fully later in the chapter. In particular, my understanding of "implied version of the film maker(s)" will be explained.

7. Gerard Genette, *Narrative Discourse*, trans. Jane E. Lewin (Ithaca: Cornell University Press, 1980), pp. 186–89.

8. For a sample of Kawin's use of this term, see *Mindscreen*, p. 19. Notice also that on p. 170 Kawin says that in *Two or Three Things I Know about Her* "Godard introduces a subtle difference, and *thinks with* images and sounds, rather than simply recording his fantasies." It is passages such as these which suggested the first reading of Kawin's claim.

9. Ibid., pp. 113–27.

10. For a good introduction to the subtleties and complexities of this topic see Thomas Nagel, "Subjective and Objective," in *Mortal Questions* (Cambridge:

Cambridge University Press, 1979), pp. 196–214, and G. E. M. Anscombe, "The Subjectivity of Sensation," in *Metaphysics and the Philosophy of Mind* (Minneapolis: University of Minnesota Press, 1981), pp. 44–56.

11. For the standard account of the concept of "implied author," see Wayne C. Booth, *The Rhetoric of Fiction*, 2d ed. (Chicago: University of Chicago Press, 1983). I believe that it was Booth who, in the original version of his book, introduced this term, although the concept, as he admits, was used, in various versions, by others before him. Booth's notion and his use of it are deservedly controversial, and I have attempted to spell out, as best I could in a short space, how I conceive of the notion and why I think it has value. I believe that my account is broadly in accordance with what I take to be the main lines of Booth's account. However, he says a great deal about implied authors which I do not accept.

12. Mark Crispin Miller, "*Barry Lyndon* Reconsidered," *Georgia Review* 30 (1976): 827–53.

13. As the next chapter reveals, the issues here are a bit more complicated because the character in question serves as a voice-over narrator in a part of the film. However, the added complications do not affect the main point.

14. For an essay that reaches similar conclusions about plot, discussed in relation to literary works, see Alexander Nehamas, "Mythology, the Theory of Plot" in *Essays on the Philosophy of Monroe C. Beardsley*, ed. John Fisher (Philadelphia: Temple University Press, 1983). I do not, however, accept Nehamas's more positive account of plot.

Chapter 8: Josef von Sternberg's The Devil Is a Woman

1. The wacky screenplay of this film is credited to John Dos Passos and Sam Winston. However, there is reason to believe that Dos Passos played very little role in the final product. However, the indirect evidence of von Sternberg's touch is considerable.

2. Josef von Sternberg, *Fun in a Chinese Laundry* (New York: Macmillan Co., 1965), p. 56.

3. For an interesting and helpful overview of this phenomenon in nineteenth-century aesthetics, see Jean Pierrot, *The Decadent Imagination, 1880–1900*, trans. Derek Coltman (Chicago: University of Chicago Press, 1982).

4. Pierre Louys is the author of *Woman and Puppet*, the novella upon which the film is loosely based. An English translation is found in *The Collected Works of Pierre Louys* (New York: Liveright Publishing, 1932), pp. 157–224.

5. See Charles Dickens, *Hard Times* (New York: New American Library, 1961), p. 198.

6. What Don Pasqual actually says is, "But they had disappeared completely—mother and daughter, bag and baggage." Presumably, the conventional reference to luggage is intended, but the special placement of the parallel construction suggests the nasty equivalences in question.

7. For example, compare these recent remarks with my briefer discussion of *The Scarlet Empress* at the end of chapter 4.

8. Von Sternberg knew when he was making *Devil* that his success as Dietrich's director was on the wane, and that Paramount was anxious to transfer her to more conventional hands.

Chapter 9: Nicholas Ray's Rebel without a Cause

1. The screenplay of *Rebel* is credited to Stewart Stern and Irving Shulman, and the story credit is given to Ray himself. However, it is well-known that such divisions of credit can present a misleading idea of the nature of the various actual contributions.

2. This quote is from the entry on *Rebel without a Cause* in *The Oxford Companion to Film*, ed. Liz-Anne Bawden (New York: Oxford University Press, 1976), p. 581. I chose this quote because it is typical of a common response to the film.

3. Barr's famous essay "Cinemascope: Before and After" is reprinted in *Film Theory and Criticism*, 2d ed., ed. Gerald Mast and Marshall Cohen (New York: Oxford University Press, 1979), pp. 140–69.

4. An early working title for *Rebel* was "The Blind Run." Presumably, this was meant to make literal reference to the film's chickie run. However, in the light of the present discussion, it should be clear how the title would have been appropriate to larger thematic concerns as well.

5. It seems to me that Ray's work in the middle to late fifties has a much greater coherence than is generally recognized. *Rebel* was released in 1955. *Bigger Than Life* (1956) deals with a man who, under the influence of cortisone, goes into mad rebellion against the narrowness and constriction of his life. It is made clear that the rebellion, despite the madness, has some genuine justification. *Wind across the Everglades* (1958) is about a representative of "civilization" who is thrown up against a group of criminals who have formed their own primitive society in the swamp. His reaction to this confrontation is ambivalent. Finally, *The Savage Innocents* (1959) examines, from an explicitly anthropological perspective, the last of a tribe of Eskimos. The film plainly draws relativistic conclusions about the moral and social codes that order human groups. Many of the concerns in these films could have been predicted from *Rebel*.

Chapter 10: Morals for Method

1. Colin McCabe, "The Classic Realist Text," *Screen* 15, no. 2 SEFT, 152–62. The article is reprinted with omissions in *Realism and the Cinema*, ed. Christopher Williams (London: Routledge and Kegan Paul, 1980), pp. 152–62. All page citations in the text are to this volume.

2. Brian Henderson, *A Critique of Film Theory* (New York: E. P. Dutton, 1980), pp. 3–4.

3. The relevant early work is found in Christian Metz, *Film Language: A Semiotics of the Cinema*, trans. Michael Taylor (New York: Oxford University Press, 1974).

4. Henderson, *Critique of Film Theory*, p. 5.

5. Ibid., p. 49.

6. Stanley Cavell, *The World Viewed* (New York: Viking Press, 1971), p. 31.

Index

George M. Wilson is professor of philosophy at the Johns Hopkins University and is the author of *The Intentionality of Human Action*.